THE MINORITY PARTY IN CONGRESS

The
Study of
Congress
Series

THE MINORITY PARTY
IN CONGRESS

CHARLES O. JONES
University of Pittsburgh

LITTLE, BROWN AND COMPANY · BOSTON

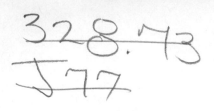

To
William O. Farber
and
Ralph K. Huitt

Foreword

The Study of Congress is sponsored by the American Political Science Association with the support of a generous grant from the Carnegie Corporation. The project was first conceived by a small group of scholars and congressmen (the latter led by Chet Holifield, D-Calif., and Thomas B. Curtis, R-Mo.) who held a series of discussion meetings on Congress with financial aid from the Philip Stern Family Fund. These discussions led to an agreement to seek support for a comprehensive study of Congress. A formal proposal was prepared by Evron M. Kirkpatrick, Executive Director of the American Political Science Association, and Donald G. Tacheron, Associate Director, which resulted in the grant by the Carnegie Corporation.

The Study of Congress gave political scientists an opportunity to cover ground in one concerted thrust which they might individually inch over in a decade. Such an opportunity was unprecedented, and it increased the urgency and importance of the basic questions: What should be the target of the study? Who should do it? How should it be done?

Reform of Congress is always in the air. Congress is criticized, even by its own members, because, as a representative body, it mirrors the weaknesses as well as the strengths of the represented. Moreover, it is powerful; almost alone among the national legislatures, it has withstood domination by the executive and has remained the coordinate branch the Founding Fathers meant it to be. What Congress does matters very much, here and abroad, and for that reason one is tempted to try to change it, to alter some procedure or structural arrangement in order to increase one's influence on the legislative product.

Nevertheless, reform is not the target of this research project. Congress does change, but slowly, adaptively in things that matter, and seldom according to blueprint. Structure and procedure are not neutral; they are used to work the will of those who control them. Moreover, alterations in them often have unforeseen consequences. This is more likely to be true when structure and rules, and to whose benefit they work, are imperfectly understood. The Study of Congress began, therefore, with a modest admission and an appropriate resolution: there are large gaps in what political scientists know about Congress and the Study would try to fill in as many as it could.

Each of the studies which make up the Study of Congress has been undertaken by a scholar already deeply immersed in the subject. The research in each case promises to produce a book, a monograph, or one or more scholarly articles. Each man is free to recommend changes in the organization and procedures of Congress, but there will be no "official" list of recommendations by the Study of Congress itself. The purpose of the Study is to produce original research studies of Congress. Like other research enterprises, the usefulness of this one will be determined by the people who use it.

The Study of Congress Series presents associated studies designed to tell interested people as much as possible about how Congress works. It provides analytical descriptions of Congress, its subsystems, and its relations with its environment. The series fills in research blanks and suggests relevant variables for future research. It provides some basis for stating the functions performed by Congress for the political system, evaluating the performance, and pointing out alternative structural arrangements and modes of action which realistically seem to be open to Congress. Until these tasks are completed, our lists of congressional reforms are little more than statements of personal preference.

In this fourth volume of the series, Charles O. Jones examines the organization and operations of minority parties in twentieth-century Congresses. As such the book is a complement to Randall B. Ripley's study of majority party leadership. Jones builds from two basic assumptions: (1) that the right to criticize and oppose is fundamental to democratic thought and practice and (2) that the principal instrument of opposition in the United States has been not third parties, but the main minority party. Thus, most of his focus has been on the Democratic party through the first three decades of this century and the Republican party since 1930. In early chapters he explores significant political factors — external and internal — which condition the range of strategies available to the minority and compares and contrasts House and Senate leadership. Just how much impact can a Joseph Martin of Massachusetts or an Everett Dirksen of Illinois have on shaping partisan issues or achieving legislative goals? In subsequent chapters he examines through a variety of historical cases the ways in which "restricted," "participating," and "unrestricted" minorities affect legislative outcomes and reduce or enhance the opportunities for the minority to become a majority party. In his concluding chapters, Jones assesses the role of contemporary Republican minorities in the House and Senate and their contributions to innovative and creative policy making.

Ralph K. Huitt
Robert L. Peabody

Preface

This book combines my interests in Congress, the Republican Party, the role of opposition in American politics, and creativity in a political system. Since these are broad concerns, I have focused on one institution — the minority party in Congress — in order to say something meaningful about them. In this book I attempt to sort out some of the significant variables that determine the political limits on minority party activity in Congress. I feel as though I have barely scratched the surface in analyzing this subject, although I have been working on it for several years.

I have incurred many debts in writing this book. The American Political Science Association's Study of Congress financed the largest part of the study from a grant by the Carnegie Corporation. The Director, Ralph K. Huitt, has been my mentor since he first defined the word "thesis" for me in graduate school at the University of Wisconsin. The Associate Director, Robert L. Peabody, has been my friend and colleague for many years. Both read the manuscript and suggested improvements. I am also grateful for support from the Institute of Government Research at the University of Arizona and its Director, Currin V. Shields. I was given a reduced teaching load during one semester and direct financial assistance by the Institute. The Brookings Institution cooperated by providing me with a Guest Fellowship during the summer of 1965. I am particularly grateful to the Brookings Library staff for their assistance.

A great many people supported the project in various ways. Then a graduate student, Professor Louis D. Hayes accompanied me to Washington in the summer of 1965 to assist in collecting data from interviews and the Library of Congress. Several congressmen and staff aides were particularly helpful. E. Y. Berry of South Dakota and his secretary, Mrs. Mavis Daly, have always been generous in assisting me in my research on Capitol Hill. Charles E. Goodell of New York, Albert H. Quie of Minnesota, Melvin R. Laird of Wisconsin, and particularly John J. Rhodes of Arizona, were all supportive along the way, as was Dr. William Prendergast, then research director for the House Republican Conference. I very much appreciate their interest and hope they find something of value in this book. Many other congressmen and staff members gave time for interviews.

On the Senate side, I particularly wish to thank Dr. Stephen Horn, formerly on Senator Thomas H. Kuchel's staff; Robert E. Berry of the Subcommittee on Intergovernmental Relations; Dr. Charles L. Clapp, formerly on Senator Leverett Saltonstall's staff; and Dr. Martin J. Clancy of the Senate Republican Policy Committee. Each in different ways helped to enlighten me about the complicated workings of the Senate. I am also appreciative of the time given me by several Senate Republican staff aides in interviews.

I also want to acknowledge the assistance of those who helped me to put this book together. Randall B. Ripley and I consulted at every stage of our research. I hope that our continuous collaboration results in books that are complementary. Mrs. Carol Hayes typed countless interviews and bibliographical notes and Mrs. Shelly Poore typed her third book manuscript for me with her usual efficiency, accuracy, and good humor. Miss Rose Marie Costello and Mrs. Kendall Stanley typed the final draft. As always, my wife Vera made it her business to create the conditions under which I could do my job both as a political scientist and as head of the Jones family.

Finally, a word about those to whom the book is dedicated. William O. Farber is a devoted teacher who has started many a young undergraduate on a career of public service. Ralph K. Huitt is a fine teacher, a respected scholar, and a talented public servant. If I am a political scientist, these men deserve the credit; if not, I accept the blame.

Charles O. Jones

Table of Contents

xiii

List of Tables

THE MINORITY PARTY IN CONGRESS

CHAPTER ONE

Introduction

The right to oppose is fundamental to democratic political thought. Political systems are measured by the extent to which this right is guaranteed in form and institutionalized in practice. The form and practice may vary widely, however, and still be labeled "democratic." Perhaps the principal institution of opposition in the United States is the minority party.[1] The subject of this book is the minority party as it operates in its principal national arena of action, the Congress. Robert A. Dahl has argued convincingly that a "distinctive, persistent, unified structural opposition" scarcely exists in the United States.[2] He might have added that to expect one is to misunderstand American political conditions. On the other hand, there is an identifiable minority party most of the time, and, more than any other institution of its size, it offers opposition, criticism, and alternatives. If not *the* opposition on all issues and at all levels of government, it is certainly one major source of opposition. But minority parties in the United States Congress have been unwilling and unable to limit themselves to this single function. Some political conditions *allow* them to be flexible in adopting strategies for achieving their goals. Other political conditions *force* them to do more than merely oppose.

My purpose in this book is to examine the political conditions, the range of strategic choices, and the choices themselves of the minority party in Congress. Specifically I will concentrate on minority party

[1] As used here "minority party" refers to the second party, the party of opposition, and not to third parties.

[2] Robert A. Dahl, ed., *Political Oppositions in Western Democracies* (New Haven: Yale University Press, 1966), p. 34.

1

activities that relate to the function of Congress in the national policy process — that of legitimizing one course of action rather than another to solve public problems. The policy process is composed of various subprocesses or stages, e.g., formulation, legitimation, administration. Following the identification of a public problem (itself a rather complex process), efforts are made to formulate solutions or, more accurately, various courses of action that will change the nature of the problem if implemented. Political executives and high-ranking bureaucrats are normally very much involved in this process, but participants from Congress and private and public groups may be involved too. Competing or complementary courses of action may be developed and proposed outside government with no one from the executive participating.

The legitimation subprocess is where certain legal requirements are met in adopting one course of action over others. Whereas the output of formulation is a course of action, the output of legitimation is "policy" — defined simply as a "legitimate course of action." In the American political system, one major form of legitimation is majority coalition building in legislatures. Legitimation is not simply selecting among courses of action that are on the agenda, however. Nor is it merely ratification. It is a process characterized by evaluation, bargaining, compromise, and coalition building. Seldom is the end-product a replica of any one course of action that has been proposed.

A third subprocess involves administering policy to the problem. The principal participants in policy administration are the bureaucrats, though others may be involved. Further, studies of administration establish that a full policy-making cycle may be authorized within administration (that is, where bureaucrats have the authority to formulate courses of action and legitimate one over the others). Perhaps administrative discretion to make policy decisions has been included in a broad policy that has been legitimated in Congress.

The emphasis here will be on legitimation, focusing on those minority party activities which facilitate or impede majority building in Congress. The minority party has goals of its own in this legitimating process. Its basic goal is majority party status. Certain requirements must be met before it can entertain the thought of achieving this goal. Richard F. Fenno, Jr., identifies two organizational requirements for the House of Representatives — establishing a decision-making structure and maintaining that structure — which apply equally well to the minority party in Congress.[3] Neither of these prerequisites is easily met in the American political system. As a result, the minority party may occasionally find itself almost completely preoccupied with maintenance, unable to devote time and effort to the maximal goal of achieving majority party status.

Under certain political conditions the minority party may divide on whether majority party status is in fact its basic goal. Certain party members may find enough individual satisfaction in minority party status that they are not inclined to pursue majority party status. Such people may even be in leadership positions.

It is evident that, as with any group, different goals for the minority party are set by different groups. Scholars may attribute certain goals to the party on the basis of logic, values, or research. Party members may define party goals in terms of their own preferences, which are influenced by constituency wishes, personal and political experience, national leadership, seniority, and other variables. Leaders may be expected to define party goals aimed at maintaining their positions.

Let me set forth my own value-based analysis of the goals of a minority party in Congress. I will tend to measure minority parties in this century by the standards implied in these goals. I think it is important for the political system that the minority party be aggressive in the legislative process. I value criticism and opposition as beneficial in the development of policies that will solve public problems. Thus, in this book one major test of the minority party's effectiveness in Congress will be the extent to which party leaders actively pursue the strategies available to them. Another test will be the extent to which these leaders aggressively pursue the more positive strategies. The effective minority party capitalizes on its advantages so as to be a creative instrument in the legitimating process of majority building in Congress.

Majority and minority parties behave differently in Congress. Despite this obvious distinction, few scholars have made an effort to define these differences in any but the most superficial manner. One of the few detailed discussions of these functional differences is contained in Jesse Macy's *Party Organization and Machinery* (1912). Macy concluded that the minority party "is likely to gather

[3] Richard F. Fenno, Jr., "The Internal Distribution of Influence: The House," in David B. Truman, ed., *The Congress and America's Future* (Englewood Cliffs, N.J.: Prentice-Hall, 1965).

to itself the adherence of a variety of dissatisfied classes." The majority party adopts a middle course, while the minority finds itself representing "the extremes of opposing positions." Thus, the minority party is the party of criticism, of those not favored by the policy decisions of the majority party. The party in power accepts all credit for whatever progress is made and thus maintains itself in power over a long period of time. When the minority party does come to power, according to Macy, it "suffers from a lack of experience in the actual conduct of public affairs" and is likely to have a "brief tenure of power." The minority party comes to power when the number of dissatisfied exceed the number of satisfied, that is, when the majority party fails to accommodate the majority.[4] There is much to commend Macy's analysis. But it does not go far enough in describing and analyzing the variety of political circumstances in which the minority party must operate. Little has been done since to explore the questions Macy raised.[5]

We will examine in detail the patterns of activities of the minority party in congressional policy making. Randall B. Ripley, in a study in this same series, has focused on the majority party and we have worked closely together in the development of our research.[6] Thus, an assumption in our research, just as fundamental as the different patterns of majority and minority party activity, is the variation in behavior for each party over time, depending on a variety of political conditions.

A number of questions are treated in this volume.

1. What political conditions are significant in determining the behavior of the minority party in Congress?

2. What strategies are available to the minority party in the process of majority building in Congress?

3. How do political conditions determine the range of strategies available to the minority party?

---

[4] See Jesse Macy, *Party Organization and Machinery* (New York: The Century Co., 1912), Ch. 20.

[5] See, however, Theodore Lowi, "Toward Functionalism in Political Science: The Case of Innovation in Party Systems," *American Political Science Review*, Vol. 57 (September, 1963), pp. 570–83; and David R. Mayhew, *Party Loyalty among Congressmen* (Cambridge: Harvard University Press, 1966). Both develop conclusions that are specifically applicable to majority-minority differences.

[6] Randall B. Ripley, *Majority Party Leadership in Congress* (Boston: Little, Brown, 1968).

4. How does the minority party organize itself to participate in the process of majority building in Congress?

5. What are the characteristics of minority party leaders?

6. What is the significance of minority party leadership and organization for determining the behavior of the minority party in Congress?

7. To what extent have minority parties realized the potential of strategies available to them in specific Congresses?

8. Does the behavior of the minority party differ in the House and the Senate? Does it differ in the Democratic and Republican parties?

9. What is the role of the minority party today?

In order to answer these questions, I have organized the study into four main sections. In the first, Chapter Two, I focus on the first three questions, outlining broadly the principal political conditions for minority parties and noting the range of strategies available. In the second, Chapter Three, I treat the organizational and leadership questions, 4–6. In the third and longest section, Chapters Four, Five, Six, and Seven, I examine the various types of minority parties classified by the range of strategies available, illustrating with minority party experience in specific Congresses (questions 3, 7, and 8). The final section, Chapters Eight and Nine, deals with the last question on the role of the minority party today and presents some concluding observations about the minority party and Congress.

I have limited the scope of this study in several ways. First, I examined Congresses in this century only, fully realizing that this omits some interesting minority party situations (particularly before 1856). Second, I have not made any serious attempt to examine the role of the minority party in foreign policy. For the most part, in examining specific Congresses, I have concentrated on domestic policy. Third, only selective illustrations of minority party action are provided.

Finally, it is inevitable that more attention will be given to the Republican Party as a minority in Congress. The Republicans were the minority party in the 90th Congress and were in the minority in sixteen of the eighteen previous Congresses. The immediate prospects of the Republicans becoming a permanent majority party do not appear very bright.[7]

---

[7] That is, as is amply supported in the survey data of the Survey Research Center of the University of Michigan, though the Republicans may win either the

SPECIAL PROBLEMS

A variety of special problems were encountered in doing the research for this book. I identify these so as to alert colleagues to the complications of this type of research — not to discourage such endeavors or to apologize for the present effort. First and foremost was the problem associated with accomplishing the overall goal of the study. My major purpose is to identify the patterns of activities of the minority party in Congress under different political conditions. I am seeking some rather broad generalizations, fitting political conditions to policy-making strategies and measuring the extent to which the minority party realizes its potential. In order to accomplish this goal, it was necessary to do some rather unscientific probing into a Congress. As the aim of the study was to develop some sense of the general patterns of minority party action, in-depth studies of action in individual Congresses were not essential. This is not to say that I have not made an effort to analyze each Congress with care. I have relied on a great diversity of materials for clues as to the political conditions, strategies, and actions of the minority party. And throughout the book I refer to literature that might be consulted for further information.[8]

A second problem is directly related to that discussed above. Throughout I have tried to focus on the minority party *qua* minority party, attempting to separate what minority party members do as individuals from what they do as a party. In particular, I have searched for those instances when the party developed policy positions, when party leaders pressed for party stands on issues, and when a party strategy as such was evident in the policy-making action on an issue. Often this search was in vain.

A third problem in accomplishing the goals of the study results from the difficulty in comparing the Democratic and Republican

---

White House or Congress (perhaps even both) on occasion, they have consistently remained the minority party in terms of voter identification. Democrats vote for Republicans, but there has been no postwar shift in numbers of Democrats or new voters who claim identity with the Republican Party; if anything, the reverse has been the case. See in particular Angus Campbell, *et al.*, *The American Voter* (New York: Wiley, 1960).

[8] For a listing of much of this literature, see Charles O. Jones and Randall B. Ripley, *The Role of Political Parties in Congress: A Bibliography and Research Guide* (Tucson, Ariz.: University of Arizona Press, 1966).

parties as minority parties. Cycles of one-party dominance nationally explain this difficulty. Presently, of course, we are in a period of Democratic Party dominance nationally. The Democrats have been in the minority in Congress twice since 1932. During the 80th Congress the Republicans had a healthy margin in the House and a narrow margin in the Senate, but Democrat Harry S Truman was in the White House. During the 83rd Congress, the Republicans had very narrow margins in both houses, and Republican Dwight D. Eisenhower was in the White House. Neither instance provides a firm base for making significant comparisons with the Republicans in their various minority party situations between 1932 and the present. One is forced to go back to the 1920's for comparisons. But the problems in comparing a Democratic minority party under certain political conditions before 1932 with a Republican minority under vastly different political conditions after 1932 are virtually insurmountable.

Fourth, I experienced more problems than I expected in collecting data for study. The data sources for Congresses in this century are uneven in quantity and quality. The Congressional Quarterly's various publications serve admirably for recent Congresses as a significant supplement to government documents, newspapers, and the many contemporary sophisticated analyses of Congress by political scientists. The literature and source materials for earlier Congresses in this century are considerably more limited, however. In some cases, accounts of events are totally unreliable because different sources provide different facts regarding the same event. Further, there may be a detailed account of a party caucus during one session of Congress, in *The New York Times* for example, and no mention of a crucial caucus during the next session of Congress.[9] Eventually, perhaps, many of the facts of congressional behavior will be neatly catalogued on computer tape so that the scholar will not have to spend most of his time digging and searching for details. That day will, indeed, be a joyful one. In the meantime, however, any analysis of the sort attempted here will have to be based on "bits and pieces" collected from a variety of sources, many of which are of questionable reliability.

Finally, it will become apparent in the next chapter that I toss more balls into the air than any juggler with five thumbs on each

[9] For a more detailed discussion of this problem, see Jones and Ripley, pp. 1–13.

hand can be expected to handle. Any one of the variables identified deserves separate and lengthy study. As the study unfolds, it is important to recall that my purpose is to identify general patterns — i.e., the political conditions under which a minority party in Congress acts, the strategies available for participating in the process of majority building, and actual performance of the minority party in various strategic situations.

CHAPTER TWO

Significant Political Conditions
for Minority Parties

The specific behavior of the minority party in any one Congress depends on a combination of conditions: constitutional arrangements, political circumstances inside and outside Congress, and the nature of specific issues. Constitutional conditions are relatively stable over time. The others are more likely to change from one Congress to the next or, particularly in the case of issues, within a Congress from one week to the next. The significance of these conditions is that they ultimately determine the range of strategies available to the minority party as it participates in the various stages of the political process. The principal emphasis here is on political conditions.

CONSTITUTIONAL CONDITIONS

When one considers the constitutional environment for political parties in this country, it is not surprising that American parties are decentralized and generally lack a guiding program. The founding fathers displayed considerable skill in distributing power throughout the political system. Federalism, representation, and separation of powers, all have the important effect of limiting what the minority party can accomplish.[1] In distributing power between a central unit and subunits, federalism, when combined with democracy, also dis-

[1] See Austin Ranney and Willmoore Kendall, *Democracy and the American Party System* (New York: Harcourt, Brace, 1956), Part 6, for discussion of the effect of the governmental system on the American party system. It should be noted that in setting limits on party activity and potential, the Constitution also provides opportunities. Thus, the term "limits" is meant only to indicate the boundaries within which parties operate in this country.

tributes elective offices throughout the land. Political parties exist to fill these offices and therefore may be expected to organize wherever elections take place.

The representation system was carefully designed to ensure representation from all the component parts of the federal system. The states are represented as sovereign units in the Senate, the numbers of people in each state not being a consideration. They are represented by population in the House and by both systems (sovereignty and population) in the Electoral College. To complicate matters further, the president, senators, and representatives were all given terms of different lengths. Thus, the system of representation "locks in" the federal condition in the national government. Political parties must live with it.

One could conceive of a political system characterized by federalism and representation but without separation of powers in the national government. The founding fathers rejected any such combination and divided power yet again. The representatives of the federal units and the nation have a significant measure of independence in exercising power, with only very limited constitutional provisions for coordinating action among the semiautonomous branches. But just in case coordination were possible, our framers included a system of checks and balances whereby each branch would have certain powers to check the other branches. A sort of "mutual suspicion" was built into the governmental process at the national level, a suspicion, and jealousy, which continues to exist and influence policy making today.

These and other constitutional conditions help to explain the decentralization, lack of cohesion, and lack of "responsibility" (as the "two-party responsibility school" defines that term) of American political parties.[2] These characteristics may be accepted as givens in analyzing the actions of the minority party in Congress.

Another constitutional condition is less national in its effect. Bicameralism is, perhaps, the most outstanding characteristic of our national legislature. The House and Senate share truly significant political power — a fact which practically assures that the Congress

---

[2] The "party responsibility" literature is familiar to students of Congress. The two principal sources are: American Political Science Association, "Toward a More Responsible Two-Party System," *American Political Science Review*, Vol. 44 (September, 1950), Supplement; and E. E. Schattschneider, *Party Government* (New York: Farrar & Rinehart, 1942).

is *sui generis* among national legislatures in the world (though many state legislatures have true bicameralism).

For present purposes, the significance of bicameralism is that minority parties exist in both the Senate and the House of Representatives. It may well be, as indeed it has been, that the party which is the minority in one house will be the majority in the other. Since 1861, there have been a total of eight Congresses in which the minority party was not the same in both houses (44th, 45th, 48th, 49th, 50th, 52nd, 62nd, and 72nd). Further, and more relevant for this study, even when the same party is the minority in both houses, the nature of the two chambers is so different that the role of the minority party is different in each. The Senate and House minority parties will vary in size, leadership, and organization; and it is likely that different political conditions will exist for each. It is necessary, therefore, to separate these two units in our analysis.

POLITICAL CONDITIONS OUTSIDE CONGRESS

I have identified four political conditions outside Congress and six inside Congress which potentially and in combination have an important bearing on minority party behavior there. Those outside Congress include: temper of the times, relative political strength of the minority party, national party unity, and presidential power.

The "temper of the times" is extremely difficult to measure with any precision. I will rely on fairly crude estimates here. Of particular interest is whether a domestic or international crisis is of such proportion as to create a mood for action in Congress and the executive. Problems obviously develop in defining a crisis and determining when it becomes a source of power for the majority party or acts to limit the minority party. Evidence abounds to demonstrate the crisis nature of the 73rd Congress, Franklin D. Roosevelt's first, and the war Congresses. In the post-World War II Congresses, however, the frequent domestic and international crises have not resulted in a clear, identifiable mood for action. Typically, therefore, the temper of the times is not a dominant condition in explaining the role of the minority party in Congress.

The relative strength of the minority party outside Congress is measured in two ways. First, I rely on the concept of voter partisan identification as developed by the Survey Research Center at the University of Michigan. The SRC analysts have concluded that "few factors are of greater importance for our national elections than the lasting attachment of tens of millions of Americans to one of the parties." [3] Before 1932, a majority of Americans presumably attached themselves to the Republican Party (though no survey data are available for that period). Since 1932, a majority of Americans presumably have identified themselves with the Democratic Party.[4] If the minority party in Congress is the majority party in terms of voter partisan preference in the nation (as was the case in 1947–1948 and 1953–1954), it is assumed that, other things being equal, the party will have an important source of strength which will make a difference in congressional policy making.

The second measure of importance is whether the minority party in Congress has a president in the White House. Again, one may expect different behavior by the minority party under these circumstances than if the congressional majority party has control of the White House.

One party has dominated the presidency, Congress, and national voter identification during forty-six years out of sixty-eight studied here (68 per cent) (see Table 2.1). The Democrats have been dominant during twenty-six years, the Republicans during twenty. There are fourteen different combinations of split control, of which six have been experienced since 1900. The most frequently occurring combinations are those where the minority party in Congress and the nation has been able to capture the White House (combinations 6 and 11) or where the majority party in the nation has been unable to control either Congress or the White House (combinations 5 and 12). Only two Congresses have been characterized by split control between the House and Senate (combination 15) and only one, the famous 80th Congress, witnessed the unusual phenomenon whereby the majority party in the nation controlled the White House but not Congress.

The third condition in this category is majority and minority party unity outside Congress. Occasionally disunity within the party among groups outside Congress has resulted in serious disunity within Congress. Indeed, the Republicans in 1912 can attribute their loss of

---

[3] Angus Campbell, *et al.*, *The American Voter* (New York: Wiley, 1960), p. 121.

[4] *Ibid.*, p. 124. See also the other voting studies: Paul Lazarsfeld *et al.*, *The People's Choice* (New York: Duell, Sloan & Pearce, 1944); Bernard Berelson, *et al.*, *Voting* (Chicago: University of Chicago Press, 1954); and Angus Campbell, *et al.*, *The Voter Decides* (Evanston, Ill.: Row, Peterson, 1954).

TABLE 2.1

COMBINATIONS OF THE TWO PARTIES SHARING DOMINANCE
OF THE HOUSE, SENATE, PRESIDENCY, AND NATIONAL
VOTER IDENTIFICATION, 1901–1969

Combi- nation	Democrats control	Republicans control	Occurring in
1	NPI, PR, HO, SE[a]	————	1933–47, 1949–53, 1961–69 (26 yrs.)
2	NPI, PR, SE	HO	————
3	NPI, PR, HO	SE	————
4	NPI, PR	HO, SE	1947–49 (2 yrs.)
5	NPI	PR, SE, HO	1953–55 (2 yrs.)
6	NPI, SE, HO	PR	1955–61 (6 yrs.)
7	NPI, HO	PR, SE	————
8	NPI, SE	PR, HO	————
9	PR, HO	NPI, SE	————
10	PR, SE	NPI, HO	————
11	PR	NPI, HO, SE	1919–21 (2 yrs.)
12	PR, SE, HO	NPI	1913–19 (6 yrs.)
13	SE, HO	NPI, PR	————
14	SE	NPI, PR, HO	————
15	HO	NPI, PR, SE	1911–13, 1931–33 (4 yrs.)
16	————	NPI, PR, SE, HO	1901–11, 1921–31 (20 yrs.)

[a] Key: NPI — national partisan identification of voters; PR — presidency; HO — House of Representatives; SE — Senate.

Congress and the White House to their inability to unite the two principal wings of the party. The 1912 disaster for the Republican Party represents the extreme in party disunity, but there are other significant examples too: Republican disunity during the 1920's, Democratic disunity in 1948, Democratic disunity in the 1960's.

The final condition is of greater constant significance as an explanatory variable than the first three. Presidential power becomes a major factor in setting limits on minority party behavior. In analyzing presidential power I rely to a considerable extent on the writings of Professor Richard E. Neustadt. A strong president is one who has available, and utilizes, a number of sources of power. Neustadt summarizes these sources as follows:

> First are the bargaining advantages inherent in his job with which to persuade other men that what he wants of them is what their own responsibilities require them to do. Second are the expectations of those other men regarding his ability

TABLE 2.2

RATING THE PRESIDENTS BY SOURCES OF
POWER, 1901–1969

SOURCES OF POWER[a]

President	Bargaining advantages	View of ability	Estimate of public view	Style	Overall rating
McKinley	X[b]	/[b]	X	O[b]	Moderately strong
Roosevelt	/	/	X	X	Moderately strong
Taft	O	/	O	O	Weak
Wilson	X	X	O	X	Strong (to weak)[c]
Harding	X	O	/	O	Weak
Coolidge	/	O	X	O	Weak
Hoover	O	/	O	/	Moderately weak (to weak)[c]
Roosevelt	X	/	X	X	Strong
Truman	/	O	O	X	Moderately weak
Eisenhower	/	O	X	O	Weak
Kennedy	X	X	O	X	Moderately strong
Johnson	X	X	X	X	Strong (to moderately weak)[c]

[a] As identified by Richard E. Neustadt in *Presidential Power* (New York: Wiley, 1960).

[b] Key: X = definitely a source of power; / = a partial source of power; O = extremely limited as a source of power.

[c] Wilson, Hoover, and Johnson experienced dramatic shifts in their sources of power. Wilson had impressive sources of power during his first term, few sources during his second term. Hoover experienced a significant shift almost immediately. Johnson's sources of power lasted from the Kennedy assassination until the 1966 elections.

and will to use the various advantages they think he has. Third are those men's estimates of how his public views him and of how their publics may view them if they do what he wants.[5]

The measure of strength in the office is not confined to whether these advantages actually exist but must include whether the man in the White House is able to make use of these advantages.

In this analysis "presidential power" is very much a dependent variable. A president may have advantages because of existing political conditions. For example, President Franklin D. Roosevelt drew strength from the temper of the times. President Dwight D. Eisen-

[5] Richard E. Neustadt, *Presidential Power: The Politics of Leadership* (New York: Wiley, 1960), p. 179.

hower was personally popular but was handicapped by not having control of Congress.

Table 2.2 represents an extremely risky, but essential, venture — the rating of presidents of this century by the Neustadt criteria. This is risky because it represents only my educated hunches about applying the measures to the man. Further, attaching an overall rating to a president is troublesome because his sources of strength may well change — e.g., Woodrow Wilson, Herbert Hoover, and Lyndon B. Johnson. The attempt is important, however, in that it gives the reader a sense of how I intend to use the term "presidential power" in this volume, and why I rate the presidents as I do.

POLITICAL CONDITIONS INSIDE CONGRESS

A large number of internal conditions may also affect minority party behavior in the legislative process. Six will receive consideration here: procedure, size of the margin, majority party leadership and organization, length of time in the minority, and relative strength of the party in the other house.

Senate and House procedures are normally quite stable; major changes occur infrequently. From time to time, however, significant procedural changes are made which influence the effectiveness of the minority party. The most significant changes in this century — perhaps in the history of Congress — occurred in 1910–1911 when the Speaker of the House lost many of his formal powers. Of course, these changes were in large measure attributable to internal disputes within the dominant Republican Party, but the result was to diffuse power in both parties. Other changes of importance were those made in 1946 for both houses,[6] the two-year experiments with the 21-day rule in the 81st and the 89th Congresses, and the series of changes affecting the House Committee on Rules between 1961 and 1965.

The size of the margin for the majority party over the minority party has varied in the House from a low of 2 for the Republicans following the 1930 elections (actually the Democrats organized the House in the 72nd Congress as a result of deaths of Republican members before the opening of Congress) to a high of 244 for the

---

[6] These were the changes in committees, staff, and procedure made in the Legislative Reorganization Act of 1946. See the forthcoming book by Joseph Cooper on congressional reform (Brookings Institution).

Democrats following the 1936 elections (see Table 2.3). In the Senate, the variation has been from the narrow margin of 1 seat in the 66th, 70th, 72nd, 82nd, 83rd, and 84th Congresses to 58 seats for the Democrats in the 75th Congress. A wide margin for the majority party normally places severe restrictions on the range of strategies available to the minority party, but under certain circumstances the minority party has flexibility despite relatively small numbers.

An otherwise disadvantageous minority party situation may be enhanced considerably by weak majority party leadership and organization, combined with strong minority party leadership and organization. As with presidential power, effective party leadership in the House and Senate depends to a great extent on the men holding leadership positions. Party organization is not inherently strong; quite the reverse. For present purposes, the effective party leader is one who understands the political context within which Congress legislates, recognizes his own sources of power, organizes his party accordingly, and takes full advantage of the openness of the system and the options available to him. Even when the minority party is hopelessly outnumbered, an imaginative and resourceful leader can assist the party to realize some of its goals.

The length of time in the minority may well have an important effect on the role of the minority party. The Republican Party has been in the majority only twice since 1930 in the House and twice since 1932 in the Senate (see Table 2.3). Only once, in the 83rd Congress, did the Republicans control both Congress and the White House. When President Eisenhower was inaugurated, only one of his congressional party leaders (Joseph W. Martin, Jr.), 15 House Republicans of 221, and no Senate Republicans, had served under a Republican President before. The President himself made reference to "the unfamiliarity of Republicans with either the techniques or the need of cooperating with the Executive." [7] Obviously, the leaders of a party in the minority over a long period of time will be members who are from safe districts and thus have been able to survive majority party landslides. The selection procedure for standing committee leadership is based on this principle. It is a perfectly reasonable hypothesis that a party that becomes accustomed to being

---

[7] Dwight D. Eisenhower, *Mandate for Change* (Garden City, N.Y.: Doubleday, 1963), p. 192.

TABLE 2.3
SIZE OF MARGIN, MAJORITY PARTY OVER MINORITY
PARTY, HOUSE AND SENATE, 1900–1968[a]

Margins

Election year	Congress	HOUSE		SENATE	
		GOP margin over Demos	Demos margin over GOP	GOP margin over Demos	Demos margin over GOP
1900	57	45	—	27	—
1902	58	29	—	26	—
1904	59	114	—	26	—
1906	60	58	—	32	—
1908	61	47	—	27	—
1910	62	—	163	—	7
1912	63	—	38	—	17
1914	64	—	66	7	—
1916	65	6[b]	—	—	11
1918	66	46	—	1	—
1920	67	168	—	22	—
1922	68	18	—	8	—
1924	69	64	—	14	—
1926	70	42	—	1	—
1928	71	104	—	17	—
1930	72	2[c]	—	1	—
1932	73	—	196	—	23
1934	74	—	219	—	44
1936	75	—	244	—	58
1938	76	—	93	—	46
1940	77	—	105	—	38
1942	78	—	13	—	19
1944	79	—	53	—	19
1946	80	58	—	6	—
1948	81	—	92	—	8
1950	82	—	35	—	1
1952	83	8	—	1	—
1954	84	—	29	—	1
1956	85	—	33	—	2
1958	86	—	129	—	32
1960	87	—	89	—	28
1962	88	—	83	—	36
1964	89	—	155	—	36
1966	90	—	61	—	28

[a] Figures represent the margins immediately following the election. Changes between the elections are not reflected.

[b] Though the Republicans had a slim majority over the Democrats following the elections, enough Progressives voted with the Democrats to organize the House.

[c] Deaths of Republicans following the 1930 election resulted in a slim majority for the Democrats by the time Congress met in 1931.

the party of criticism, obstruction, and opposition may develop a "minority party mentality." Those who survived over a long period of time may even substitute individual satisfactions gained from opposing or accommodating the majority party for the politically rational goal of attaining majority party status. The minority may find itself in the anomalous position of perpetuating *itself* in a semipermanent minority status. The implications of these developments for the legislative system are fascinating to ponder.

The antidote to a developing "minority party mentality" is the constant influx of new blood — of freshman minority party members. Old members die, retire, or are defeated in primaries; Democrats are replaced by Republicans and vice versa. These new members of the two houses temper the trend toward the "minority party mentality"; if enough of them are elected at any one time, they may be successful in changing the whole nature of the party (including the leadership). At the same time, as with every social institution, a socialization process occurs in the minority party which may include developing the "minority party mentality."

The last internal condition to be considered here is the relative strength, leadership, and organization of the party in the other house. This would not normally be a major factor in determining the role of the minority party, as wide discrepancies in the relative size of the margin between the two houses are infrequent. Exceptions exist, however, and these will be discussed. Also in rare instances the strength of leadership in one body becomes a factor in the role of the party in the other house.

ISSUE CONDITIONS

The role of the minority party during a congressional session may also vary depending on the issues before Congress. Certain issues divide the majority, making minority party behavior crucial to the outcome. Other issues divide the minority, neutralizing its potential influence on the outcome (e.g., civil rights for the Democrats, foreign trade for the Republicans). Some issues are determined by leaders to be of significance for minority party goals, while others are not.

No systematic attempt has been made here to analyze the variation in minority party behavior by issues. I will illustrate strategies employed on different issues, but I have not undertaken the enormous task of analyzing issues as independent variables in determining either party actions or the political conditions for a Congress.

MINORITY PARTY STRATEGIES

A number of strategies are available to the minority party, depending on the combination of conditions that exist at the time. These strategies range from those which are very limited in terms of goal achievement to those perceived to be highly contributory. Certain of them are relied on in the early stages (subcommittee and committee stages); others are employed in the later stages (final committee stage, calendar stage, floor stage).

When I speak of "relying on" or "employing" a strategy, I am referring to party leadership behavior. But party leaders' efforts are not always very well coordinated. The party leader in a standing committee (including the important House Committee on Rules) or a subcommittee is normally its ranking minority member. Party leaders for the House or Senate minority party are the floor leaders, whips, party committee and conference chairmen. A strategy employed within a committee or subcommittee may or may not (usually not) be the result of consultation among all party leaders in the chamber. Further, the party plays no role at all in many matters before Congress, either because of the nature of the issue, or because of the rules of the game in the committee, or for some personal reason.[8] As a result, a number of strategies are employed by different party leaders at various stages of the legislative process. And these strategies are not always compatible.

The following list of strategies incorporates those typically employed by the minority party in the process of majority building in

[8] Most students of Congress accept the conclusion that the influence of party is generally pervasive in Congress, though the problems of sorting out its precise influence are duly noted by all. See David R. Mayhew, *Party Loyalty Among Congressmen* (Cambridge: Harvard University Press, 1966); Julius Turner, *Party and Constituency: Pressures on Congress* (Baltimore: Johns Hopkins Press, 1951); David B. Truman, *The Congressional Party: A Case Study* (New York: Wiley, 1959); Malcolm E. Jewell and Samuel C. Patterson, *The Legislative Process in the United States* (New York: Random House, 1966), Ch. 17; William J. Keefe and Morris S. Ogul, *The American Legislative Process: Congress and the States* (Englewood Cliffs, N.J.: Prentice-Hall, 1964), Ch. 8.

Congress. The particular combination relied on depends on political conditions.

Support — The minority party actually supports the majority-building efforts of the majority party, contributing votes and, in some cases, leadership.

Inconsequential opposition — The minority party opposes, but its efforts are largely inconsequential to the majority party.

Withdrawal — The minority party simply does not attempt to take a position on a significant issue, probably because of intraparty divisions.

Cooperation — The minority party cooperates with the majority party in building majorities, including taking the initiative in efforts to formulate courses of action in such a way as to gain acceptance in committee and on the floor.

Innovation — The minority party develops courses of action on its own and attempts to build majorities in favor.

Consequential partisan opposition — The minority party opposes the coalition-building efforts of the majority party but does not counter with proposals of its own.[9]

Consequential constructive opposition — The minority party opposes the efforts of the majority party and counters with its own proposals for acting on the problem at hand.

Participation — The minority party is in the position of having to build majorities consistently because it controls the White House.

A minority party may employ several of these strategies during a single session of Congress. One measure of the minority party's strength is the extent to which its leaders are able to adapt the strategy to the policy-making situation. Further, different strategies may be employed on the same piece of legislation as it works its way through the stages of the legislative process. For example, cooperation or innovation may be employed during the formative stages (subcommittee and early committee action), and partisan opposi-

---

[9] In his paper presented to the American Political Science Association, Professor Robert L. Peabody illustrates the partisan opposition strategy when quoting a House Republican: "When the party gets the scent of blood, it wants to deal a death blow. It wants to knock out what the other side is proposing, completely." See Peabody, "House Republican Leadership: Change and Consolidation in a Minority Party," paper prepared for delivery at the 1966 Annual Meeting of the American Political Science Association, Statler-Hilton Hotel, New York City, September 6–10, 1966, p. 26.

tion or constructive opposition or support may be relied on during the later stages (final committee and floor action).

The classification of each Congress in Tables 2.4 and 2.5 is based on my examination of the existing political conditions and their effect on the minority party's strategic options. Typically, party unity and presidential power among the external conditions, and size of margin and party leadership among internal conditions, were important in my classifications. In some cases resourceful party leaders

TABLE 2.4
RANGE OF STRATEGIES FOR THE MINORITY PARTY
IN THE HOUSE OF REPRESENTATIVES,
57TH–90TH CONGRESSES

Congress	Year	Minority party	Range of strategies
57	1901–2	Democratic	Restricted
58	1903–4	Democratic	Restricted
59	1905–6	Democratic	Restricted
60	1907–8	Democratic	Moderately unrestricted
61	1909–10	Democratic	Unrestricted
62	1911–12	Republican	Participating (weak)
63	1913–14	Republican	Severely restricted
64	1915–16	Republican	Restricted
65	1917–18	Republican	Unrestricted
66	1919–20	Democratic	Participating (weak)
67	1921–22	Democratic	Restricted
68	1923–24	Democratic	Unrestricted
69	1925–26	Democratic	Moderately unrestricted
70	1927–28	Democratic	Unrestricted
71	1929–30	Democratic	Unrestricted
72	1931–32	Republican	Participating (weak)
73	1933–34	Republican	Severely restricted
74	1935–36	Republican	Severely restricted
75	1937–38	Republican	Severely restricted
76	1939–40	Republican	Moderately unrestricted
77	1941–42	Republican	Moderately unrestricted
78	1943–44	Republican	Unrestricted
79	1945–46	Republican	Unrestricted
80	1947–48	Democratic	Participating (moderate)
81	1949–50	Republican	Moderately unrestricted
82	1951–52	Republican	Unrestricted
83	1953–54	Democratic	Unrestricted
84	1955–56	Republican	Participating (weak)
85	1957–58	Republican	Participating (weak)
86	1959–60	Republican	Participating (weak)
87	1961–62	Republican	Unrestricted
88	1963–64	Republican	Unrestricted
89	1965–66	Republican	Restricted
90	1967–68	Republican	Unrestricted

TABLE 2.5
RANGE OF STRATEGIES FOR THE MINORITY PARTY
IN THE SENATE, 57TH–90TH CONGRESSES

Congress	Year	Minority party	Range of strategies
57	1901–2	Democratic	Restricted
58	1903–4	Democratic	Restricted
59	1905–6	Democratic	Restricted
60	1907–8	Democratic	Restricted
61	1909–10	Democratic	Moderately unrestricted
62	1911–12	Democratic	Unrestricted
63	1913–14	Republican	Moderately unrestricted
64	1915–16	Republican	Restricted
65	1917–18	Republican	Moderately unrestricted
66	1919–20	Democratic	Participating (weak)
67	1921–22	Democratic	Restricted
68	1923–24	Democratic	Moderately unrestricted
69	1925–26	Democratic	Moderately unrestricted
70	1927–28	Democratic	Unrestricted
71	1929–30	Democratic	Unrestricted
72	1931–32	Democratic	Unrestricted
73	1933–34	Republican	Severely restricted
74	1935–36	Republican	Severely restricted
75	1937–38	Republican	Severely restricted
76	1939–40	Republican	Restricted
77	1941–42	Republican	Restricted
78	1943–44	Republican	Moderately unrestricted
79	1945–46	Republican	Moderately unrestricted
80	1947–48	Democratic	Participating (moderate)
81	1949–50	Republican	Moderately unrestricted
82	1951–52	Republican	Unrestricted
83	1953–54	Democratic	Unrestricted
84	1955–56	Republican	Participating (weak)
85	1957–58	Republican	Participating (weak)
86	1959–60	Republican	Participating (weak)
87	1961–62	Republican	Moderately unrestricted
88	1963–64	Republican	Restricted
89	1965–66	Republican	Restricted
90	1967–68	Republican	Moderately unrestricted

were able to overcome other restrictive conditions and increase the options available to the minority.

GOAL ACHIEVEMENT

It is assumed that the minority party in Congress will act in such a way as to achieve the ultimate goal of majority status. What should a minority do in order to reach this goal? No one can say for certain.

TABLE 2.6

SUMMARY OF CONGRESSES, 57TH–90TH, CLASSIFIED BY RANGE
OF STRATEGIES AVAILABLE TO THE MINORITY PARTY

	Number of Congresses	
Category	House	Senate
Severely restricted	4	3
Restricted	6	10
Participating (weak)	6	4
Participating (moderate)	1	1
Moderately unrestricted	5	10
Unrestricted	12	6
	34	34

Indeed, one of the principal decisions for minority party leaders is to determine what strategies to employ under varying circumstances. My interest here is in trying to discover what decisions are made and can be made given various combinations of working conditions in Congress for the minority party and its leaders. What seem to be optimum strategies for achieving majority party status may turn out not to be so in fact. For example, the minority party may lose heavily at the polls following a Congress in which it had a wide range of strategies and, by other criteria, employed brilliant strategies frequently resulting in minority party victories. What party leaders think is necessary to elevate the minority party to majority status often differs from what actually will make it happen. If the history of elections is any guide, it seems apparent that the congressional record of the minority party is only one of many factors that may result in majority status. Most of these other factors *cannot be controlled by the minority party and its leaders.*

Minority party leaders face an interesting dilemma in their efforts to meet expectations. Consider, for example, the following expectations. On the one hand, the party is expected to behave in the policy process so as to win majority status — a rational political action. On the other hand, it is expected to behave "responsibly" in the policy process, contributing to majority building so that a particular public problem will be solved. To satisfy the first demand, party leaders may seek glamorous issue stands or headline-grabbing victories on policy. Leaders feel pressure to win spectacular victories or at least go down dramatically. If alternatives are to be offered, they should have enough appeal so that the press will pay attention. Ironically, unless the majority party happens to be in trouble by its own making, often much of this public relations activity in the policy process is of very little assistance in winning congressional elections. But party leaders are expected to react in this way, nevertheless.

This activity is very likely to work to the detriment of meeting the second expectation — a responsible and effective role in policy making. The high probability is that the spectacular victory for the minority party will be an essentially "destructive" victory, i.e., a defeat for the majority party, notably for the president.

Given the political context of Congress, in order to meet the second set of expectations, minority party leaders will have to settle for victories that are not dramatic, victories that come in subcommittees and committees, in having clarifying amendments adopted, in minor concessions in conference committees. And it may be that victories of this type result in general satisfaction with the performance of the majority. In the long run, therefore, the so-called constructive opposition ensures that it will not achieve the goal of majority party status. Given the fact that the public retains party loyalty over a long period of time and that only cataclysmic events shake this loyalty, it is easier to stay in office than to gain office. Thus, goal achievement for the minority party is considerably more challenging than for the majority party. The majority party may lack creativity and remain in office; the minority party may be creative and responsible and *not only remain the minority party but even ensure the continued success of the majority party.*

All this analysis suggests a very frustrating existence for the minority party and its leaders. It is no wonder that the study of minority party leadership does not reveal any outstanding leaders. The fact is that the minority party in the American political system is not a very creative instrumentality — and for good reason.

CHAPTER THREE

Leadership and Organization

Until the minority party establishes a viable organization with able leadership, it cannot think of taking part in the majority-building process in Congress. If it builds and maintains an effective organization, it may well escape the restrictions imposed by immediate conditions such as strong presidential leadership, large margin, and procedure. What has been the minority party's experience in getting effective leadership and organization in this century? Can we discover differences between the House and Senate that affect the establishment and maintenance of party organization? Do the two parties differ in their methods?

Effective leadership for the minority party cannot be precisely measured. Party unity in Congress is one test, and it will be relied on here, but other measures can be used. First, an effective leader must be able to rely on some sources of power: national party unity, sizable party membership, members' and opponents' estimates of his ability, personality, and prerogatives of the office. Second, one can evaluate whether the leader in fact capitalized on the sources of power available to him and took full advantage of the strategic options open to the minority party at the time. Third, one can examine the extent to which a party leader succeeds in making the minority party a creative instrument in policy making. By this measure, party leaders go beyond those strategies which existing political conditions permit to develop policy proposals rather than merely reacting to those offered by the majority party or the executive.

THE HOUSE

The House is so much larger than the Senate, or practically any other legislative body in the United States, that it poses special leadership and organizational problems for the political parties:

> There are significant differences between the legislative party in the House and that in the Senate, differences in degree if not in kind which may make the larger group functionally more inclusive, more critical for the survival of its members. Fundamentally, these differences are traceable to the greater size of the House. In a body four and one-half times as large as the Senate, whose parties are larger than those in the upper chamber by approximately the same proportions, the individual member is scarcely visible to the electorate. . . . Even in the Washington arena, where the chance of such association is generally greater than in the geographically nearer seats of government in the states and the localities, a representative, in contrast to a senator, is more likely to be perceived as one member of a party than as a name and a person in his own right.
>
> A member of the House, in short, is almost certainly more dependent than a senator. His dependencies may be many, but one of them is the party, and especially the legislative party.[1]

The greater numbers in the House demand a more formal, centralized organization than is required in the Senate, and yet this size presents a problem in developing that organization. Majority party leaders in the House have been severely limited for this reason, since the revolt of 1910, and minority party leaders have always been tightly limited. Under the best of circumstances, House party leaders lack basic sanctions for enforcing their decisions. Majority party leaders have varied sources of influence over their followers, such as committee assignments, control over the scheduling of legislation, special favors, and control of the rules. But they do not have the ultimate sanction — that of denying the member's reelection to the House.[2] The individual member potentially has an important source

[1] David B. Truman, *The Congressional Party: A Case Study* (New York: Wiley, 1959), p. 194.
[2] See Charles O. Jones, "Joseph G. Cannon and Howard W. Smith: An Essay on the Limits of Leadership in the House of Representatives," *Journal of Politics*, Vol. 29 (August, 1968), pp. 617–46.

of power, too — his option to help form the majority on an issue. Thus, leader-follower relationships in the House are characterized by bargaining, and no majority party leader can afford to take his majority for granted.

The situation is even more precarious for minority party leaders. Though they too have sanctions — e.g., committee assignments, special favors — their range is more restricted than that of majority party leaders. As with the majority leaders, they must persuade followers to "go along" by relying on party appeals. Their most useful argument may well be the essentially negative one (which is in fact highly dubious in its logic and insupportable by evidence) that if enough majority party proposals are defeated, the electorate will turn to the minority party.

Conditions in the House of Representatives limit the options available to party leaders. The successful party leader in the House needs the skills of the cautious negotiator who is not excessively issue-oriented. Flamboyant ideologues of either party do not usually lead the House. On the other hand, if the minority party's goals are to be achieved, party leaders must vigorously and imaginatively pursue them.

PARTY LEADERS. The types of minority party leaders in the House of Representatives are (1) elected party leaders (floor leader, whip, Caucus chairman, Steering or Policy Committee chairman); (2) those who have seniority (most of them will be ranking members of standing committees); and (3) those who have expertise or gain a following for other personal reasons. The first two are of interest in this study.

Elected leaders in the minority party have at their disposal only the most limited sanctions for developing a strong minority party. Even more than the majority party leaders, they must be accommodators and can seldom force compliance with their decisions. Further, their party is plagued with discohesive forces. Individual members are anxious to do what is necessary to stay in office, particularly when the majority party is gradually capturing marginal seats. Thus, they may ignore the pleas of party leaders in favor of satisfying constituents. Majority party leaders may need minority party votes on a proposal and may attract them by relying on the special favors available to them. The minority party that has long been in that position in Congress may well become frustrated with its leadership and change it frequently, resulting in instability.

TABLE 3.1
LEGISLATIVE EXPERIENCE AND SENIORITY RANK OF HOUSE MINORITY
FLOOR LEADERS, 1901–1969, AT ELECTION

Democrats	Age	Years in House	Party seniority rank[a]	Years served in majority
James D. Richardson, Tenn. (1901–2)	55	14	2	8
John S. Williams, Miss. (1903–8)	48	10	13	2
James B. Clark, Mo. (1909–10)[b]	58	14	7	2
James B. Clark, Mo. (1919–20)	69	24	1	8
Claude Kitchin, N.C. (1921–22)	51	20	3	6
Finis J. Garrett, Tenn. (1923–28)	47	18	5	6
John N. Garner, Tex. (1929–30)[b]	60	26	2	6
Sam Rayburn, Tex. (1947–48)[b]	65	34	3	20
Sam Rayburn, Tex. (1953–54)[b]	71	40	1	24
Republicans				
James R. Mann, Ill. (1911–18)	54	14	22	12
Bertrand H. Snell, N.Y. (1931–38)	60	16	28	12
Joseph W. Martin, Jr., Mass. (1939–46)[b]	54	14	23	6
Joseph W. Martin, Jr., Mass. (1949–52)[b]	64	24	7	8
Joseph W. Martin, Jr., Mass. (1955–58)	70	30	4	10
Charles A. Halleck, Ind. (1959–64)	58	24	8	4
Gerald R. Ford, Mich. (1965——)	51	16	13	2

[a] Calculated by number of terms served and alphabetical order.
[b] Served as Speaker in a subsequent Congress.

Among the elected leaders, the floor leader has traditionally been *the* leader of the minority. Twelve men have served in this capacity since 1900 — seven Democrats and five Republicans. Although seniority is not a formal requirement for the position, both parties usually elect members with many years in the House and with relatively high seniority rank (see Table 3.1). Democratic minority floor leaders in this century have had an average of 19.4 years of House service prior to being selected; Republican leaders, 16.8 years. The average age of minority leaders elected in this century has been 58.2 for Democrats and 58.7 for Republicans. Floor leaders come from areas that have traditionally been safe for the party — Democrats from the South, Republicans from the Midwest and Northeast. Of the minority floor leaders in this century, only Charles Halleck of Indiana represented a somewhat marginal congressional district.[3]

[3] In the five elections up to 1968, Halleck's average percentage of the two-party vote in his district was 55.5, ranging from 52.2 in 1958 to 57.6 in 1962.

Republicans have been in the minority for twenty-one of the thirty-four Congresses since 1900. Quite naturally then, a Republican holds the record for longevity as minority floor leader. Joseph W. Martin, Jr., served sixteen years in that capacity. James R. Mann and Bertrand H. Snell each served eight years. Only two Democrats, John S. Williams and Finis J. Garrett, served more than two terms each as minority floor leader. Each served six years.

Though Republican minority floor leaders have had longer average tenure than Democrats, they have more frequently ended their service by defeat in the House Republican Party. Of the five Republican minority floor leaders in this century, three were ousted by their colleagues. Mann was defeated for the speakership by Frederick H. Gillett of Massachusetts when the Republicans organized the 66th Congress, despite the fact that Mann had served eight years as the party's leader.[4] Martin was defeated by Halleck in 1959 in a battle for floor leadership and Halleck in turn was defeated by Gerald R. Ford in 1965. Of those who have completed their service, only Snell was able to retire voluntarily. Of course, Martin twice served as speaker.

The Democrats, on the other hand, have ousted none of their minority leaders in this century. The leaders have either retired voluntarily (Richardson, Williams, Garrett), been elevated to the speakership (Clark the first time, Garner and Rayburn twice), died (Kitchin), or been defeated for reelection (Clark the second time).

The eleven minority whips in this century, six Republicans and five Democrats, have been considerably less senior than the leaders upon election — 9.8 years of service on the average for the Democrats and only 6.8 years for the Republicans.[5] As with the floor leaders, they have usually come from the party's strongest regions. The minority whip at this writing, Leslie C. Arends of Illinois, has the longest service in this capacity, twenty years (he also served

---

[4] On the defeat of Mann by Gillett, see Chang-wei Chiu, *The Speaker of the House of Representatives Since 1896* (New York: Columbia University Press, 1928), pp. 25–27. Mann was challenged both on his close association with Cannon and on his dedication to the war effort. The caucus vote was: Gillett 138, Mann 69, others 18.

[5] See Randall B. Ripley, "The Party Whip Organizations in the United States House of Representatives," *American Political Science Review*, Vol. 58 (September, 1964), pp. 561–76. See also Lyn Shepard, "Cracking the Whip in the House," *Christian Science Monitor*, January 27, 1968, p. 9.

four years as majority whip). Only one other minority whip, Harry Englebright of California, served more than four terms. In neither party has the minority whip been defeated for reelection as whip, though Arends was seriously challenged in 1965. The Republicans and Democrats differ in one respect in whip selection. The Democrats have had the former majority leader, John W. Mc-Cormack, assume the whip's position when they were in the minority. The Republicans kept Arends as whip when they reverted to the minority following the 1948 and 1954 elections.

The Caucus or Conference chairman has not been a major figure in either party until recently. The Democrats traditionally have changed their chairman in each Congress, using the position to honor a member. The Republicans have usually given their chairman longer tenure. The record holder is Roy O. Woodruff of Michigan, who served in this capacity for seven terms, once as majority Caucus chairman. In recent years, the Republican Conference chairman has become a major party figure. In 1963, a number of younger members organized a revolt, ousted the incumbent chairman, Charles B. Hoeven of Iowa, and elected Gerald R. Ford of Michigan in his place. These members argued that the Conference had the potential of becoming a useful policy unit. In 1965 Ford successfully challenged Halleck for the post of floor leader and Melvin R. Laird of Wisconsin became the Conference chairman. Generally recognized as an important leader in the Republican Party, nationally as well as in the House, Laird organized the Conference into a number of task groups for doing research on major public problems.

Although it has received much attention from congressional re-formers, the Steering or Policy Committee has never gained much favor with the members themselves. The Democrats as a minority have never relied on such a group. The Republicans used one during the second Wilson administration, with the floor leader serving as chairman. In 1949 the House Republicans created a Policy Committee with the floor leader as chairman. It was not until 1959, however, that this unit developed any significance. At that time, House Republicans separated the positions of floor leader and Policy Committee chairman. The House Republican Policy Committee has since become a major party unit and was involved in the intraparty power struggles during the 1960's. Like the Conference, it has been used by younger members as a mechanism for expressing themselves. Only two men, John W. Byrnes of Wisconsin and John J. Rhodes of Arizona, have served as chairman since 1959.

Ranking minority members of standing committees have become major party leaders since the speaker's power was curbed in 1910–1911. Formerly the speaker could appoint chairmen, and though seniority was relied on as an important criterion for appointment, the speaker could remove chairmen and violate seniority in appointments. Speaker Joe Cannon of Illinois chose to do so frequently in the 61st Congress.[6] The speaker could also appoint minority members to committees. Partly to divide the minority, Cannon agreed to allow it to perform this task while John S. Williams was minority leader, as Cannon and his cohorts concluded that the minority leader "would become involved in all sorts of petty difficulties with his followers."[7] When the seniority system was established as the primary means of selecting chairmen and ranking minority members, committee chairmen gained extensive autonomy.

Until the 61st Congress, it was the custom to have the minority leader also serve as the ranking minority member on the two most powerful committees, Rules and Ways and Means. Thus, coordination was built in between party leadership on the floor and these two major committees. Since that time, the diffusion of leadership has often resulted in a lack of coordination between the leadership on the floor and in committees. Only in recent years, with the development of the House Republican Policy Committee, has any attempt been made to establish formal coordination among these various leaders, and even this effort has been weak.

As with other party leaders, the ranking minority members of standing committees are from regions that are party strongholds. Since 1900, sixteen men have served as ranking minority members on the Committee on Rules — six Democrats and ten Republicans. Of the six Democrats four were from the South and one was from

---

[6] For significant studies of seniority, see George Goodwin, "The Seniority System in Congress," *American Political Science Review*, Vol. 53 (June, 1959), pp. 412–36, and Nelson W. Polsby, *et al.*, "The Growth of the Seniority System in the United States House of Representatives," *American Political Science Review*, Vol. 63 (September, 1969), pp. 787–807. For observations on Cannon, see Jones, *Journal of Politics*, Vol. 29 (August, 1968), pp. 619–24.

[7] William R. Gwinn, *Uncle Joe Cannon, Archfoe of Insurgency: A History of the Rise and Fall of Cannonism* (New York: Bookman Associates, 1957), p. 97.

Chicago; of the ten Republicans four were from the Northeast and five were from the Midwest. A similar pattern emerges for the sixteen men who have served as ranking minority member of the Committee on Ways and Means and the nine men who have served as ranking minority member of the Committee on Appropriations since 1900.

Until recently the principal leadership posts in the minority party were those of floor leader and ranking minority members of the standing committees. Members in these positions have been senior, from safe areas, and with a relatively high average age upon election. They have survived the many minority party defeats. They are what is left. Interestingly, these same characteristics apply to majority party leaders. The fact is that the House has been led by old men who seldom needed to worry about reelection. For the minority party these characteristics have special meaning. By definition the minority party has a number of disadvantages, but some of these can be overcome by vigorous, imaginative, and resourceful leadership. For the most part, these have not been characteristics of minority party leaders in this century; quite the reverse.

Other party posts were not of great significance in either party until the 1960's, when the Republicans attempted to find uses for both the Conference and the Policy Committee. Younger members especially have relied on these units to revitalize the House Republican Party.

PATTERNS OF LEADERSHIP. Randall B. Ripley identifies three patterns of minority party leadership in the House: "minority leader," "disorganized," and "collegial." [8] By minority leader, he means that leadership is essentially centered in the floor leader; disorganized refers to a "lack of purposeful leadership"; and collegial describes the situation where a group of leaders is in control (see Table 3.2).

These patterns are reasonably reliable and informative, but some refinements are necessary. Leadership may be focused in the floor leader and yet his sources of power may be quite weak. In the Congresses early in this century, the minority party continued to gain strength as the majority party became more and more divided, but the speaker continued to dominate the House. When James R. Mann became minority leader in 1911, he had few sources of power.

[8] Randall B. Ripley, *Party Leaders in the House of Representatives* (Washington, D.C.: The Brookings Institution, 1967), pp. 102–10.

TABLE 3.2

PATTERNS OF MINORITY PARTY LEADERSHIP IN THE
HOUSE OF REPRESENTATIVES, 1901–1969

Congress	Minority party	Minority leader	Pattern of leadership[a]
57	D	Richardson	Disorganized (lack of leadership)
58–61	D	Williams, Clark	Minority leader (weak)
62–65	R	Mann	Minority leader (weak to moderately strong)
66–71	D	Clark, Kitchin, Garrett, Garner	Disorganized (lack of leadership)
72–75	R	Snell	Disorganized (lack of leadership and weak in numbers)
76–79, 81–82, 84–85	R	Martin	Minority leader (strong)
80, 83	D	Rayburn	Minority leader (strong)
86–88	R	Halleck	Collegial (involuntary)
89–90	R	Ford	Collegial (voluntary)

[a] Based on categories in Randall B. Ripley, *Party Leaders in the House of Representatives* (Washington, D.C.: The Brookings Institution, 1967), with refinements suggested by the specific circumstances of the Congresses in question.

His party was seriously divided and few in numbers. During his last term, on the other hand, Mann had more resources — somewhat greater party unity, more House Republicans, a weakened President Wilson. Joseph W. Martin had several advantages. He was elected floor leader following the first major Republican comeback in 1938 (when they increased their numbers by 80 seats). During the eight terms Martin served as minority leader, the House Republicans averaged 188 members (ranging from 162 to 209). During two of his terms, Martin served a Republican president. Despite these strengths, serious questions about his effectiveness arose, particularly during his last four years.

The other minority floor leader who fits this first category is Sam Rayburn. He, too, had many sources of strength. During his first term as minority leader he served a Democratic president. During his second term, he headed a strong minority party in Congress, one that was only temporarily out of power.

Although the individual leader may well fit the minority leader pattern of leadership, any leader has strengths and weaknesses that should be accounted for in describing patterns. We may suggest gradations of this category according to the strength of the minority leader. Rayburn would certainly be classified a strong minority leader, as would Martin for most of his career. Williams and Clark had some strengths, but they led their party when the speaker had unusually impressive powers. Mann ranged from weak to moderately strong.

Ripley's other categories are also very useful as general descriptions but need refinement. Certainly the disorganization of the Democrats during the 1920's differs from that of the Republicans during the 1930's. With the exception of the 67th Congress, when they had only 132 members, the House Democrats were strong in numbers and because of the Republican Party's continued divisiveness. The Democrats had an average of 187 members during the 68th–71st Congresses. Although their effect is difficult to measure because of the low production of these Congresses, they were certainly more important as a minority than the Republicans during the early 1930's.

Bertrand H. Snell had almost no sources of strength as minority leader between 1931 and 1939. The average membership of the House Republican Party under Snell was 131. Including only the 73rd to 75th Congresses, the average membership was 103 out of 435. Disorganization describes Snell's reign because there was very little to organize or to organize about.

Again, disorganization can be of two kinds: internal party conditions (disunity, weak leadership) and a hopelessly weak second party. These situations are quite different and produce different minority party behavior.

Finally, the collegiality of the Halleck period is somewhat different from that of the Ford reign, as Ripley points out. Halleck had collegiality forced on him as part of the bargain for gaining support from younger members in the revolt against Martin. Ford was then a part of this "set" and therefore was generally more congenial to this pattern of leadership than Halleck. How much many of the insurgents wanted Halleck in the first place is questionable, so Halleck's position in the party was always somewhat tenuous. The collegiate pattern under Ford represents the triumph of several young and energetic House Republicans. If they continue to work with one another, perhaps the collegial pattern will remain. It certainly represents an optimum in reflecting the varied interests within the House Republican Party. One junior member very much in evidence in

the leadership changes of the 1960's analyzed the Republican leadership situation in an interview:

> The minority leader has lost some power but when the party
> is split and there are frequent leadership changes, you expect
> this. It is like the leadership situation [in the Soviet Union]
> when Stalin died. Many leaders took over until one leader
> emerged. This will probably happen to us. We need a leader
> with the toughness of Mel Laird, as well liked as Gerry Ford,
> and as studious as Charlie Goodell. Until he comes along we
> will be split up among several leaders.

ORGANIZATIONAL UNITS. As the minority party in the 90th Congress,
House Republicans relied on an elaborate organization. In addition
to the minority leader and his personal staff of thirteen, there were
the Conference, Policy Committee, Research and Planning Committee with a number of task forces, Committee on Committees, Campaign Committee, and an extensive whip organization. This complex
system is a departure for minority parties in this century. Traditionally, the minority party has had very little structure. It usually
has reduced the number of organizational units when it became the
minority, apparently on the assumption that the minority does not
have very much to do. But if the minority party is to be effective, it
needs as elaborate an organization as does the majority.

The minority leader has always found some organizational units
upon which he could rely for information and leadership. Whips,
conferences and caucuses, and campaign committees have existed
since the turn of the century. In the early part of the century, the
whip was normally a trusted lieutenant of the minority leader, but
no extensive whip organization was developed by the minority party
until 1931. At that time, Carl G. Bachmann (R-West Virginia) appointed assistant whips responsible for regions and a "key man" for
each state.[9] He relied on these men to poll the Republicans on important legislative issues. This system continued to develop under
Bachmann's successors, Harry L. Englebright (1933–1943) and Leslie
C. Arends (1943——). The minority party whip system now includes a deputy whip, three regional whips, and twelve assistant

[9] Ripley, *American Political Science Review*, Vol. 58 (September, 1964),
p. 565.

whips. The Democrats apparently had never relied greatly on the whip prior to 1921, as a minority or as a majority. They did develop a whip system during the 1920's and by 1929 the whip had a number of assistant whips. The system was further developed when they became the majority party in 1931.

The caucus or conference has always been used to select party leaders and occasionally to develop party positions on legislation. During the 1920's the Democrats met in caucus to discuss legislation and established minority party positions on bills before the House.[10] Beginning in 1939, the Republicans began to meet more often in conference, though generally not for deliberation. Normally, the leadership would simply use the Conference to urge members to support them on legislation.

Though the ouster of Hoeven as Conference chairman in 1963 was to result in changes, little was done during the 88th Congress to utilize the Conference. Considerable effort was made in the 89th Congress under the chairmanship of Melvin R. Laird to establish a conference bureaucracy, however. The Conference staff now worked on specific research projects and public relations. The House Republican Conference became a significant organizational unit, more significant than any conference or caucus for either the majority or the minority since the majority party caucus in the 63rd Congress.

The minority party Campaign Committee and organization has seldom been involved in policy making in the House and therefore deserves little attention here. It focuses on getting members reelected and on increasing the number of minority party members in the House. The Campaign Committee served a minor policy role for the Republicans before the Policy Committee was revitalized in 1959. Since their goal was electing Republicans to the House, the Committee got involved in the policy record of the House Republican Party. In their attempts to publicize the record or defend it, research and discussion were necessary. Thus, the Committee, its leadership, and staff (the only extensive party committee staff on the House side) has had a minor policy role. Even after the Policy Committee was revitalized, coordination between the Policy Committee and the Campaign Committee was assured through some overlap-

---

[10] This was a rather weak carry-over from the early Wilson Congresses when, under the majority leadership of Oscar W. Underwood, the House Democrats relied extensively on the caucus for legislative purposes.

ping membership and making the chairman of the Campaign Committee an ex officio member of the Policy Committee.[11] In an
interview, a Campaign Committee staff member summarized the
Committee's policy role in comparing the House Committee with
the Senate Committee:

> We are more service-oriented. We have to perform more
> services than the Senate Committee. They have a policy com-
> mittee over there which gets Senate appropriations. Senators
> can rely on that for a lot of the kind of work that we have to
> provide on the House side. In the past we have played some-
> what the same sort of role that the policy committee plays on
> the Senate side. Of course, [Chairman Bob] Wilson is a
> member of the joint House-Senate leadership group and the
> House Republican Policy Committee and so he gets involved
> in policy. But mostly we have gotten into policy because of
> the void.

Of the other organizational units in the minority party during the
1960's, the Committee on Committees has the longest history. It
came into existence following the revolt against Speaker Cannon in
1910. In 1911, the Democratic majority in the House, with progressive Republican support, stripped the speaker of his power to appoint
committees. The Democratic Party assigned this responsibility to the
Democratic members of the Committee on Ways and Means "because of the fear that each member, in the case of a . . . [separate
Committee on Committees], would appoint himself chairman of a
great committee." [12] The Republicans at first authorized their minority leader, James R. Mann, to appoint committees. In 1917, however,
following much criticism and some open opposition to Mann, a
special seventeen-member Committee on Committees with Mann as
chairman was established to make minority appointments to committees.[13] This procedure has continued.[14]

---

[11] A useful history of the House Republican Campaign Committee may be
obtained from the Committee headquarters: Henry M. Maggenti, *One Hundred
Years: A History of the National Republican Congressional Committee* (Washington, D.C.: Judd and Detweiler, 1966).

[12] Paul D. Hasbrouck, *Party Government in the House of Representatives*
(New York: Macmillan, 1927), p. 43.

[13] *The New York Times*, April 1, 1917.

[14] See Nicholas Masters, "Committee Assignments in the House of Representatives," *American Political Science Review*, Vol. 55 (June, 1961), pp. 345–57.

Although they have existed on occasion in both parties, until the 1960's policy or steering committees were not heavily relied on by the minority party. In 1949, the Republicans converted their moribund Steering Committee into a Policy Committee. Under the chairmanship of Joseph W. Martin, Jr., however, the new committee was only slightly more active than the old one. In 1959, Martin was defeated by Halleck and the party named a separate chairman of the Policy Committee, John W. Byrnes of Wisconsin. This move was insisted on by some of the younger members who wanted to see a more vigorous minority party. During the next six years, the Policy Committee became an important party unit, holding weekly meetings to discuss pending legislation, issuing policy positions, creating task groups to examine specific policy problems, and hiring a small staff to do research. By this effort the Republicans attempted not only to discover some basis for consensus on legislation, but to begin the much more difficult task of trying to build constructive alternatives to majority party proposals — or even perhaps take the initiative in some policy areas. The latter was a break from the past for minority parties.

In 1965, when the Republicans had another leadership struggle, the Policy Committee's role was lessened somewhat. The Committee had come to be important in internal party politics and 1965 was no exception. When the new minority leader, Gerald R. Ford, was unable to get his choice as Policy Committee chairman, he established a Committee on Research and Planning as a part of the Republican Conference. This new committee, chaired by Charles E. Goodell of New York (Ford's choice for Policy Committee chairman), assumed the research functions formerly performed by the Subcommittee on Special Projects of the Policy Committee. Thus, though the Policy Committee had to share its previous functions with a new committee — an arrangement of questionable efficiency — it is significant that a procedure for developing Republican policy proposals continued to exist. During the 89th Congress, the Research and Planning Committee was active in research and publicity (see Chapter Eight).

From this brief sketch of organizational units, we can see that traditionally the minority party has taken a rather narrow view of its role in Congress. The historical record is sketchy on organizational developments in congressional parties, but the evidence indicates that the minority party has not considered it necessary, or a part of its function, to establish mechanisms within the party for offering alternative policy proposals or initiating policy proposals. Only since 1959 have the Republicans consciously attempted to create a procedure for generating proposals of their own.

THE SENATE

I have heard students argue that Congress is *sui generis*. Not even our more important state legislatures, they point out, are enough like Congress to make comparisons fruitful. If, indeed, the Congress is unique, a major reason is the nature of its upper chamber. Nowhere in the world is there a body quite like it. It is vastly different from the House of Representatives in size, representation, style, procedure, output, norms, leadership. One might expect therefore that the *modus operandi* of the minority party in the Senate would be quite different from that in the House.

Many of the characteristics of the Senate can be traced to two basic features: its small size and the prestige and responsibility of representing an entire state. The Senate reflects federalism, with its concept of state sovereignty, better than any other institution at the national level. The senators from New York and California represent more than sixty times as many people as do the senators from Alaska and Nevada and yet all are presumed to be equal in the Senate chamber. The courtesy each senator extends to his colleagues is like the diplomatic courtesies extended in international conclaves. Though seniority has become as important in the Senate as in the House, every United States senator is assumed by his colleagues, the press, and the nation to be an important public figure.

These characteristics of the Senate help to determine the role of the minority party in that body. The informality, courtesy, and prestige of individual members result in increased policy participation for minority senators. They have a better opportunity than House members to communicate their ideas, to influence the precise composition of the compromise, and to receive credit for their contributions. At the same time, minority party leaders in the Senate must negotiate more with their own followers than their counterparts do in the House since they are dealing with a body of men who have more independent sources of power. Thus, it does not necessarily follow that the party as a whole will be more significant in the Senate than in the House. That is, individual minority senators may be more influential, but the party may be less so.

PARTY LEADERS. Unfortunately, it is not possible to determine the identity of certain minority leaders in the early part of this century or whether, in fact, the leadership position existed. Here again, party records are either nonexistent or not available to the scholar. Of the elected leaders, the most complete listings are those for minority floor leaders and the whips.

Until 1911, both the majority and minority parties elected a different floor leader in every session of Congress. Eight Democrats served as minority floor leader during the first ten years of this century and six Republicans served as majority floor leader during the same period. Since 1910, thirteen men have served as minority leader and thirteen men have served as majority leader. Clearly, the floor leadership post was not of major significance before 1910. The chairman of the minority party Caucus served as floor leader, but apparently he was a leader in name only. The Senate was dominated by Nelson W. Aldrich (R-Rhode Island) during the early part of this century.

The practice of passing the floor leadership around in every session was changed in 1911. Since no sources discuss the development of the floor leadership, one can only speculate that a combination of circumstances resulted in the change. Until 1910, the majority Republicans were led by a cabal variously composed of William B. Allison, Iowa; John C. Spooner, Wisconsin; Orville H. Platt, Connecticut; Eugene Hale, Maine; and dominated by Nelson W. Aldrich. By the time the 62nd Congress convened, these men were no longer in the Senate.[15]

With Aldrich and his cohorts gone, and progressivism rising in the party, a leadership vacuum developed in the Republican Party. Senator Shelby M. Cullom (R-Illinois), who served in the Senate for thirty years, concluded that no one led the party.

> The question is often asked, "Who has succeeded Aldrich as leader of the Senate?" No one. Practically, there are three parties in the Senate, consisting of thirty-seven Regular Republicans, forty-one Democrats, and thirteen Insurgent Re-

[15] For an excellent discussion of Senate leadership before the turn of the century, see David J. Rothman, *Politics and Power in the United States Senate, 1869–1901* (Cambridge, Mass.: Harvard University Press, 1966). See also George H. Haynes, *The Senate of the United States: Its History and Practice* (Boston: Houghton Mifflin, 1938).

publicans. In caucus, the Insurgents act with the Regulars, but in legislation, they more frequently line up with the Democrats. The consequence is that no party is in control, therefore that no party can dictate the course of leadership. Under such circumstances, real leadership is out of the question. Senator Penrose [Boies Penrose of Pennsylvania] succeeds Senator Aldrich as Chairman of the Committee on Finance, and is proving thoroughly competent for his work in that capacity. If emergency should arise throwing the direction of affairs into the hands of the Republican Party, he might also succeed the Rhode Island Senator to the leadership of the Republican forces, but until such emergency presents itself, no one can see whether that position would fall to him or to some other Republican.[16]

Senator Cullom's reference to the insurgents in the Senate suggests another reason why the Republicans began to elect a permanent floor leader. As Cullom points out, the Progressives in the Senate, led by Robert M. La Follette of Wisconsin, had become an important third force. The Republican Party had no leader who could control the party from behind the scenes. In their biography of La Follette, Belle and Fola La Follette state that the heir apparent to leadership among the old guard Republicans was Jacob H. Gallinger of New Hampshire. Gallinger was proposed as president pro tempore following the resignation of William P. Frye of Maine. The insurgents had their own candidate, however, and were successful in blocking Gallinger's election.[17] Six senators, including one Democrat, actually served as president pro tempore during the 62nd Congress and during several months no one served. Some served for a few days only, depending entirely on the majority that happened to exist at any one time.

Although they had difficulty electing Gallinger permanently to the position of president pro tempore, the regulars were still a majority in their party and therefore could elect him to the majority floor leadership. Never a strong leader, Gallinger served as majority floor leader for two sessions of the 62nd Congress (Shelby M. Cullom served in this capacity during the third, lame-duck, session) and as

---

[16] Shelby M. Cullom, *Fifty Years of Public Service: Personal Recollections of Shelby M. Cullom* (Chicago: A. C. McClurg, 1911), pp. 425–26.

[17] Belle C. and Fola La Follette, *Robert M. La Follette* (New York: Macmillan, 1953), pp. 323–24.

minority floor leader for the next three Congresses (totaling eight regular sessions and two special sessions). Only two Republican leaders, Allison and Hale, had previously served two consecutive sessions in this century.

Thus, on the Republican side, the floor leadership, as a position held more or less permanently over a period of time, emerged during the 62nd and 63rd Congresses. Its power, however, did not become of major importance until after the Republicans had healed the wounds of the 1912 presidential nominating convention.

The Democrats appeared to change their pattern at about the same time as the Republicans. Prior to the election of Thomas S. Martin of Virginia as minority leader in the second session of the 62nd Congress, only two Democrats, Francis M. Cockrell and Henry M. Teller, had served two consecutive sessions. But the establishment of a permanent and influential floor leader came in the 63rd Congress when the Democrats became the majority party. Apparently until that time leadership in the Senate Democratic Party was wielded by a group of southern Democratic senators much in the manner of the regular Republicans (though no figure dominated the Democratic Party as Aldrich dominated the Republican). When Woodrow Wilson was elected in 1912, however, he intended to lead the Congress and he wanted leaders who favored his program. Though Martin was still in the Senate, the Democrats selected John W. Kern of Indiana as their leader. Though prominent in Democratic Party politics for many years, Kern had been in the Senate only two years when selected. Claude G. Bowers explains why he was chosen:

> Never before in the history of the Senate had any member been called to the leadership of the majority of that body after only two years of service in it. There were many reasons entering into the selection. The first qualification and the one of prime importance was that the leader should be known nationally as a progressive in complete harmony with the Baltimore platform and with the program of the incoming president. No member of the Senate met these requirements more fully. His entire life politically was in harmony with the program, and he had been chairman of the Committee on Resolutions at the national convention.[18]

[18] Claude B. Bowers, *The Life of John Worth Kern* (Indianapolis: Hollenback, 1918), pp. 287–88.

And Bowers wrote later in his autobiography:

> When . . . the militantly progressive Senator Kern displaced Senator Tom Martin, the ultraconservative Virginian, from his long-held position of Democratic floor leader [sic], it became crystal clear that the Democratic Party — was experiencing a rebirth and rejuvenation.[19]

The characteristics of minority floor leaders in this century can best be described by dividing them into two groups — those serving before the 63rd Congress and those after. The post was simply passed around among southern Democrats (with one exception) before 1913. The Democratic floor leadership changed hands eleven times in twelve years. These were old men (an average age of seventy-three) with considerable seniority (see Table 3.3). Two of them, Morgan (during his second term as leader) and Pettus were over eighty.

After 1913, and particularly post-Gallinger, minority leaders were younger and seniority was clearly less important. When the Democrats returned to minority status after World War I, Martin, Hitchcock, and Underwood served for a short time (Hitchcock only as acting leader), and then Joseph T. Robinson of Arkansas was elected leader. Robinson served five Congresses as minority leader, becoming the first Democrat to serve more than two. He also served two Congresses as majority leader. The only other Democratic floor leaders in this century, Barkley and Johnson, served only one term each as minority leader but led their party as majority leader during the Democratic Party dominance in the Senate — Barkley from 1937 to 1946 and Johnson from 1955 to 1960. The Democratic pattern of electing southern Democrats continued; only one, Hitchcock of Nebraska, was from outside the South, and he served only a short time as acting leader.

The Republicans have had only seven men serve as minority leader in this century (though during the rapid changeover of leaders between 1901 and 1913 they also changed leaders eleven times). Three men — Gallinger, McNary, and Dirksen — have served more than two Congresses as minority leader. Gallinger was a member of the old guard and his election followed the pattern of electing old men with much seniority. Gallinger was 81 and still minority

---

[19] Bowers, *My Life: The Memoirs of Claude Bowers* (New York: Simon and Schuster, 1962), p. 70.

TABLE 3.3
LEGISLATIVE EXPERIENCE AND SENIORITY RANK OF SENATE
MINORITY FLOOR LEADERS, 1961–1969, AT ELECTION

Democrats	Age	Years in Senate	Party seniority rank[a]	Years served in majority
John T. Morgan, Ala. (1901–2)	77	24	2	4
James K. Jones, Ark. (1902–3)	63	17	4	2
Arthur P. Gorman, Md. (1903)	64	18[b]	22	2
Francis M. Cockrell, Mo. (1903–5)	69	28	1	4
John T. Morgan, Ala. (1905–6)	81	28	1	4
Edmund W. Pettus, Ala. (1906–7)	85	9	10	0
Henry M. Teller, Calif. (1907–9)	77	28[c]	1	20
Hernando D. Money, Miss. (1909)	70	12	7	0
Augustus O. Bacon, Ga. (1909–10)	70	14	2	0
Hernando D. Money, Miss. (1910–11)	71	13	4	0
Augustus O. Bacon, Ga. (1911)	71	16	1	0
Thomas S. Martin, Va. (1911–13)	64	16	1	0
Thomas S. Martin, Va. (1917–19)	72	26	1	8
Gilbert Hitchcock, Nebr. (1919–20)[d]	59	8	13	6
Oscar W. Underwood, Ala. (1920–23)	58	6	29	4
Joseph T. Robinson, Ark. (1923–33)[e]	51	10	12	6
Alben W. Barkley, Ky. (1947–48)[e]	70	20	3	14
Lyndon B. Johnson, Tex. (1953–54)[e]	45	4	31	4

Republicans				
Jacob H. Gallinger, N.H. (1911–18)[e]	76	22	1	20
Charles McNary, Ore. (1933–44)	57	16	5	14
Wallace White, Me. (1944–47)[e]	66	13	8	2
Kenneth Wherry, Nebr. (1949–51)[e]	56	6	14	0
H. Styles Bridges, N.H. (1952)	54	15	1	0
William Knowland, Calif. (1955–58)[e]	46	10	11	2
Everett M. Dirksen, Ill. (1959–69)	63	8	18	2
Hugh Scott, Penn. (1969——)	68	10	14	0

[a] Calculated by number of terms and alphabetical order.

[b] Gorman served from 1881 to 1899, was defeated, and returned to serve in the Senate from 1902 to 1906.

[c] Teller served 18 years as a Republican; 6 of them were as an Independent Silver Republican. If only his Democratic service is counted, his seniority rank would be 19.

[d] Hitchcock was never formally elected as floor leader. He served as acting leader between Martin's death and the election of Underwood.

[e] Also served as majority leaders.

leader when he died. The "deans" among Republican minority floor leaders have been Charles L. McNary and Everett M. Dirksen. Mc-Nary served for eleven years, Dirksen served for ten and was reelected to that capacity for the 91st Congress but died before completing his term. No geographical pattern appears among Republican minority leaders: three have been from New England, two from the Midwest, and two from the West.

Whereas House Republicans have ousted three of their five minority leaders in this century, removal from office has not been the pattern in the Senate in either party. For the Republicans, four leaders died in office (McNary, Gallinger, Wherry, Dirksen), one became majority leader and then left the Senate (White), one left the Senate to run for governor of California (Knowland), and one was not an active candidate for reelection to the post (Bridges). On the Democratic side, after 1913, Martin died in office, Underwood declined to serve again, Robinson and Johnson became majority leader, and Barkley left the Senate for the vice-presidency.

The whip system in the Senate differs markedly from that in the House. Obviously the task of the Senate whip is much less complex.[20] Normally, therefore, the minority whip has not had an organization and he seldom finds it necessary to perform the so-called whip functions. The whips have tended to act as assistant floor leader in both parties. In fact, it was the practice for a time in the Republican Party (1922–1935) for the whip to serve also as vice-chairman of the Caucus.

Apparently the first whip for the Democrats was selected in 1913 and for the Republicans in 1915. There is no record of whips for earlier Congresses. Since that time there have been eleven minority whips, seven Republican and four Democratic. The first minority whip was James W. Wadsworth (R-New York), a freshman senator who served only seven days in that capacity. Why he was selected and why he served such a short tenure is not clear. Seniority definitely has not been a criterion in selecting whips. Only three minority whips have had more than six years of service in the Senate when selected. Two had only one year and two had two years. Clearly, the whip post has often been awarded to younger members who show promise and/or, as with Thomas Kuchel (R-California), to provide a balance in ideology among party leaders.

No whip has been defeated for reelection to that post. Seven of the twelve minority whips have accepted other leadership posts, three becoming minority floor leaders (Wherry, Dirksen, and Scott),

---

[20] For a brief description of the whip's duties, see *Congressional Quarterly Weekly Report*, Sept. 25, 1964, pp. 2251–52.

two majority whips (Charles Curtis, R-Kansas, who later served as vice-president under Coolidge, and Earle C. Clements, D-Kentucky), one Conference chairman (Leverett Saltonstall, R-Massachusetts), and one majority floor leader (Scott Lucas, D-Illinois). Three others were defeated for reelection as senators (Peter G. Gerry, R-Rhode Island; Felix Hebert, R-Rhode Island; and Thomas Kuchel, R-California).

Until the 79th Congress, the Senate Caucus or Conference chairman served as the floor leader for both parties. The Democrats continue this practice but the Republicans, since the 79th Congress, have elected separate Conference chairmen. Since the separation, the chairmanship in the Senate Republican Party has gone to a senior party member. The chairman does have important appointive powers since he chooses the membership of the Committee on Committees, Policy Committee, and Campaign Committee. His other powers are extremely limited, however. As with most party posts, the Republican Conference chairmanship potentially is important, depending on who fills the slot. None of the four Republicans — Arthur H. Vandenberg, Michigan; Eugene Millikin, Colorado; Leverett Saltonstall, Massachusetts; or Margaret Chase Smith, Maine — has been assertive in the exercise of this position.[21]

The Policy Committee is a relatively recent party organizational unit. It was created by legislation in 1947 and received appropriations from Congress. The chairmen have been important leaders in the party. The Democrats traditionally have had their floor leader serve in this capacity, whereas the Republicans, who have relied on collegial leadership in recent years, have elected a separate chairman.

Seniority has been relied on in the Senate for committee assignments and chairmanships longer than in the House, since "this body was reluctant to give its presiding officer, the Vice President, the appointment power." [22] Thus, the ranking minority positions on major committees have gone to senior Democrats and Republicans who normally represent areas of great strength for the two parties. In the important committees on Finance and Appropriations, only three men were under fifty when they assumed the ranking minority spot. As the most important in the Senate, the Committee on Ap-

---

[21] See Rothman, p. 44, for background material on Senate caucus chairmen.
[22] Goodwin, *American Political Science Review*, Vol. 53 (June, 1959), p. 417. See also Haynes, *The Senate of the United States*, pp. 249–55 regarding president pro tempore.

propriations has very low turnover; the average age of its ranking minority members is high, significantly higher than for Finance. Five ranking minority members on Appropriations were seventy or over when they assumed that post. Obviously, the South is well represented among Democratic ranking minority members on these two committees — five of six on Finance, and five of seven on Appropriations. The Republicans have been principally from the Northeast and Midwest (six of seven on Finance and five of six on Appropriations).

House and Senate minority party leaders operate in significantly different environments. One would not expect that Senate party leaders, in either party, would have the controls that their counterparts in the House would have. It seems evident that though Senate party leadership is more formal and centralized now than at the turn of the century, the key position of floor leader is still not as institutionalized as it has been in the House for some time.

PATTERNS OF LEADERSHIP. If one accepts the generalization that power is more widely shared in the Senate and therefore overall one expects more collegialism, four types of leadership can be identified in this century. The first pattern characterized the first ten years of this century. As a group of southern Democrats controlled the minority party, it is appropriate to label this period "leadership by cabal or faction." It continued the type of leadership described as predominant in the Senate in the latter years of the nineteenth century.[23] The Senate was dominated, however, by Nelson W. Aldrich, the unofficial leader of the Republican Party. The Democrats were never able to challenge his leadership successfully. Indeed, the eventual challenge to Aldrich came from the progressive wing of his own party.

Aldrich was well suited for his time in the Senate. He was brilliant, tough-minded, affable, "clubby," persuasive, domineering. According to Claude G. Bowers, he had "a lofty contempt for the masses," [24] and therefore could be expected to recoil incredulously from the trend toward progressivism. To him, the Senate was not a "public place." Aldrich was called "the manager of the United States" and

---

[23] Rothman, Ch. 2.
[24] Bowers, *Beveridge and the Progressive Era* (New York: Literary Guild, 1932), p. 318.

the "schoolmaster of the Senate." [25] He was accused of carrying a
chloroform bottle: "It is invisible. . . . He sits down beside a Senator and the first thing that the Senator knows he has been chloro-
formed, and is completely under the Aldrich influence." [26] Bowers
describes his power in the Senate:

> No one in the entire history of the Senate has ever domi-
> nated it more autocratically through sheer will power than
> Nelson W. Aldrich. A member of that body for many years,
> he had, from the beginning, made himself indispensable to
> the party organization there, rising step by step as the elders
> passed out, until in the end he made himself the dictator of
> a cabal which for a time was the master of the Government.[27]

How did he accomplish this feat? Apparently he led by his force-
ful personality and the ability of "The Four," consisting of Aldrich,
Allison, Platt, and Spooner.

> The Four in those days worked together with systematic regu-
> larity. Their meeting place "for thrashing over the next step in
> some legislative programme" was likely to be the little apart-
> ment of the Platts at the Arlington. Miss Lawler attended
> these sessions and took stenographic notes. . . . The Four
> kept very sharp ears wide open for rumors. What the world
> outside thought or did not think seldom troubled any of them
> but Mr. Allison. What Washington thought was another
> story. The rumors that deserved most attention concerned
> the President and it was frequently Platt who was the one to
> warn him. "When other men had informed him of their
> fears he would seek out Miss Lawler's room for the con-
> fidential dictation, thus wise: 'Dear Mr. President . . . :
> There is a rumor about the Capitol — of course it is only a
> rumor — that you are going to do so-and-so. I wish you would
> hold this matter in abeyance until I have an opportunity to
> see you. Very truly yours.' Then Mr. Platt would turn to
> Miss Lawler and say, 'Send it by mounted messenger.'
> Within a trice the reply from Roosevelt would come, 'My

[25] See David S. Barry, *Forty Years in Washington* (Boston: Little, Brown,
1924), p. 152; and Chauncey M. Depew, *My Memories of 80 Years* (New York:
Scribner's, 1922), p. 180.

[26] Quoted in Arthur W. Dunn, *From Harrison to Harding*, Vol. II (New
York: Putnam's, 1922), p. 64.

[27] Bowers, *Beveridge*, p. 314.

> dear Friend: Of course, I will withhold action. When can I
> see you? Sincerely.' " [28]

Aldrich and his cohorts had the ability, the organization, and, with
Aldrich "close to the source of campaign supplies," the money to
wield power in the Senate:

> Thus, symbolizing material power, a genius in the art of legis-
> lative bargaining, a master of senatorial organization, the
> head of the little clique that determined legislative programs
> and organized committees, his position was commanding
> beyond that of almost any other senator in generations.[29]

What did all this mean for the minority party? First, Aldrich so
thoroughly dominated the Senate that practically everything and
everyone was measured in relation to him. In 1911, when the Democrats were selecting a new chairman of the Caucus, *The New York
Times* included a table indicating the extent to which the various
candidates had voted with Aldrich in the previous Congress.[30] Interestingly, Thomas S. Martin of Virginia, who had voted most often
with Aldrich, was elected (much to the chagrin of the titular leader
of the Democratic Party, William Jennings Bryan). Then, of course,
Aldrich "was always ready to do legislative favors to senators on the
opposite side."

> Once when Senator Tillman was — or thought himself —
> in danger of missing re-election because of his failure to
> secure an appropriation for the Charleston Navy Yard, it was
> Senator Aldrich who saved his place for him by pushing
> through the desired appropriation.[31]

The minority, as a result, was an extremely weak opposition party
controlled by senior southern Democrats who often supported Senator Aldrich. Opposition to the ruling clique developed within each
party and eventually caused serious intraparty splits.

The second minority party pattern appears in the post-Aldrich
Republican Party. During two periods since that time the Republicans have served in the minority — during 6 of the 8 years of the

[28] Nathaniel W. Stephenson, *Nelson W. Aldrich: A Leader in American Politics* (New York: Scribner's, 1930), p. 204.

[29] Bowers, *Beveridge*, p. 321.

[30] *The New York Times*, April 7 and 12, 1911.

[31] Stephenson, p. 205.

Wilson administration and during 32 of the 36 years since 1933. During the earlier period, the Senate Republican Party was seriously split between the Progressives and the regulars. Although the regulars were in the majority, and therefore were able to elect the Caucus chairman/floor leader, they were not able to maintain control over the insurgents. With Aldrich gone, and the Progressives gaining in strength in the Senate, the Republican Party in 1911 entered a period of disunity that continued until 1932, though they were in the minority for only six years of this period. The problems causing disunity were not resolved in 1932 (nor have they been even today); instead, the party then sustained such an enormous defeat that its attention was diverted from internal disputes.

The regulars were given ample warning of what was to ensue when they tried to organize the Senate in 1911. The Republican margin in the Senate was narrow — a mere seven seats — and the Progressives held the balance of power. Led by Robert M. La Follette of Wisconsin, eight Progressives refused to attend the Republican Caucus that elected Jacob Gallinger of New Hampshire chairman. This same Caucus proposed Gallinger as president pro tempore to succeed William P. Frye of Maine, who announced his intention to resign the post due to ill health. La Follette's group supported Moses E. Clapp, Progressive from Minnesota, for president pro tempore. The result was a stalemate.

Gallinger, then, headed a party he never really led. The Progressives did not accept his leadership and he had to share leadership of the regulars with others, notably Boies Penrose of Pennsylvania, Henry Cabot Lodge of Massachusetts, Charles Curtis of Kansas, and others.

The third pattern is found in the Republican Party since 1932. For the most part, this period has been characterized by collegialism. During the early years of the Roosevelt administrations, the Senate Republicans were a small, unhappy, and impotent family. What they did as a minority made very little difference. They were led by Charles L. McNary of Oregon. He adopted an unaggressive strategy, hoping that the Democrats might eventually begin to fight among themselves.[32] It was after McNary's long reign that the party began to divide all the various leadership posts among the members. The

---

[32] Malcolm Moos, *The Republicans: A History of Their Party* (New York: Random House, 1956), pp. 406–7.

floor leadership and Conference chairmanship posts were separated for the first time in 1945. Since that time, the Senate Republicans have awarded leadership posts to many members. The eight posts in the 89th Congress were floor leader, whip, Conference chairman, Policy Committee chairman, Campaign Committee chairman, Committee on Committees chairman, Personnel Committee chairman, and Calendar Committee chairman. And every Republican in the Senate served on at least one party committee.

It is quite possible, of course, to have a number of members serving in leadership positions and still have the party dominated by one man, but generally this has not happened in the Senate Republican Party. Not all leadership positions are of equal weight (the chairmanships of the Personnel and Calendar committees are inconsequential), but the party has been led from within this group. Some leaders have been particularly influential (Robert A. Taft of Ohio, H. Styles Bridges of New Hampshire, Everett M. Dirksen of Illinois), but none has dominated as much as some majority leaders (notably Aldrich and Lyndon B. Johnson).

The fourth pattern of leadership is that in the Democratic Party following their tenure as the majority party during the Wilson administrations. Martin was reestablished as majority leader when Kern was defeated for reelection to the Senate in 1916. He became minority leader when the Democrats lost control of the Senate in 1918, but died on November 12, 1919. Gilbert M. Hitchcock of Nebraska then served as acting leader (having been vice-chairman of the Democratic Caucus) until April 27, 1920, when Oscar W. Underwood of Alabama was elected leader. Underwood served until 1923, resigning because of ill health and pressure. Since that time, the Democrats have had only six floor leaders (majority and minority) and four of these — Robinson, Barkley, Johnson, and Mansfield — have served for twenty-one of the twenty-three Congresses.

Three of the six Democratic floor leaders since 1923 have served as minority leaders — Robinson, Barkley, and Johnson. Though the Democratic floor leader is not always an all-powerful figure, he does have more prerogatives than his Republican counterpart. The floor leader continues to be chairman of the Caucus, Policy Committee, and Committee on Committees, so that leadership in the Democratic Party has been centered much more in the minority leader than it has in the Republican Party.

Thus, though collegialism is more general in the modern Senate than the modern House, at least four patterns of minority party leadership are discernible: weak leadership by southern Democratic cabal during Aldrich's domination of the Senate and before the direct election of senators, divided leadership during the Wilson administrations, Republican collegialism after 1932, and Democratic centralism after 1923.

ORGANIZATIONAL UNITS. As one might expect, less elaborate organization is needed in the Senate minority party. Even a minority party with the maximum number of senators is not a large group. The principal units have been the Caucus, Committee on Committees, and, more recently, the Policy Committee. The Caucus, or Conference as the Republicans have called it since 1913, elects the leadership and determines party organization and therefore has been the scene of many internal struggles in the minority party.[33] The Caucus has also been used for discussing legislation from time to time — by the Democrats during the 1920's and the Republicans in recent years. The principal purpose of the Caucus, however, has been discussion rather than decision. The binding caucus has not been used regularly in recent years by either party.

The Committee on Committees has traditionally been an important unit in both parties. The floor leader chairs the Democratic Committee and appoints its members. The Democrats have also traditionally relied on it as a steering committee. Though evidence is scanty, it appears that the Republicans have always had separate committees — a committee on committees and a steering committee — when they were in the majority. They apparently dropped the Steering Committee, however, when they were in the minority (at least during the Wilson administration). The floor leader would serve as chairman of the Steering Committee but a separate chairman was appointed for the Committee on Committees. (*The New York Times* listed the membership of both committees for the majority Republican Party in 1911.)[34] Senator Cullom, as chairman of the Caucus during the first session, appointed both committees.

[33] Technically the caucus and the conference differ. The caucus is presumably binding, if a specified number of members (generally two thirds) vote in favor of a policy position, whereas the conference is not binding. As Hasbrouck writes: "After the Cannon regime, the Republicans for a time gave up the caucus form of meeting, and substituted the conference, which was not strictly binding upon those who participated." p. 31.

[34] *The New York Times*, April 12, 1911.

He chaired the Steering Committee but Gallinger chaired the Committee on Committees. Unfortunately no mention is made of either committee in the *Times* in 1913, when the Senate Republicans became the minority party. It is assumed that the minority party did not rely on a Steering Committee, as the Committee's function was principally to determine the order of business; it primarily served at that time as a majority party committee.

The Democrats continued to call their Committee on Committees a steering committee even when they were in the minority, but it did not function in that capacity.[35] For the most part, when either party was in the minority, they viewed their function as being one of opposition and criticism, not of policy development. Senator Robinson's statement in 1923, upon his election as minority leader, is revealing:

> While we are not prepared, and do not propose at this time, to assume the responsibility which devolves upon the majority to take the initiative respecting the details of legislation, it is expected that our organization will stand for a material reduction in taxes and for aggressive measures to effectuate retrenchment in public expenditures.[36]

Not until 1947 was a committee formed to enable the minority party to coordinate policy activities. Both parties were authorized by Congress to form "policy committees," which were to "plan the legislative program, coordinate and guide committee activity, focus party leadership, and strengthen party responsibility and accountability." [37] Neither party has used its policy committee in these ways. The precise function of the Republican Committee has depended on the chairman. Taft was a strong chairman, as was Bridges. Both used the Committee as a base for their leadership in the party. Neither relied on it to accomplish the purposes intended by the reformers who pressed for its adoption. In recent years, the Committee has facilitated communication (though as we have seen communication among so few people is not a major problem in the Senate minority

---

35 Haynes, pp. 483–87. See in particular the Mondell proposal for House and Senate steering committees, which would hold joint meetings occasionally with the president. Apparently four joint meetings were held in 1919, but the plan was soon abandoned. Haynes, pp. 485–87.

36 *The New York Times*, December 4, 1923.

37 George B. Galloway, *The Legislative Process in Congress* (New York: Crowell, 1955), p. 335.

party), and its staff has engaged in research, publicity, speech writing, bill drafting, and other services. The appropriations for staff principally provide individual senators with additional staff assistance. Very little attempt is made to direct the staff toward research that would result in policy formulation.

The other organizational units are of little consequence. The Campaign Committee can be used as a power base but normally is not. Often, because his principal responsibility is to raise money, the chairman is a senator who is well known nationally. The Committee staff, led by the late Victor Johnston for several years, has always been very small. Its responsibilities are minor compared to those of its counterpart in the House.

SUMMARY

For the most part the minority party in Congress retreats into itself, taking a comparatively nonaggressive view of its responsibilities. Minority parties in this century have been led mostly by senior members who apparently are important in determining the party's role. Normally the apparatus relied on by these leaders has been a sort of organization for existence, that is, organizational units that perform very basic functions so that the party will survive. Until recently, little or no effort has been made to develop units that are less preoccupied with survival, or mere partisan opposition, and more with developing policy alternatives. In short, it appears that congressional minority parties in both houses and for both parties have not begun to approach their potential in the majority-building process in Congress.

Some qualifications to these generalizations about minority party leadership and organization are necessary. First, the House Republican Party in recent years has made serious attempts to assume a more aggressive and dynamic role (see Chapter eight). Second, the precise role of the minority party always depends on the several variables previously discussed (see Chapter two). Third, it appears that many of the restrictions on the minority party are self-imposed. Though the majority party does have a number of advantages, the minority party has great latitude in selecting a role for itself. There is much to discourage the minority party from taking a more constructive role in policy making, but little to prevent them from doing so.

CHAPTER FOUR

Restricted Minorities
in the House and Senate

In this book twentieth-century Congresses are classified by the extent to which political conditions affected the strategies available to the minority party. Examination of individual Congresses will begin with those where the minority party was most limited. For each class of Congress there is a description of: (1) the external and internal political conditions that appear important in determining the strategies the minority party can use in a specific Congress; (2) the strategies available in these Congresses; (3) the degree of realization of the potential of each situation; and (4) significant differences between the House and Senate.

THE HOUSE

The Congresses analyzed in Table 4.1 have a number of characteristics in common. In all, party control was unambiguous at the national level: one party controlled both the White House and Congress. In eight of the ten, the dominant party was also the majority party in national partisan identification (see Table 2.1). Second, national party unity was typically weak; in three Congresses, the 63rd, 64th, and 89th, intraparty divisions were important in explaining the party's impotence. Third, in all but one (the 67th), the president had impressive sources of power and, for the most part, employed these in congressional policy making. Most students of the presidency would agree that Wilson, the two Roosevelts, McKinley, and Johnson were the most effective presidents in this century. And an effective president (defined as one who is able to

55

TABLE 4.1
CHARACTERISTICS OF RESTRICTED MINORITIES IN THE HOUSE OF REPRESENTATIVES

				EXTERNAL CONDITIONS				INTERNAL CONDITIONS			
Congress	Minority party	Temper[a]	Majority-minority combination[b]	Minority party unity	President[c]	Procedure	Margin[d]	Majority leadership	Minority leadership	Years in minority	Minority party in Senate
SEVERELY RESTRICTED MINORITIES											
63	R	3	12	Weak	Strong (WW)	Major changes	Large	Strong	Weak	2	Moderately unrestricted
73	R	4	1	Moderate	Strong (FDR)	No changes	Large	Weak	Weak	2	Severely restricted
74	R	4	1	Moderate	Strong (FDR)	No changes	Large	Weak	Weak	4	Severely restricted
75	R	4	1	Moderate	Strong (FDR)	No changes	Large	Weak	Weak	6	Severely restricted
RESTRICTED MINORITIES											
57	D	2	16	Weak	Moderately strong (WMcK)	No changes	Small	Weak	Weak	6	Restricted
58	D	2	16	Weak	Moderately strong (TR)	No changes	Small	Strong	Moderate	8	Restricted
59	D	1	16	Weak	Moderately strong (TR)	No changes	Large	Strong	Moderate	10	Restricted
64	R	3	12	Weak	Strong (WW)	No changes	Small	Moderately weak	Weak	4	Restricted
67	D	1	16	Weak	Weak (WGH)	No changes	Large	Weak	Weak	2	Restricted
89	R	3	1	Weak	Strong (LBJ)	Minor changes	Large	Moderately weak	Moderately weak	10	Restricted

a Key: (1) No dominant crisis, mood — inaction; (2) No dominant crisis, mood — unclear; (3) No dominant crisis, mood — action; (4) Dominant crisis, mood — action; (5) War crisis.
b See Table 2.1.
c See Table 2.2.
d Key: Large — over 100; moderate — 50–99; small — 0–49.

maximize his sources of power) is of major significance in determining the strategies available to the minority party.

Two other characteristics seem important for this type of Congress. The margin in the House has generally been large, e.g., 219 in the 74th Congress and 244 in the 75th Congress. Often it has been large in the Senate at the same time. Minority party leadership in the House was often weak during these Congresses, although strong leadership might have lessened the impact of restrictive conditions. But majority party leaders were not particularly strong during these Congresses either. The most impressive were Joseph G. Cannon and his cohorts (58th and 59th) and Oscar W. Underwood and his cohorts (63rd and 64th). Where House majority leaders were weak, either the president was strong (Franklin D. Roosevelt) or the minority's listlessness was fully matched by that of the majority and its president (Warren G. Harding).

RANGE OF STRATEGIES. What strategies are available to the "restricted" minority party? Although theoretically it could employ any strategy, for the most part during these Congresses it has limited itself to the weak strategies of support, inconsequential opposition, and withdrawal.

Two Congresses during which the minority party was severely restricted (the 63rd and 73rd) and three during which it was more moderately restricted (59th, 67th, and 89th) are discussed in detail here; the others listed in Table 4.1 receive much less attention.

SEVERELY RESTRICTED MINORITIES. The minority party in the 63rd and 73rd Congresses, the Republican Party, was rendered practically immobile by political conditions. But as the salient conditions for the minority party in the two Congresses were quite different, it employed different strategies. During the 63rd Congress, the most prominent condition was the party's disunity, which was responsible for most of the other limiting conditions as well. A Democrat was in the White House, the Democrats had an overwhelming margin in the House (largest for either party to that date), major changes had been made in House procedure, and House Republican leadership had been weakened — all primarily attributable to internecine warfare in the party. Further, President Wilson could draw strength from Republican disunity.

The condition most severely limiting the Republican Party during the 73rd Congress was the economic crisis facing the nation. In four

years, the Republican Party went from triumph to disaster. Few
would have predicted the downfall of the majority party following
the 1928 election. Hoover had won more electoral votes (444) and
popular votes (more than 21 million) than any other president in
history, the second highest percentage of electoral vote (84 per cent),
and the second highest percentage of popular vote (58 per cent)
since 1856 and the establishment of the modern two-party system.
Republicans had also won commanding majorities in both the House
and Senate. In 1932, Roosevelt broke most of Hoover's records — a
phenomenal accomplishment. Further, after the 1932 election, the
Republicans had only 117 members in the House of Representatives
(a loss of 150 seats over 1928), and 36 members in the Senate (a loss
of 20 over 1928). Certainly, no president in modern times had such
a clear mandate from the American people.

Few strategies were available to the minority Republicans in these
Congresses. During the 63rd Congress, House Republicans were
preoccupied with their internal divisions and stymied by the policy
procedures developed by the Democrats. For the most part, the party
could offer only inconsequential opposition to the legislative proposals
of the majority. Practically, the only alternative available to impotent
opposition was to withdraw completely if an issue divided the minority. During the 73rd Congress, particularly in the first session, House
Republicans were forced to support the legislative proposals of the
majority on occasion — an even weaker strategy than those employed
during the 63rd Congress. During the second session they turned to
inconsequential opposition and withdrawal.

Minority party behavior did differ between these two Congresses.
During the 63rd Congress, the primary restrictive condition, disunity,
could be remedied within the Republican Party, which was still the
majority party in national partisan preference. If the party were successful in eliminating its internal divisiveness, the restrictions on its
strategic options in Congress would be only temporary. If it could
not heal the breach, it could well disappear as a major party. Thus,
the stakes in seeking a rapprochement were large.

Given the characteristics of the American party system, this reunion might best be accomplished very simply by less aggressive behavior on both sides. That is, since the Republican Party was the
majority party in national partisan preference and preference is a
rather stable characteristic of the American voter, the party might
accomplish a partial healing by "holding on," ensuring that the

divisiveness would not go further and that the disagreements that did exist would not be advertised so broadly. The party in fact halted the trend toward divisiveness and glossed over disagreements, and the situation repaired itself.[1]

During the 73rd Congress, the Republican Party faced quite differ-ent conditions. It was not within the party's power to produce remedies; events were out of control. The party was pared to its members from the safest districts and, owing to a series of defeats, was denied the constant influx of new membership from marginal districts (or districts normally held by the other party) that it needs to stay alive. For the first time in the history of the modern two-party system, the party out of power lost seats in four consecutive elections — 1930, 1932, 1934, and 1936. By 1937, only 89 Repub-licans were left in the House, representing the last bastions of Repub-licanism in the nation. During the 75th Congress (1937–1938) the Republicans controlled only 7 of 48 state delegations in the House (three others were evenly divided). These were states in the North-east (Vermont, Maine, and Massachusetts), Midwest (Michigan and Wisconsin), and the Plains States (North Dakota and Kansas).

During the 63rd Congress the Democrats were forced to develop new procedures in enacting legislation. The revolt against Speaker Cannon in 1910 and its aftermath resulted in important rules changes intended to disperse power in the House. It was inevitable that a period of democratization would follow. President Wilson had an extensive program that he was determined to have enacted, however, and House Democrats had to develop some procedure that would also meet his demands. House Democrats had one Congress, the 62nd, in which they could develop procedures and yet not be fully responsible for the passage of the executive program (as Taft was still president). By the 63rd Congress, they had worked out a most interesting party procedure.

With the speaker's power diminished in 1910–1911, and collegial-ism and personalism rejected as leadership styles, Speaker Champ Clark of Missouri could not expect to wield power equal to that of his illustrious predecessor. Clark was almost perfectly suited to this situation. Affable, personable, and beloved, Clark reportedly said in the 61st Congress, "Although I am going to be Speaker next time, I

---

[1] Though the disagreements were "papered over," they were not resolved. The Republican Party continued to have serious divisions as a majority party in the 1920s.

am going to sacrifice the Speaker's power to change the rules." [2] He referred to himself as "Dean of the Faculty." Randall B. Ripley classifies his style of leadership as "collective," essentially sharing power with others.[3] Clark's majority leader, however, was Oscar W. Underwood, the brilliant Congressman, later Senator, from Alabama. Underwood also served as chairman of the powerful Committee on Ways and Means, and therefore of the Democratic Committee on Committees. He became the principal Democratic leader in the House.

Underwood capitalized on the pressure for democratization by establishing the caucus as a policy-setting group. Though the evidence on Underwood's techniques is still scanty, it is possible to describe the procedure that developed.[4] Following the introduction of major bills, and their assignment to committees, the Democratic Caucus would meet to debate the legislation, sometimes for two weeks. A vote would be taken, making the bill a party measure. Unless they recused themselves, Democrats were bound to vote for the bill and to vote against all amendments except those supported by the party leaders. The bill would then be brought before the appropriate committee, hearings would be held at the discretion of the Democratic leadership, and the bill would be sent to the House floor for debate. The Republicans played a very minor role in these proceedings.[5]

Even with all these disadvantages, it is conceivable that the minority party's options could be increased simply because of the strength, imagination, and style of its leaders. But the House Republicans in 1913 could not rely on their leadership as a source of power. They were led principally by old-guard leaders, all of whom had supported

[2] Quoted in Chang-wei Chiu, *The Speaker of the House of Representatives Since 1896* (New York: Columbia University Press, 1928), p. 303.

[3] See Randall B. Ripley, *Party Leaders in the House of Representatives* (Washington, D.C.: The Brookings Institution, 1967), p. 16.

[4] For one of the few analyses of Underwood's leadership during this period, see James S. Fleming, "Oscar W. Underwood: Leader of the House of Representatives, 1911–1915," (unpublished Master's thesis, University of Arizona, 1968).

[5] Various sources may be relied on for a more complete description of this procedure. See Chiu; Fleming; and also George R. Brown, *The Leadership of Congress* (Indianapolis: Bobbs Merrill, 1922); Paul D. Hasbrouck, *Party Government in the House of Representatives* (New York: Macmillan, 1927); Arthur S. Link, *Wilson: The New Freedom* (Princeton: Princeton University Press, 1956); Wilder H. Haines, "The Congressional Caucus of Today," *American Political Science Review*, Vol. 9 (November, 1915), pp. 696–706.

Cannon in the speakership fight. The minority leader was James R. Mann of Illinois, an interesting, rather enigmatic figure. He was closely identified with Cannon and won the minority floor leadership post in 1911 because the old-line Republicans still maintained a majority in the House Republican Party. Mann apparently was precise, humorless, and brilliant in his own way, a sort of "thinking man's H. R. Gross" (the taciturn representative from Iowa in recent Congresses). He seemed to be a transitional figure for the House Republicans; he was not very well liked by his colleagues but he was charged with the responsibility of holding the party together until they recaptured control of Congress. When the party did gain a majority in the House in 1919, Mann was defeated for the speakership by Frederick H. Gillett of Massachusetts.

This combination of external and internal political conditions neutralized the House Republican Party. Republicans were limited to inconsequential opposition. That is, they opposed the principal aspects of Wilson's program but could do little more than try to have amendments accepted, attempt to have the legislation recommitted, and then oppose final passage. Only if the Democrats were seriously split on an issue could the Republicans affect the outcome, and these instances were rare.[6]

The pattern of frustration for House Republicans can be illustrated by the three major pieces of legislation that passed during the 63rd Congress: the Underwood-Simmons Tariff, the Federal Reserve Act, and the Clayton Anti-trust Act. Each passed in the same way. Once the legislation was introduced and a binding Caucus vote obtained, the standing committee met merely to endorse it.

In spite of some controversy within the Democratic Party, when the party and President Wilson reached agreement, the bills passed the House by large margins (281–139 for the tariff, 286–85 for the banking bill, and 277–54 for the antitrust bill). Republicans complained about this procedure. Sereno E. Payne (New York), ranking Republican on the Committee on Ways and Means and former majority leader under Speaker Cannon, made the following state-

---

[6] One such instance was the legislation to repeal the exemption to American coastwise shipping under the Panama Canal Act of 1912. Speaker Clark and Majority Leader Underwood opposed President Wilson on repeal but, with some Republican support, Wilson was able to build a majority without their endorsement. See Link, *Wilson: The New Freedom*; and James M. Leake, "Four Years of Congress," *American Political Science Review*, Vol. 11 (May, 1917), pp. 252–83.

ment in the minority report on the Underwood Tariff: "In this statement we shall not attempt to analyze this bill or to criticize it in detail. *Our acquaintance with it is too brief to permit this.*" [7] The minority report on the Federal Reserve Act expressed the same frustrations:

> The undersigned regret that when the Committee on Banking and Currency met finally to consider H.R. 7837 they found the majority members of the committee so *bound by their caucus action that they could not consider amendments* to the bill which, if adopted, would have eliminated its unsound and questionable provisions.
> Such changes . . . are fundamental and vital. The majority members of the committee refused to favorably consider them on the ground that they involved matters of Democratic party policy settled *by the caucus.*[8]

Floor debate was generally *pro forma.* Republicans complained about the binding caucuses, the failure to hold hearings on the legislation itself, the so-called gag rule whereby Democrats were bound by the Caucus not to accept any amendments except those supported by their leaders, and other tactics. But the size of the Democratic majority and their unity overwhelmed all Republican efforts in the House. Only one Republican amendment was accepted on these three bills. On September 18, the Republicans introduced an amendment to the Federal Reserve bill endorsing the gold standard. This move was an effort to embarrass Secretary of State William Jennings Bryan. Bryan agreed to the amendment, however, and it was included in the bill.

In the 73rd Congress, the majority party leadership was principally located in the White House. It was fortunate for the Democrats that presidential leadership was strong, the margins were large, and the popular mood favored action. Neither the speaker, Henry T. Rainey of Illinois, nor the majority leader, Joseph W. Byrns of Tennessee, was a strong leader. Randall B. Ripley classified Rainey as a figurehead who was conservative in his use of power.[9] He classifies Byrns's speakership in the 74th Congress in the same way. The

---

[7] U.S. Congress, House, Committee on Ways and Means, House Report No. 5, 63rd Cong., 1st Sess., 1913, p. 1v (emphasis added).

[8] U.S. Congress, House, Committee on Banking and Currency, House Report No. 69, 63rd Cong., 1st Sess., 1913, p. 133 (emphasis added).

[9] Ripley, p. 16.

Democratic whip for the 73rd Congress was Arthur H. Greenwood of Indiana. Greenwood established an extensive whip system that became an important part of the party organization. The Democrats did use the Caucus but, for the most part, they did what President Roosevelt wanted them to do.[10]

If Democratic Party leadership in the House was weak, Republican Party leadership was weaker. Gone was the strength of Nicholas Longworth of Ohio and John Q. Tilson of Connecticut, who had led the House during the Coolidge and Hoover administrations. The minority floor leader in the 73rd Congress was Bertrand H. Snell, a staunchly conservative businessman from upstate New York, who was never very effective in his eight years as minority leader (though it must be said that he led under extremely difficult circumstances). The whip was Harry L. Englebright of California. Ripley indicates that Englebright continued the efficient whip system established by his predecessor, Carl G. Bachmann of West Virginia.[11] We have very little evidence that the leadership relied on either the Caucus or the Steering Committee to any great extent.

For these reasons, the minority party in the 73rd Congress varied between the weak strategies of supporting the majority-building efforts of the president and inconsequential opposition. The emergency was there, the president had won an overwhelming mandate, and the Republican Party had little claim to public support. House Republicans could only add a voice to the consensus, which served to legitimize unprecedented legislative actions.

President Roosevelt understood that the first days of his new administration were critical. Complicated governmental procedures could be set aside temporarily to catch up with rapid social change, but "politics as usual" would soon reappear. Thus, in the famous "Hundred Days," the president

> sent fifteen messages to Congress, guided fifteen major laws
> to enactment, delivered ten speeches, held press conferences
> and cabinet meetings twice a week, conducted talks with
> foreign heads of state, sponsored an international conference,

---

[10] The caucus apparently proved useful in canvassing opinion and organizing the great numbers of new Democrats. See E. Pendleton Herring, "The First Session of the 73rd Congress," *American Political Science Review*, Vol. 28 (February, 1934), pp. 65–83. The Democratic Caucus minutes for this period are available in the Library of Congress.

[11] Ripley, p. 36.

made all the major decisions in domestic and foreign policy, and never displayed fright or panic and rarely even bad temper.[12]

I have selected four pieces of legislation out of the vast quantities passed during the 73rd Congress to illustrate the minority party's strategies. Three were passed in the first session, the Emergency Banking Act, the Agricultural Adjustment Act, and the National Industrial Recovery Act; and one was passed in the second session, the Reciprocal Trade Act.

Most Republican support came very early in the first session. The Emergency Banking bill was introduced, debated, and passed in both houses March 9, the opening day of the 73rd Congress. Majority Leader Byrns asked for and got a unanimous consent agreement to limit debate to forty minutes *even though members had not seen the bill.* Minority Leader Snell expressed the hope that Republicans would not object to this procedure.

> The house is burning down, and the President of the United States says this is the way to put out the fire. And to me at this time there is only one answer to this question, and that is to give the President what he demands and says is necessary to meet the situation.[13]

The bill passed by a voice vote.

No other legislation would go through the House with such ease. But the legislative process by no means returned to normal. House Democrats pushed through legislation at a record pace by relying on closed rules, which restricted amendments. Ten closed rules were employed during the first session, compared to an average of two such rules a session for other Roosevelt Congresses. As a detailed study of the House Committee on Rules points out: "Hardly a single important bill having to do with the economic recovery program of the President was considered by the House except under the restrictions imposed by a so-called gag rule." [14] Despite these tactics — so dreaded and heavily criticized by the minority — sizable numbers of Republicans supported the legislation.

---

[12] Arthur M. Schlesinger, Jr., *The Coming of the New Deal* (Boston: Houghton Mifflin, 1959), p. 21.

[13] *Congressional Record,* 73rd Cong., 1st sess., March 9, 1933, p. 76.

[14] Lewis J. Lapham, "Party Leadership and the House Committee on Rules" (unpublished Ph.D. dissertation, Harvard University, 1954), p. 52.

Both the Agricultural Adjustment bill and the National Industrial Recovery bill were brought to the floor with closed rules. Representative William Bankhead (D-Alabama) met the chorus of criticisms from Republicans on the agriculture bill with the argument that:

> The Committee on Rules is the political and policy vehicle of the House of Representatives to effectuate the party program and the party policy. . . . The House of Representatives is now controlled by the Democratic Party. This is a part . . . of the Democratic program.[15]

Edward W. Pou (D-North Carolina), chairman of the Committee on Rules, argued the case for the National Industrial Recovery bill. He seemed somewhat defensive (and well he might since many Democrats were upset by now with the frequency of closed rules), saying, "It is what I understand the President of the United States desires. . . . Friends of the administration in charge of this measure do not wish the bill imperiled." [16] Arthur H. Greenwood (D-Indiana), the majority whip, pointed out that "these unusual rules are offered for the purpose of taking care of unusual situations." [17] Following brief debates, both bills passed with large margins (315–98 for the agriculture bill and 325–76 for the recovery bill).

During the second session of the 73rd Congress, House Republicans gave much less support to Roosevelt's efforts. They assumed the slightly more aggressive strategy of inconsequential opposition. Thus, with the trade bill, they issued a minority report listing twenty-four reasons why Republicans could not support the bill. It was extremely rare for House Republicans to issue a minority report in the first session. When the bill reached the floor, Allan T. Treadway (Massachusetts), ranking Republican on the Committee on Ways and Means, served mild notice that Republicans would offer less support in the future.

> In making critical remarks I wish to say that they are in no way reflections on the personality of the President of the United States. I hold the President in the very highest esteem. I have voted with him as far as I could, consistently with my conscience, in his program of recovery; but I claim that when our stern convictions differ from those of the Pres-

[15] *Congressional Record*, 73rd Cong., 1st sess., March 21, 1933, p. 666.
[16] *Ibid.*, May 25, 1933, p. 4188.
[17] *Ibid.*, p. 4189.

ident of the United States, there is but one course for us to pursue.[18]

Treadway's remarks were very circumspect, however, and caused the president no great worry; Roosevelt had a sizable and dependable majority without Republican support. The bill passed, after some committee amendments were accepted, 274–111. Only two House Republicans voted in favor.

The 63rd and 73rd Congresses represent very unusual minority party situations. In both, political conditions required that the minority party rely on a limited range of strategies in congressional policy making. House Republicans in both Congresses had the more immediate problem of survival as a political party.

The Republicans had little relief during the 74th and 75th Congresses. Franklin D. Roosevelt and the Democrats continued to dominate American politics. House Republicans either withdrew into silence or offered inconsequential opposition. As so often happens in Congress, the majority party soon became top-heavy. Thus, the Republican strategy became one of biding time, waiting for the Democrats to argue among themselves. Eventually, of course, the southern Democrats were offering as much active opposition to the president's program as the Republicans.

LESS RESTRICTED MINORITIES. Three Congresses, the 59th, 67th, and 89th, will be used in this study to illustrate the moderately restricted minority. Some distinctions must be made between these Congresses and those in which the minority party was severely restricted. Often these distinctions are subtle, as many of the same conditions seem to exist in both situations. As before, there are important differences among the Congresses according to the conditions that determined the restrictions on the minority party.

A number of similarities characterize the minority party in the 59th and 67th Congresses. In both it seems apparent that insofar as one can identify a national mood (always a difficult problem), that mood seemed to favor limited governmental action. This mood has been well established and identified in the 67th Congress and is summarized by the phrase "return to normalcy." But a similar sort of mood appeared during 1905–1907. In his introduction to Volume I of Theodore Roosevelt's letters, E. E. Morison describes the entire

---

[18] *Congressional Record*, 73rd Cong., 2nd sess., March 23, 1934, p. 5262.

Roosevelt era in the White House as a period of "normalcy." [19] And one of Roosevelt's biographers states that:

> In 1905 the United States was heady with the wine of prosperity and the prophets proclaimed, as prophets always do, that this blessing would last forever. Even the farmers were happy.[20]

In both Congresses, the minority Democrats suffered devastating defeats at the hands of the Republicans. In 1904, Roosevelt had won a smashing victory over Judge Parker, gaining more electoral votes than any previous presidential candidate. The House Republicans had a 114-seat margin over the Democrats. Their 250 seats represented a new high for either party. The Republican margin in the Senate was comfortable too.

In 1920, the nationally predominant Republican Party returned to power following the two Wilson administrations. Harding's victory was complete, garnering 76 per cent of the electoral vote and 60 per cent of the popular vote. In the House, the Republicans won 300 seats — the first time in history that a party had even approached that mark (the previous high was 250 in 1904). Their margin was 168 seats. The Democrats had never been so outnumbered and have not been since. As in 1904, the Senate margin was sizable (22 seats).

Another important similarity between the two Congresses was that the majority Republicans not only were divided but seemed to lack any unifying purpose that might result in an extensive program of legislation. Of course, this characteristic probably was related to the general mood of the country.

Other differences between these two Congresses determined the behavior of the minority party. Aside from the differences in margin and size of victory, changes occurred in the relative positions of Congress and the executive, and both presidents, Roosevelt and Harding, viewed their responsibilities differently.

The relative position of Congress changed greatly between 1905 and 1921. The principal event, of course, was the revolt against Speaker Cannon. The revolt itself, plus the election of Woodrow Wilson, a major supporter of "presidential government," resulted in a

---

[19] Elting E. Morison, ed., *The Letters of Theodore Roosevelt* (Cambridge: Harvard University Press, 1951–54), Vol. 5, p. xxiv.

[20] Henry F. Pringle, *Theodore Roosevelt: A Biography* (New York: Harcourt, Brace, 1931), p. 367.

decline in the power of Congress in relation to the executive. The House still had not recovered in 1921. In 1905, "congressional government" still characterized national policy making. In 1921, however, despite Harding's weakness, Congress (particularly the House) had not recovered from the decentralizing of its leadership and therefore could not reassert itself in policy making.

Harding took a very limited view of his position. To him, government was "a simple thing," [21] and he opened his inaugural address with these words: "Our supreme task is the resumption of our onward, normal way." [22] His analysis of himself is revealing: "I know my limitations. I know how far removed from greatness I am." [23] Despite his enormous margin in Congress, and the fact that Wilson had increased the power of the presidency, Harding's own view of his responsibilities kept him from being more assertive.

Roosevelt, on the other hand, was not modest. Before his inauguration in 1905, he reportedly announced: "Tomorrow I shall come into my office in my own right. Then watch out for me!" [24] Roosevelt's accomplishments in the 59th Congress may now seem unimpressive, but he did intend to lead. As E. E. Morison observes, "A great many things happened from 1901 to 1909, but after forty years not much, at first glance, seems to be left." [25] Still, Roosevelt dominated what was there to dominate.

Though the Democrats were seriously outnumbered in both Congresses, in neither instance were they as restricted as the Republicans during the 63rd and 73rd Congresses. The reasons are different for the two Congresses (the 59th and 67th). During the 59th, an energetic president was somewhat thwarted by lack of crisis and mood for action, intraparty divisions, and the fact that "congressional government" (in Woodrow Wilson's words) was still very much alive. During the 67th Congress, a lethargic president, who conceivably had greater prerogatives than Roosevelt, willingly adapted himself to what he thought was the mood of the country. Further, the congressional reforms of 1910–1911 had weakened majority party leadership in Congress — a weakness heightened by the continued internal party disputes among Republicans.

[21] Lindsay Rogers, "The First (Special) Session of the 67th Congress," *American Political Science Review*, Vol. 16 (February, 1922), p. 41.

[22] Willis F. Johnson, *The Life of Warren G. Harding* (New York: Johnston, 1923), p. 102.

[23] *Ibid.*, p. 12.

[24] Pringle, p. 359.

[25] Morison, p. xiv.

One might very well question whether the minority party in the 59th and 67th Congresses had greater influence on public policy making than the minority party in the 63rd and 73rd. Is a minority party with slightly greater options during periods of low output more influential in policy making than a minority party with fewer options during periods of high output? This is a very difficult question to answer. For the present, it is enough to say that the minority party's role is slightly different.

So little legislation was enacted during the 59th Congress (Congress was in session for only ten months during the two years) that it is difficult to select issues to illustrate our thesis. The very fact that the session was so short and so little was done is partial evidence, however. Much of Roosevelt's energy during this period was directed to foreign policy, notably the Russo-Japanese War and the Panama Canal. Henry F. Pringle refers to these as the "Imperial Years" in his biography of Roosevelt. Domestically, the principal legislation included the Hepburn Act, the Pure Food and Drug Act, and the Meat Inspection Act — all passed in 1906. The principal subject of domestic legislation during this period, the tariff, received limited attention. Apparently Roosevelt favored a downward tariff revision but was persuaded not to push it in Congress. Joe Cannon takes the credit for dissuading him.

> Roosevelt's mind was ever active, and there were times when he was more ready to listen to agitators and theorists with wild schemes than to take sober counsel of men of practical experience who preferred to let well enough alone rather than go tilting at windmills or chasing rainbows. I have already said that after Mr. McKinley's death Roosevelt was full of tariff revision. Now economics was a subject of which he knew nothing.[26]

According to Cannon, Roosevelt called him to the White House to discuss whether he should include tariff revision in his inaugural address. After asking the others around the room, the president asked for Joe's opinion. Cannon said that he agreed with Senator Platt of Connecticut in opposing any tariff revision. Thus, according to Cannon, the president:

> saw tariff revision would provoke a long and acrimonious debate and interfere with other legislation in which he was

[26] L. White Busbey, *Uncle Joe Cannon: The Story of a Pioneer American* (New York: Holt, 1927), pp. 208–9.

much more interested, and the wisest course was to drop the tariff, with all its dangers, and take up other subjects more popular and attended with fewer risks.[27]

On other legislation, cooperation and support frequently came from the minority Democrats. On the Hepburn bill, designed to increase the powers of the Interstate Commerce Commission in fixing railroad rates, the Democrats, despite their numbers, were able to have amendments adopted in committee. As Minority Leader Williams said in the floor debate:

> Mr. Chairman, the attitude which the House of Representatives holds to this bill is a rather remarkable one. It is very seldom that the two Parties in this House, crossing swords day by day, with partisanship always tense, though sometimes concealed, will unite publicly in presenting a common measure to the country, with the view of having an effect upon public sentiment in the country and upon other legislative quarters for the benefit of the people, regardless of party.[28]

The Hepburn bill passed the House by the overwhelming margin of 346-7. Minority Leader Williams even asked one of his Democratic colleagues to withdraw his motion of recommittal, stating, "We do not want to recommit this bill, of course." [29]

This pattern suggests another reason why the minority Democrats had more options than the Republicans during the 63rd and 73rd Congresses. Many of the programs favored by President Roosevelt that he was successful in getting past his own "old guard" were also favored by a number of Democrats. Thus, he could expect support and cooperation from the minority, conceivably as much as from his own party. Again, Williams' remarks on the Hepburn bill are revealing: "I congratulate the Democratic party, because, although in the minority, by constant driving and constant reiteration, a very much cherished Democratic policy is about to triumph under a Republican administration." [30]

During the 67th Congress, a major cause of inaction and dissension among the majority Republicans was the growth of an agricultural bloc in both houses that pressed for action by the federal government

---

[27] *Ibid.*, pp. 213–14.
[28] *Congressional Record*, 59th Cong., 1st sess., February 7, 1906, p. 2248.
[29] *Ibid.*, p. 2270.
[30] *Ibid.*, p. 2248.

to solve a serious farm economic crisis. President Harding was unwilling to support subsidies, which he considered "socialist doctrine." Harding recalled his own experiences on the farm:

> There is no remedy which will eliminate hardships which attend the inevitable hazards of farming. I can remember, in my early youth, there were many relatively barren years on the farm, but in those days nobody expected relief through the government. Farmers accepted their fortunes as they came and would economize and deny and seed again and look forward to a helpful harvest.[31]

This division in the Republican Party, plus the continual split between the Progressives and the regular Republicans, made it possible for the Democrats to increase their options somewhat as a minority party.

Obviously, if the Republicans could work together, there was very little they could not accomplish. Their margins in both houses were enormous and the president could rely on his popularity in the nation as expressed in the 1920 election. The potential strength of their position was demonstrated in the passage of the Fordney-McCumber Tariff in 1922. A major tariff revision was highly likely with the Republicans controlling Congress and the White House for the first time in eight years. An upward revision of the Underwood Simmons Tariff passed the Republican-controlled 66th Congress but was vetoed by President Wilson. In the 67th Congress, the tariff was even billed as "farm policy." Although farmers needed greater markets, a high tariff was offered as a palliative for their economic problems.[32] Thus, on this issue, the Republican Party was unified. As Andrew Sinclair observed: "For once, country and city, Capitol Hill and the White House were agreed. The products of both farm and factory were protected." [33] When the Committee on Ways and Means settled down to working out the details of the tariff schedules, they excluded the Democrats from their deliberations — an indication of how much power they had if they were united enough to use it.[34] The tariff passed the House by the large margin of 288–127.

[31] Andrew Sinclair, *The Available Man: The Life Behind the Masks of Warren Gamaliel Harding* (New York: Macmillan, 1965), p. 250.
[32] Lawrence H. Chamberlain, *The President, Congress and Legislation* (New York: Columbia University Press, 1946), p. 120.
[33] Sinclair, p. 250.
[34] Chamberlain, p. 121.

Despite the enormous margins amassed by the Republican Party in the 1920 elections, the 67th Congress did little to solve the major domestic problems facing the country after the war. With its great numbers, the Republican Party had to represent too many diverse interests to reach accord on what should be done. A crisis might have forced the party to pull together. But in 1921, no crisis came and Harding, who liked to think of himself as a "party man," [35] never succeeded in leading his party in Congress.

As Table 4.1 shows, the 89th Congress differed considerably from the 59th and 67th. A mood for action in policy making had been generated in part by Kennedy's assassination, in part by the reaction to the negativism about the Goldwater candidacy in the Republican Party, and in part by the overwhelming mandate given to President Lyndon B. Johnson. The result was that Johnson had impressive sources of power in dealing with Congress — the most impressive since Franklin D. Roosevelt's early Congresses. Although Johnson's victory at the polls did not break all election records, it was as astounding as any because there was no general crisis to explain it. In addition to his own victory, Johnson was able to negotiate with a Congress in which the Democrats had margins reminiscent of the early depression Congresses. And he deserved credit for these margins.

Thus, the important condition for the 89th Congress was the strength of the president following the 1964 elections. The result was an unparalleled outpouring of legislation during the first session. The minority party was rendered nearly impotent during this session, though not always as much as conditions seemed to suggest. The first and second sessions of the 89th Congress were markedly different. Despite their numbers, the minority party became a significant factor in much legislation during the second session. No parallel appears in the modern Congress for so sharp a distinction in the minority party's role between two sessions of the same Congress. The explanations for this phenomenon may be that so much was done during the first session that the majority wanted to take a breather, that the president's mandate was not quite real (i.e., many voters were voting against Goldwater rather than for Johnson),[36] or that Democratic congressmen were afraid of the label "rubber-stamp Congress," particularly with the upcoming midterm elections in 1966.

[35] See Johnson, Ch. 22.
[36] See Philip E. Converse, *et al.*, "Electoral Myth and Reality: The 1964 Election," *American Political Science Review*, Vol. 59 (June, 1965), pp. 321–36.

All these factors are important in explaining the differences between these two sessions. But an additional factor is of particular importance. The minority party began to develop a more positive role for itself in policy making. In the House the younger, more energetic members, who had pressed for a more constructive opposition party, continued their efforts to assume control of the party. They took advantage of the fact that their party was in disarray and won a number of leadership posts, including the floor leadership. Despite the disunity in the national Republican party, House Republicans especially decided to develop policy alternatives. Despite their numbers, they presented a minority "state of the union" appraisal in 1966. Thus, the minority party in the 89th Congress was not the same kind of impotent, leaderless, and generally disorganized minority party of the 63rd and 73rd, or even the more moderately restricted minority party of the 59th and 67th Congresses. In fact, these two sessions can be distinguished by the strategies available to the minority party — moderately restricted during the first session and moderately unrestricted during the second session.

So much legislation was passed during both sessions of the 89th that a detailed analysis of the minority party's role is not possible in this book. An entire book should be written on this remarkable Congress. The most that can be done here is to summarize the actions of the minority party in the two sessions on some of the more significant legislation so as to illustrate the range of strategies.

During the first session, Johnson set many records. He submitted 469 proposals and had 323, or 68.9 per cent, approved. On roll calls in the House, where the president's stand was clear, he was on the winning side 94 per cent of the time — a phenomenal statistic! The list of legislation is impressive: medical care for the aged, aid to elementary and secondary education, enforcement of voting rights for Negroes, immigration reform, housing, regional economic planning and development, establishment of a Department of Housing and Urban Development, highway beautification, air and water pollution control, a constitutional amendment on presidential continuity, agricultural programs, among the more important measures. Although the minority Republicans frequently were limited to inconsequential opposition, one can identify major instances of innovation (medical care for the aged), cooperation and support (voting rights for Negroes), consequential partisan opposition (rent supplements), and constructive opposition (several proposals). Though restricted overall, the minority party in the 89th Congress demonstrated that it can have a definite, active role in policy making despite limiting conditions.

The second session of the 89th Congress found the Democrats less unified — an important condition for increased minority party influence. The Democratic record is still impressive; President Johnson submitted 371 proposals and had 207, or 55.8 per cent, approved, and he won 91 per cent of the roll calls in the House where his stand was clear.[37] In nearly every case, however, the margins were narrower and the threat posed by a unified minority seeking support from dissident members of the majority was important.

THE SENATE

Since many of the same Congresses are involved in analyzing restricted minorities in the Senate, the similarities among external conditions would remain — strong president (with the exception of Harding), one-party dominance, weak national minority party unity. Among the internal conditions, the margins were large, the majority leadership somewhat stronger than for the House, and the minority leadership generally weak.

SEVERELY RESTRICTED MINORITIES. As with the House, only the Senate Republicans have been severely restricted in this century. During the 73rd Congress, Senate Republicans had not as yet received the full brunt of the changes among the electorate. Since only one third of the Senate is elected every two years, dramatic changes among the electorate affect that body somewhat less rapidly. It was not until 1936, and the 75th Congress, that party change was fully reflected in the Senate. Conversely, it took the Senate Republicans somewhat longer to recover than House Republicans.

During the 73rd Congress, the Democrats had a relatively moderate margin of twenty-three over Republicans. But the margin is not always critical in determining the limits on the minority. The voters had clearly indicated their mood in House elections, and the meaning of these returns was not lost on Republican senators. In almost every piece of major legislation during the dramatic first session, opposition was only slightly greater among Senate Republicans than House

[37] These percentages are from the Congressional Quarterly. See *Congressional Quarterly Almanac*, Vols. 21 and 22, 1965, 1966.

TABLE 4.2
CHARACTERISTICS OF RESTRICTED MINORITIES IN THE SENATE[a]

| | | | EXTERNAL CONDITIONS | | | | | INTERNAL CONDITIONS[a] | | | |
Congress	Minority party	Temper[b]	Majority-minority combination[c]	Minority party unity	President[d]	Margin[e]	Majority leadership	Minority leadership	Years in minority	Minority party in House
SEVERELY RESTRICTED MINORITIES										
73	R	4	1	Moderate	Strong (FDR)	Moderate	Strong	Weak	0	Severely restricted
74	R	4	1	Moderate	Strong (FDR)	Large	Strong	Weak	2	Severely restricted
75	R	4	1	Moderate	Strong (FDR)	Large	Strong	Weak	4	Severely restricted
RESTRICTED MINORITIES										
57	D	2	16	Weak	Moderately strong (WMcK)	Large	Strong	Weak	4	Restricted
58	D	2	16	Weak	Moderately strong (TR)	Large	Strong	Weak	6	Restricted
59	D	1	16	Weak	Moderately strong (TR)	Large	Strong	Weak	8	Restricted
60	D	1	16	Moderate	Moderately strong (TR)	Large	Strong	Weak	10	Moderately unrestricted
64	R	3	12	Weak	Strong (WW)	Moderate	Strong	Weak	2	Restricted
67	D	1	16	Weak	Weak (WGH)	Moderate	Moderate	Moderately weak	2	Restricted
76	R	4	1	Strong	Strong (FDR)	Large	Moderately strong	Weak	6	Moderately unrestricted
77	R	5	1	Strong	Strong (FDR)	Large	Strong	Weak	8	Moderately unrestricted
88	R	2	1	Strong	Strong (LBJ)	Large	Moderately weak	Moderately strong	8	Unrestricted
89	R	3	1	Weak	Strong (LBJ)	Large	Moderately weak	Moderately strong	10	Restricted

[a] Since no significant procedural changes were made in these Senates, this condition is omitted.
[b] For key, see Table 4.1.
[c] See Table 2.1.
[d] See Table 2.2.
[e] Key: Large, over 25; Moderate, 14–24; Small, 0–13.

Republicans, and overall the amount of support for measures that the party had traditionally opposed was amazing. With the Emergency Banking bill, Senator Arthur Vandenberg (R-Michigan) expressed the view of most Republicans when he advised his colleagues that "the new administration is fresh from a popular mandate. It is entitled to an unhampered chance to save the crisis." [38] On the National Industrial Recovery bill, more opposition was expressed by Senator Huey Long (D-Louisiana) than practically all the Senate Republicans. He referred to it as "the most tyrannical law that I have ever seen proposed since I have been in the United States Congress." [39] Yet even Senator Long voted for the bill.

The Senate Republicans reacted much as did their brethren in the House during the second session of the 73rd Congress. They were more belligerent but to no avail. Republicans strongly attacked the Reciprocal Trade bill during the lengthy debate, but Senator Long once again was most vehement. With this bill, "we have made the bold experiment of doing away with legislative government." [40] Only 5 Republicans voted for the bill, 28 against. Senator Long and four other Democrats also voted against.

The Senate Republicans were only beginning their plummet in the 73rd Congress. They were reduced to 25 in the 74th Congress and to 17 in the 75th Congress. It was during the 75th Congress that Minority Leader McNary and his 16 colleagues adopted the "operation silence" strategy. "Let the boys across the aisle do the talking," was his advice.[41] Certainly no minority party in this century was more severely restricted in developing strategies than were the congressional Republicans in both houses from 1933 to 1939.

LESS RESTRICTED MINORITIES. Two generalizations apply to our cases of less restricted minorities during the 59th, 67th, and 89th Congresses. The president in each case had more difficulty with his own party in the Senate than in the House, and the minority in the Senate potentially had greater options than its counterpart in the House.

In the 59th Congress, President Theodore Roosevelt had great problems in working with the small clique of Republican senators

---

[38] *Congressional Record*, 73rd Cong., 1st sess., March 9, 1933, p. 62.
[39] *Ibid.*, June 7, 1933, p. 5183.
[40] *Congressional Record*, 73rd Cong., 2nd sess., May 17, 1934, p. 9012.
[41] Malcolm Moos, *The Republicans: A History of Their Party* (New York: Random House, 1956), pp. 406–7.

that controlled that body. This was the period when Nelson Aldrich and his advisers dominated. Roosevelt's progressivism and general demeanor irritated Aldrich. When the Hepburn bill, a major Roosevelt proposal, got to the Senate, Senator Davis Elkins (R-West Virginia), chairman of the Committee on Interstate Commerce, refused to sponsor it. Senator Aldrich secured adoption of a resolution that put a Democrat, Senator Benjamin (Pitchfork Ben) Tillman (D-South Carolina), in charge of the bill. Tillman and Roosevelt disliked each other intensely. It was only by clever manipulation and bargaining with his own party that Roosevelt was able to get the bill passed in a form reasonably acceptable to him.[42]

Because of the difficulties between the president and his own party leadership in the Senate, and the lack of unity among Republicans, the minority Democrats were influential in majority building during the 59th Congress. Yet the potential was even greater; many options were available to the minority Democrats. If they had been more unified, elected strong leadership, and organized with strength, they might have been able to adopt strategies in majority building that would have projected them into the center of policy making. For several reasons they did not. First and foremost, this is not the way minorities behaved at that time. Second, the majority party leadership was awesome in its power. The minority party simply did not have leaders to match those of the majority. Indeed, Aldrich and his colleagues were so persuasive that many Democrats supported them. Third, the nation's mood probably would not have supported an innovative and vigorous minority.

Much of the same description applies to the 67th Congress. Harding had his greatest difficulty with the Senate, where progressivism and agricultural radicalism had strong representation in his party.

> Harding's immediate trouble was an old one. His relationship
> with the Senate grew worse and worse. He felt himself every
> inch a President — except in his dealings with Capitol Hill.
> As he told the National Press Club at the close of his first
> full year in office, he felt as if he had been "President for
> twenty years. Life since I came to the White House has been
> so full there is scarcely an impression left of the life before.

[42] For accounts of action on this legislation see Pringle, pp. 420–25 and Chamberlain, pp. 415–20.

There is only one distinct one. I recall my previous con-
ception of the Senate as compared with the one I have today,
but no unkindliness is meant by that." The unkindliness was
all on the side of the Senate, and Harding was puzzled by the
hostility of that once-friendly body.[43]

Again, had the minority been able to take advantage of this situation,
their share in policy making would have been considerably greater.
But their leadership was generally weak and their organization nonexistent, so that the options available, cooperation, innovation, constructive opposition, were generally not exercised.

During the 89th Congress, on the other hand, the Senate Republicans did exercise some of their options. Though he had much
greater success with the Senate than had Theodore Roosevelt or
Harding, President Johnson still found that body less likely to give
him support than the House. During the remarkable first session,
Johnson received almost equal support in the Senate and the House
(93 per cent of roll calls won in the Senate compared to 94 per cent
in the House). When one examines support from the average Democratic senator compared to the average Democratic representative,
however, the difference is striking. The composite score for Senate
Democrats was 64 per cent, for House Democrats 74 per cent.
Senate Republicans, on the other hand, supported the president more
than did their colleagues in the House.

In the second session, the president's stand on roll calls was supported only 69 per cent of the time in the Senate, compared to 91 per
cent in the House. The composite score for Senate Democrats
dropped to 57 per cent, compared to 63 per cent for House Democrats.[44]

Remarkable as it may seem, President Johnson found it necessary
on occasion to rely on Republican support. The most impressive
instance, of course, was with the Voting Rights bill of 1965. As with
the Civil Rights Act of 1964, the legislation so seriously divided
Democrats that the minority party found itself adopting a participating strategy even though a Democrat was in the White House. The
filibuster in the Senate could not have been broken without the
cooperation and support of the Senate Republicans. In other instances, on key roll call votes, Senate Republican support enabled the

[43] Sinclair, p. 248.
[44] See *Congressional Quarterly Almanac*, Vols. 21 and 22, 1965, 1966.

president to win — e.g., military assistance funds, rent subsidies, and foreign farm workers' legislation in 1965, and rent supplements funds, foreign aid, and the minimum wage bill in 1966.

Despite the unusually close and cordial relationship between Minority Leader Everett M. Dirksen of Illinois and the president (almost without precedent in the history of the Senate), Senate Republicans did not always cooperate, support, and participate. They also opposed vigorously — sometimes constructively, sometimes not; sometimes consequentially, and sometimes not. On many of the major Johnson proposals, individual Republican Senators attempted to get alternative proposals adopted. And on some major legislation, Republicans were able to garner enough Democratic support to defeat the president. Notable among these in 1965 was the attempt to repeal the section of the Taft-Hartley Act permitting states to enact "right-to-work" laws. In 1966, the Senate Republicans balked at supporting the civil rights legislation of that year, and as a result no bill was passed.

It seems probable that no minority party so restricted by the political conditions of the time can expect to have more influence in policy making in either House of Congress than did the Republicans in the 89th Congress. For the most part, this influence was gained by the resourcefulness of the minority party leaders and the development, particularly in the House, of an organization designed to reshape the minority party's role in Congress.

HOUSE-SENATE COMBINATIONS

In four of the Congresses discussed above, the 59th, 67th, 73rd, and 89th, the minority party was restricted in both houses. At times the minority party may be restricted in one house and not in the other. Whereas the minority Republicans in the House recovered dramatically in the 1914 elections, gaining 66 seats and narrowing the margin to 38 seats, the Senate Republicans lost an additional 5 seats. This loss, plus their own internal divisions, restricted their strategies in the 64th Congress.[45] Roughly the same circumstances prevailed in the 1938 election. House Republicans rebounded from their successive defeats to gain 80 seats. Senate Republicans did not gain the full

---

[45] Even with their gains, the House Republicans were restricted by their continued disunity.

benefit of the Republican revival and thus gained only 6 seats. Therefore, even with the ever increasing internal rifts in the Democratic Party, the Senate Republicans were not able to take full advantage because they still had only 23 members, 46 fewer than the Democrats.

Conversely, the minority party in the House may be restricted when the minority party in the Senate is not. The classic instance in this century occurred during the 63rd Congress. Again, because of the election of only one third of the senators every two years, the Senate Republicans did not lose as heavily in 1912 as did their colleagues in the House. The Democratic margin over the Republicans in the House was 163 seats, but in the Senate it was only 7 seats. President Wilson had problems with all his major proposals in the Senate, though he was remarkably successful. Party leaders in the Senate and the split in the Republican Party were the principal reasons for his victories.

These minority party combinations between the Senate and the House do increase the party's overall role in Congress by providing somewhat greater strategic options. It may well be that having a moderately unrestricted minority in the other house increases the options available to the restricted minority. During the later Roosevelt Congresses, the Republican revival was being reflected in the House elections, certainly boosting morale in the Senate party, too, even though this revival was not as dramatically reflected in Senate results. The exception appeared in the 63rd Congress, where the major cause of minority party decline was disunity. The relatively greater number of options available to the Senate Republican Party in the 63rd Congress seemed to make no difference at all for the House Republican Party.

SUMMARY

Several observations can be made as a result of this survey of restricted minorities. First, there may be important differences in influence and effectiveness among minority parties that are restricted. As has been illustrated, minority parties are virtually immobilized by political conditions; others are restricted but do have some strategies available if they are able to muster the energy to use them. Second, it is clear that some conditions primarily determine how restricted the minority party will be. Particularly burdensome is the kind of party disunity experienced by the Republicans between 1910 and 1920. Third, the minority party in the past has not realized even the limited potential of the restricted situation. Fourth, a significant change has appeared (particularly in the 89th Congress) in the minority party's aggressiveness, suggesting that even a restricted minority party can have influence in policy making. Finally, because the Senate reflects electoral shifts more slowly than the House, strategic situations can be quite different for the minority party in the two bodies.

CHAPTER FIVE

Participating Minorities

In an attempt to institutionalize their values, the founding fathers made possible highly ambiguous political combinations at the national level. The two political parties can split control of the House, the Senate, the White House, and national partisan identification of voters. Fourteen combinations of split control among these four are possible; twelve of these involve splits between House, Senate, and presidency. Fortunately, however, this nation has been spared experiencing all twelve. Only four of the twelve have occurred in this century (combinations 4, 6, 11, and 15 in Table 2.1).

These four combinations of split control represent special policy-making circumstances because the minority party in Congress (or in one house) controls the presidency. Naturally the president turns first to his party leaders in attempting to build the majorities necessary for the legitimation of his proposals. For this reason, the minority party's major strategy is limited in these circumstances to participating in majority building. Potentially, this strategy is significant for the party, particularly if the minority party president has an extensive legislative program and his congressional party leaders have important sources of power. As it turns out, however, participating minorities in this century have been rather restricted.

THE HOUSE

The Congresses with participating minorities share a number of political characteristics (see Table 5.1). First and foremost is the weakness of the president. While some, notably Taft and Hoover, have been weaker than others, all have suffered from limited sources of power. Second, the majority party often had stronger House leadership than the minority party. Finally, the margin was usually not large and the minority party had only recently lost majority status in the House.

Several important differences among these Congresses affected the minority party. The 62nd and 72nd Congresses were least like the others. In both the majority party, the Republican Party, was in decline. The party began to lose ground in the House elections of 1910 and 1930, losing control of the House in each of the two mid-term elections but retaining a majority in the Senate. In the 62nd Congress, the Democrats had a majority of sixty-six seats in the House, while the Republicans enjoyed a seven-seat majority in the Senate. In the 72nd Congress, the Democrats were slightly in the minority in the House after the elections, but by the time the House organized in 1931, they had a narrow margin because several House Republicans had died. The Republicans had a one-seat margin in the Senate.

In the Eisenhower Congresses, 84th, 85th and 86th, and Wilson's last Congress, the 66th, the president was a member of the minority party. Eisenhower was able to win through personal charisma. But his assets at the polls were not particularly helpful in dealing with Congress. Wilson won because of the split in the Republican Party, and his victory in 1916 was extremely narrow.

During the 84th and 85th Congresses, the president and the party had some important sources of power which resulted in a rather significant policy-making role for the Republicans in Congress. During the 66th and 86th Congresses, however, majority party leaders in Congress (and nationally) began to sense that their return to the White House was imminent. In both, the majority party was almost totally uncooperative with the president and a virtual stalemate developed between the executive and legislative branches of government.

The final Congress in this set is the notorious 80th Congress. The Democrats were the participating minority in both houses, as the Republicans had gained control for the first time in eighteen years. In this instance, the majority party nationally and in the White House was in the minority in Congress. A policy-making situation developed that was quite unlike that of the 62nd and 72nd Congresses where the majority party was in the process of being deposed. During the 80th Congress the Democratic Party had reasonably good prospects of returning to power in Congress in 1948. Thus President Truman and the minority party leadership were quite aggressive.

TABLE 5.1
CHARACTERISTICS OF PARTICIPATING MINORITIES IN THE HOUSE OF REPRESENTATIVES

			EXTERNAL CONDITIONS			INTERNAL CONDITIONS					
Congress	Minority party	Temper[a]	Majority-minority combination[b]	Minority party unity	President[c]	Procedure	Margin[a]	Majority leadership	Minority leadership	Years in minority	Minority party in Senate
62	R	3	15	Weak	Weak (WHT)	Major changes	Moderate	Moderately strong	Weak	0	Demos in minority (Unrestricted)
66	D	5	11	Moderate	Moderately weak (WW)	No changes	Small	Moderately weak	Moderately weak	0	Participating
72	R	4	15	Moderate	Weak (HH)	No changes	Small	Moderately weak	Weak	0	Demos in minority (Unrestricted)
80	D	2	4	Weak	Moderately weak (HST)	Major changes	Moderate	Moderately strong	Moderately strong	0	Participating
84	R	2	6	Strong	Moderately weak (DDE)	No changes	Small	Strong	Moderately weak	0	Participating
85	R	2	6	Strong	Moderately weak (DDE)	No changes	Small	Strong	Weak	2	Participating
86	R	2	6	Strong	Weak (DDE)	No changes	Large	Strong	Moderate	4	Participating

a For key, see Table 4.1.
b See Table 2.1.
c See Table 2.2.

POLICY MAKING. The natural tensions between Congress and the president are amplified when Congress (or one of its chambers) is controlled by the other party. Productivity is not likely to be great under such conditions, but it need not be low. For example, though the 62nd and 72nd Congresses were similar in many respects, the product was different. The minority Republicans in the House were virtually impotent in the 62nd Congress. The relatively moderate margin enjoyed by the Democrats was enhanced by the serious split in the Republican Party. Further, President Taft, who never had great personal sources of strength, was especially weak at this time. His prestige continued to decline, his party was hopelessly divided, and Taft endorsed a limited view of presidential power. Consequently little legislation of significance passed. The Democrats preoccupied themselves with organizing the House and holding hearings on legislation that they intended to enact when they gained full control in the 63rd Congress. The Republicans continued to fight among themselves, offering little as a party to cope with the social and economic problems that the Progressives warned were on the horizon. The president appeared to mark time. It was almost as if the Republicans were waiting for their inevitable defeat.

During the 72nd Congress, on the other hand, no set of decision-makers could ignore the need for some type of action. Though President Hoover and the House Republicans may have convinced themselves earlier that the economy was undergoing a major adjustment and would right itself eventually, by 1931 it was apparent that a boost was needed. President Hoover did not mark time. He proposed a series of corrective measures and was frustrated by the slowness with which the Congress acted. Hoover could rely on a considerably stronger House Republican party than Taft, both in numbers and in unity, even though the death of Nicholas Longworth deprived Hoover of strong leadership in the House. Longworth's successor, Bertrand H. Snell of New York, was unable to provide the kind of leadership needed.

President Hoover was able to have major legislation enacted in the House because he used his sources of power effectively and both parties acknowledged the need for action. Notable among these actions was the passage of the Reconstruction Finance Corporation Act of 1932. Hoover called congressional leaders of both parties together to gain support for this legislation and urged speed in its adoption. Naturally he relied most on Republican leaders in the House. In his

account of the passage of this legislation, Professor Lawrence H.
Chamberlain notes that speed in passage became "almost an obses-
sion with [Hoover]."

> On December 26 [1931] he let it be known that no matter
> how irresponsible Congress might be he could not afford to
> indulge in the luxury of idleness while the nation was in
> peril. He announced tersely that he planned to spend the re-
> mainder of his holiday holding numerous individual confer-
> ences with congressmen, both Democrats and Republicans,
> in an effort to gain . . . speedy action.[1]

The House finally passed the measure on January 15, 1932, with wide-
spread support from both parties — 94 per cent of the minority
Republicans and 78 per cent of the majority Democrats voting in
favor. This pattern of bipartisan support was typical of that part of
Hoover's recovery program that was enacted into law.

The Congresses under a minority party president (66th, 84th, 85th,
and 86th) differed in output too. Least productive were the 66th
and 86th Congresses, the last for the Wilson and Eisenhower administrations respectively. By the 66th Congress, Président Wilson
faced a Congress controlled by the opposition party. In the House,
the Republicans had a 46-seat margin over the Democrats. With the
president's strength waning politically and physically, few expected
the minority party Democrats in the House to take up the slack. By
1919, Champ Clark, never a strong leader, was nearly seventy and
would himself be defeated for reelection to the 67th Congress. The
Democrats were weakening, as the Republican Party began to reestablish itself as the majority party in Congress.

During the 66th Congress House members had relatively free
reign in determining the precise nature of legislation. Accommodations were arrived at between the two parties, with the president playing almost no role at all. Chamberlain concluded about the National
Defense Act, the most important military measure between the two
wars, that "perhaps the most striking aspect of the bill throughout its
history was the absence of any strong or sustained presidential support behind it." Of the Transportation Act of 1920, Chamberlain
observed, "Congress was left to deal with the railroad issue in its
own way." The President, for his part, signed the bill with little

---

[1] Lawrence H. Chamberlain, *The President, Congress, and Legislation* (New
York: Columbia University Press, 1946), p. 289.

enthusiasm: "[The bill is] so unsatisfactory that I could accept it, if at all, only because I despaired of anything better." [2] Thus, the participating minority party Democrats in the House had very little to participate in as the president finished his term in ill health. For the most part, contemporary evaluations of the 66th Congress were unflattering. That of Professor Lindsay Rogers is typical.

> Congress left many problems half completed or untouched. The Senate continued to spend a great part of its time on the Peace Treaty, and both the Senate and the House thought primarily of the effect of their activities on the presidential campaign rather than of efficient legislation; partisanship and hostility to the President were the dominant *motifs* of the session.[3]

Except for the hostility to the president, the Rogers remarks fit the 86th Congress. In 1919–1920, President Wilson was physically unable to lead with strength. In 1959–1960, President Eisenhower faced overwhelming odds in enacting his program because of the large Democratic majorities in both houses. The Republican Party suffered a much greater defeat in 1958 than the Democrats did in 1918. The Democrats had a margin of 129 seats in the House in the 86th Congress. Though there had been considerable cooperation between the administration and the House Democrats in the 84th and 85th Congresses, this cooperation did not characterize the 86th Congress. With the upcoming 1960 presidential election, the Democrats did not want to help the Republicans establish a record of achievement.

Very little major legislation was enacted during the 86th Congress. Of the 411 proposals President Eisenhower submitted, Congress approved 149 or 36 per cent (40.8 per cent in the first session and 30.6 per cent in the second).[4] To be enacted into law, presidential proposals had to be supported by many Democrats. But the President risked loss of Republican support in gaining Democratic votes — a familiar pattern during the 84th and 85th Congresses.

An important difference between the Wilson and Eisenhower administrations is that whereas Wilson's party controlled three of his

---

[2] *Ibid.*, p. 209; p. 428; quoted in *ibid.*, p. 431.
[3] Lindsay Rogers, "American Government and Politics: The Second Session of the 66th Congress," *American Political Science Review*, Vol. 14 (November, 1920), pp. 659–60.
[4] See *Congressional Quarterly Almanac*, Vols. 15 and 16, 1959, 1960.

four Congresses, Eisenhower's party controlled only one of his four Congresses. The Republicans were a participating minority in the 84th, 85th, and 86th Congresses. Until the 86th the Republicans in both houses had considerable strength. In the 84th, the Democratic majority in the House was twenty-nine seats; in the 85th, thirty-three. In both Congresses, Eisenhower was reasonably successful in gaining support for his proposals: 46 per cent were enacted into law during the 84th Congress and 42 per cent during the 85th.[5] Though production was high in the 84th and 85th Congresses compared to other Congresses with participating minorities, a close examination of the legislative record of the two Congresses reveals a pattern of confusion and frequent stalemate. The 85th Congress will be examined here in some detail.

In 1956, President Eisenhower was reelected by record margins. The minority party in Congress was faced with conflicting demands and expectations: enacting the popular president's program while opposing congressional Democratic leadership. Since the margins in both the House and Senate were narrow, three conditions — one external, two internal — could have strengthened the minority party. The external condition, would have been a president with several sources of power other than a majority in Congress. President Eisenhower did have one such source of power — his phenomenal popularity among the public. Several factors prevented Eisenhower from turning this advantage into success in policy making, however. First, no compelling crisis or general mood for action existed to rally legislators in support of the president. Second, Eisenhower's background, an asset at the polls, did not give him the necessary skills for majority building in these circumstances.[6] Third, the president did not appear to acknowledge the need for legislation in many areas and therefore did not offer an extensive program.

The internal conditions strengthening the minority party would have been weak majority party leadership combined with strong minority party leadership. If House Democratic leaders had been inept and House Republican leaders had been exceptional negotiators, it is conceivable that the minority party would have been

---

[5] See *Congressional Quarterly Almanac*, Vols. 12 and 14, 1956, 1958.

[6] Again, I rely on Neustadt's analysis in *Presidential Power* to a considerable extent in discussing a president's sources of power. Neustadt concludes that Eisenhower was unaware of his "natural advantages" for getting things done; in short, he did not understand presidential power (pp. 163–65).

highly successful in building majorities for a Republican program. But this was not the case during the 85th Congress.

In the House, the Democrats were able to rely on Sam Rayburn as speaker and John W. McCormack as majority leader. Rayburn was serving his twenty-second term as a member of the House and his seventh full term as speaker. Though Rayburn apparently lost some of his characteristic alertness in later Congresses, in the 85th Congress he led his party with strength. Rayburn approached the perfect model of the effective speaker of the House. He knew the rules and how to use them, he maintained contact with all of the various wings of the House Democratic Party, and he was very protective of his procedural majority, sensing when he might have gone too far with any members. He also retained a fine sense of compromise, and relied on techniques of leadership which emphasized party unity.[7]

McCormack was serving his fifteenth full term in the House and his ninth term as the second-ranking leader in his party, seven as majority leader and two as minority whip. Though generally considered more partisan than Rayburn, McCormack had proved himself a durable and generally well-liked leader.

Rayburn and McCormack did not rely on either the Caucus or a steering committee. They maintained a relatively efficient whip system as a formal system of communication (led by Carl Albert of Oklahoma in the 85th Congress), but both relied more heavily on informal methods of contact than on the formal whip system. Meetings of Democrats to set party policy were discouraged, as both leaders feared that such meetings would be divisive.

House Republicans were not so fortunate in getting strong leadership. Joseph W. Martin, Jr., of Massachusetts, led the party. He was experienced in leading House Republicans, having done so since the 76th Congress. As contrasted with his long-time friend, Sam Rayburn, however, Martin was losing contact with many of the younger members. In addition, his health was failing. At the opening of the 86th Congress Martin was defeated for the minority leadership post by Charles A. Halleck of Indiana.

Like Rayburn, Martin relied on personalism as a leadership technique. But he was never as successful as Rayburn. Conditions in the Republican Party (e.g., less sectional diversity) favored greater use

---

[7] For a useful, but disappointing, biography of Rayburn, see C. Dwight Dorough, *Mr. Sam* (New York: Random House, 1962).

of party caucus and committee action than for the Democrats. Republicans were generally more unified and could gain publicity from such meetings. Martin, however, continued to rely on a coterie of advisers. Halleck was one of these in earlier times, but Martin had grown to distrust him. Leslie C. Arends of Illinois served as his whip.

Thus, House Republicans had uninspired leadership in the 85th Congress. Martin's greatest sources of strength were his friendship with Rayburn and his long experience in the House. But many young members considered his friendship with Rayburn more harmful to the party than helpful and his experience no longer relevant. They wanted to establish a more positive image for the party and were frustrated under the leadership of Martin, Arends, and ranking committee members like Clarence Brown (Ohio) of the Committee on Rules. These dissatisfied members made many changes in the House Republican Party in later years.[8]

These and other factors prevented the minority party from achieving maximum effectiveness in the 85th Congress. In some cases, as with the Civil Rights Act of 1957, the two parties worked together, with the Republicans providing most support. More often, however, the policy results were characterized by confusion, ambiguity, and stalemate. Sometimes a presidential proposal divided House Republicans and Eisenhower's efforts to unify them risked the loss of needed Democratic support. Efforts to gain Democratic support further divided Republicans. The president had a mixed record on such issues. On reciprocal trade and national defense education, he and his party leaders were able to build a sufficiently large coalition for passage. On federal aid to education, not only was Eisenhower unsuccessful in mustering support, but he apparently had doubts about the bill himself. And who can know how many proposals were never offered because of the ambiguity of the congressional situation? The president himself was discouraged following the first session: "I am tremendously disappointed that so many of these bills have not been acted on, and in some cases, not even have held hearings [*sic*]." [9]

---

[8] For a discussion of the frustrations of House Republicans under Martin's leadership, see Charles O. Jones, *Party and Policy-Making: The House Republican Policy Committee* (New Brunswick, N.J.: Rutgers University Press, 1964), Ch. 2.

[9] Quoted in *Congressional Quarterly Almanac*, Vol. 13, 1957, p. 87. The comment of the editors of the *Congressional Quarterly* about the second session of the 85th Congress applied to both sessions: "Adjournment of the 85th Congress . . . brought to a close a second session as remarkable for what it didn't do as for what it did do." *Congressional Quarterly Almanac*, Vol. 14, 1958, p. 57.

The last Congress of this type to consider is the 80th Congress where the Democrats were in the minority for the first time in fourteen years. President Truman was completing Roosevelt's fourth term and had limited sources of power. For the most part this Congress was characterized by major warfare between an aggressive president and an aggressive Republican majority, a majority that became convinced that the tide was finally moving in their direction. Both President Truman and Republican leaders were intent on producing a record for the 1948 presidential elections. Neither hesitated to introduce legislation to block the other's efforts. The Republican majority ignored some presidential proposals and amended others. The Democratic president vetoed Republican measures or let them become law without his signature. The Republican majority, plus a number of Democrats, overrode many vetoes.

Again, the minority party in the House was relatively weak. Though overall the policy output of this Congress was greater than others of this type, the minority party could not claim much credit for this output. The Republicans had a respectable fifty-eight–seat margin in the House and had relatively strong leadership in Martin and Halleck. The Democrats, on the other hand, reduced the potential effectiveness of their normally able leaders, Rayburn and McCormack, because of Truman's aggressiveness and their own divisiveness.

The 80th Congress produced a mixed bag of legislation. President Truman had some spectacular successes where he was able to combine strong participation and support from his own party with impressive support from the majority Republicans. The two outstanding cases were the passage of the Truman Doctrine, offering aid to Greece and Turkey, and the Economic Cooperation Act of 1948, the Marshall Plan. The president got the support of 92.5 per cent of the House Democrats and 57.5 per cent of the House Republicans who voted on final passage of the Truman Doctrine. He got 93.5 per cent support from his own party on the final vote for the Marshall Plan and a most impressive 73.7 per cent support from those House Republicans who voted. These two measures alone made the 80th more than a "do-nothing" Congress.

On other proposals, the president was successful in getting legislation through a hostile Congress but not in the form he wanted. Truman was far from satisfied with the Housing and Rent Acts of 1947 and 1948, and the Displaced Persons Act of 1948. In all three the Republicans successfully amended the president's proposals and rejected Democratic counteramendments. In all three, the House Democrats were seriously split, providing important support for the Republicans. Of course, as is typical in such instances, President Truman and House Democratic leaders had to decide whether to risk opposing the Republican changes when the result might be no legislation at all. As President Truman said in signing the Rent Control Act in 1947, it was the "lesser of two evils." [10] He was considerably more vocal in his opposition of the Displaced Persons Act of 1948, but he signed it too.

Finally, the majority Republicans passed legislation which the president opposed. The most spectacular case was the Taft-Hartley Act in 1947. The bill passed the House by an overwhelming margin, 319–47. President Truman vetoed the measure, but the House overrode the veto with 95 per cent of the Republicans and 60 per cent of the Democrats voting to override. The House also passed a bill to reduce income taxes. The president vetoed this bill too and again the House overrode the veto, but the Senate did not. In 1948, the House again passed a tax reduction bill, the president vetoed it, and both houses overrode the veto by large margins. The House also passed the Mundt-Nixon bill in 1948 to require registration of communist organizations, but this bill did not pass the Senate.

Overall, the 80th Congress was characterized by intense political competition. The Republicans were obviously anxious for a complete victory in the 1948 elections and President Truman was fighting for his political life. Truman faced a basically hostile Congress and considerable disunity in his own party. He vetoed seventy-five bills and resolutions during both sessions. Six of these became law over his veto, five in the second session (a modern record for vetoes overridden in one session). On one other bill, the tax reduction bill in 1947, the House overrode the veto but the Senate did not. Despite this open warfare between the Republican-controlled Congress and the Democratic president, policy output was rather high, higher than for any of the other participating Congresses. This higher rate of production can be attributed more to the aggressiveness of the president and the majority Republicans than to the minority party organization and leadership in the House. The minority Democrats

[10] Quoted in Congressional Quarterly, *Congress and the Nation* (Washington, D.C.: Congressional Quarterly Inc., 1965), p. 350.

were often seriously split on major legislation, frequently lending support to the majority Republicans in their efforts to pass legislation that Truman opposed. Obviously, the Republicans could not override vetoes without Democratic support. As a consequence, majority building was an extremely complicated process for the president, more complicated than normal because of his own party's disunity and the fact that the majority Republicans were unified, actively seeking to build majority coalitions of their own, and able to capitalize on the president's lack of popularity in his own party.

THE SENATE

Fewer Congresses fit this category for the Senate than for the House (see Table 5.2). During the 62nd and 72nd Congresses, the Republicans were a participating minority in the House and a participating majority in the Senate. The minority Democrats in each Congress were relatively unrestricted in adopting strategies. Obviously, one of the sources of strength for the Democrats in each case was their majority status in the House.

The characteristics of these Congresses for the Senate minority party are similar to those for the House minority party — weakness of the president, greater strength of majority party leadership over minority party leadership, and, with one exception, the small margin of the majority over the minority. The five Congresses can be categorized in the same way for the Senate as for the House. The three Eisenhower Congresses (84th–86th) and the last Wilson Congress (66th) were of that special type where the minority party in the nation has temporarily captured the White House but does not control Congress. The 80th is that rare instance of where the majority party nationally has control of the White House but is in the minority in both the House and Senate.

POLICY MAKING. It is possible to be brief in summarizing minority party behavior in the Senate during these Congresses. In each case, the pattern varied only slightly from that in the House. The least productive Congresses were the 66th and 86th. During the 66th, the weakness of the president was not compensated for by strong Democratic leadership in the Senate. The Democrats were all but leaderless with the death of Thomas Martin (Virginia) and the hassle over his successor. Further, the majority Republicans were adversely

TABLE 5.2
CHARACTERISTICS OF PARTICIPATING MINORITIES IN THE SENATE

			EXTERNAL CONDITIONS					INTERNAL CONDITIONS			
Congress	Minority party	Temper[a]	Majority-minority combi-nation[b]	Minority party unity	President[c]	Procedure	Margin[d]	Majority leadership	Minority leadership	Years in minority	Minority party in House
66	D	5	11	Moderate	Moderately weak (WW)	No changes	Small	Moderately strong	Weak	0	Participating
80	D	2	4	Weak	Moderately weak (HST)	Major changes	Small	Moderately strong	Moderately strong	0	Participating
84	R	2	6	Strong	Moderately weak (DDE)	No changes	Small	Strong	Weak	0	Participating
85	R	2	6	Strong	Moderately weak (DDE)	No changes	Small	Strong	Weak	2	Participating
86	R	2	6	Strong	Weak (DDE)	No changes	Large	Strong	Moderately weak	4	Participating

a For key, see Table 4.1.
b See Table 2.1.
c See Table 2.2.
d For key, see Table 4.2.

affected by their continuing disunity. They did not develop proposals of their own, as did the Democrats in the 86th and the Republicans in the 80th.

In the 86th Congress, President Eisenhower retained his popularity in the country and among congressional leaders (even Democrats); the Republicans were outnumbered nearly two to one in the Senate; and the Democrats were assuming an aggressive election-year posture (with their majority leader, Lyndon B. Johnson of Texas, one of the principal candidates for the Democratic nomination for president). Because of the wide margin and the strength of the Senate Democratic leadership, the president had to do more than simply count his own party and add the requisite number of Democrats. He had to work with the majority leadership nearly as much as with his own. The results were mixed. Eisenhower was granted his routine requests, a major civil rights bill (not entirely to his liking), and a major labor-management relations bill. On many other matters, however, the Senate Democrats presented him with legislation that bore little resemblance to his requests. He was not reluctant to veto in these cases.

In short, the minority parties in the Senate in both the 66th and 86th Congresses had limited strategic options in forming majority coalitions because of the weakness of the president and the general political situation. The differences between the minorities in the House and Senate in each case were minimal, though the minority Republicans in the Senate of the 86th Congress did provide more support for the president than did their colleagues in the House.

The more productive Congresses in this set of low-output sessions were the 80th, 84th, and 85th. During the 84th and 85th Congresses minority party behavior in the House and Senate was very much the same. Minority party leadership was relatively weak in both houses for both Congresses, majority party leadership was strong, and the margins were small. The Senate Republicans consistently offered somewhat greater support to the president at the roll-call stage than did House Republicans, and though both minority leaders (Martin in the House and Knowland in the Senate) participated in decision-making, and offered their support to Eisenhower's program, Knowland was more vocal in his opposition to certain aspects of the president's foreign policy.

The pattern was also much the same in the Senate as the House during the 80th Congress. Truman had important triumphs, particularly in foreign policy, but the Republicans pressed for their own policy record. The majority leader, Wallace White, was relatively weak, but other Senate Republicans exerted strong leadership, notably Robert A. Taft of Ohio as chairman of the Policy Committee, Arthur Vandenberg of Michigan as president pro tempore, and Eugene Millikin of Colorado as chairman of the Republican Conference. Overall, the minority leaders were somewhat weaker in that they had fewer sources of strength. They had to contend with an unpopular president and a divided party. The policy results were like those in the House. Frequent conflict was inevitable, as President Truman could not and would not work with the Republicans and they did not want to build a record of cooperation with him.

POSSIBLE STRATEGIES

For maximum policy output, the model participating minority would probably have the benefit of strong leadership in the House and Senate, a small margin between the two parties, weak majority party leadership in both houses, and, perhaps most importantly, a strong, imaginative president who generously interprets his powers as chief executive while fully realizing the need to work with congressional leaders. The record of participating minorities in this century does not reveal any such models. Congresses in this set were generally unproductive. Though more active and influential than under restricted conditions, the minority parties seldom had great impact in the policy process.

Model conditions are not necessary for the minority party to be a positive force in policy making, however. Leaders could develop constructive policy proposals rather than waiting for executive initiative. Such instances could be cited for each of the Congresses discussed here. Typically, however, these Congresses were characterized by highly ambiguous political circumstances. The minority party was not well equipped to take the initiative. Indeed, during certain of the Congresses in this category, notably the 62nd, 66th, 72nd, and 86th, the minority party was on its way out of the White House as well. And during the 80th, most people, including congressional Democrats, expected that Truman would lose the next election. The political conditions of a participating minority in Congress suggest that the minority will do little more than participate in whatever ambiguous process can be devised to build majorities for a presidential program designed simply to conserve rather than create.

Two additional observations are germane. Under certain circumstances (e.g., the 80th and 86th Congresses, and, to a lesser extent, the 62nd and 72nd) the majority party in Congress takes the initiative to build majorities for its own program. If the majority party is presenting policy proposals, the minority party adopts strategies in response. While participating with the president in building majorities for his program, party leaders must decide whether to support, cooperate with, withdraw from, or offer constructive or partisan opposition to the program of the majority party. They may be pardoned for developing a touch of schizophrenia under these circumstances. And public confusion is understandable. The minority party had to develop this dual set of strategies in both the 80th and 86th Congresses. The instances were less frequent and less serious during the 62nd and 72nd Congresses because the minority party in the House controlled the Senate.

The president may also overcompromise with the majority party in order to get his program adopted. Perhaps, as frequently happened with President Eisenhower, he could count on as much or more support from the majority party as from his own party if he made certain concessions. That is, he could build a majority if he were willing to rely more on the majority party than on his own party. In this situation, it is perfectly conceivable that the minority party may not participate at all. In fact, the party may, unofficially perhaps, actually oppose its own president's efforts. Again, the minority party is not limited to participating, even if their man is in the White House.

It is possible that all of these circumstances may occur in any one session of Congress, depending on the issue. The minority party may be participating actively in developing a majority on one issue, offering its own proposals on other issues, supporting or opposing the majority on their proposals, opposing their own president on certain of his proposals. It is not surprising that policy output is low in these most ambiguous policy-making situations.

CHAPTER SIX

Unrestricted Minorities in the House

In half the Congresses in this century, political conditions have not unduly restricted the strategic options available to the minority party. Most often the principal condition facilitating increased alternatives for minority party leaders is weakness of the president. Perhaps the president takes a limited view of the office, as with Taft, Harding, Coolidge, Hoover, and Eisenhower. Perhaps he takes an expansive view of the office but is preoccupied with war crises, as with Wilson, Roosevelt, and Johnson. Perhaps his own party is divided, as with Taft, Harding, Coolidge, Roosevelt, and Truman. Or, perhaps the president must contend with more than one of these disadvantages.

An unrestricted minority party can potentially choose from the full range of strategies in the subcommittee and committee, as well as on the floor. Because of the seniority system, however, party leaders at these early stages are different from, and virtually independent of, the elected House and Senate party leaders. Their choices may conflict with those of floor leaders. This matter of strategic options at various stages in the legislative process opens an enormous research topic with many complications, few of which can be attended to here. For example, as Professor Richard F. Fenno, Jr., describes, minimal partisanship characterizes the House Committee on Appropriations and is essential to a well-integrated committee.[1] Minimal partisanship may reduce the strategic options available to the minority party in that committee, while increasing the impact individual minority members have in policy making. If partisanship is deem-

---

[1] Richard F. Fenno, Jr., *The Power of the Purse: Appropriations Politics in Congress* (Boston: Little, Brown, 1966).

phasized, the minority party has difficulty maintaining its distinctiveness. To the extent that committee norms of nonpartisanship overshadow party norms of partisanship, party becomes less significant as a determinant of behavior.

The active, unrestricted minority party has impact beyond its success in adopting one or another strategy in the process of building majorities. Minority party policy proposals may be adopted by majority party policy formulators. Or minority party victories in defeating the president may force executive policy formulators to rethink a proposal. Minority party research into administration of a policy may result in new legislation. And the general expectation that the minority party will oppose with strength, and has certain rights to criticize presidential proposals, may induce caution, precision, and careful consideration in policy formulation and administration. *In short, an unrestricted minority party can be of major significance in all phases of the policy cycle.*

CHARACTERISTICS

Congresses with unrestricted minority parties have a number of characteristics in common. First, the majority party in the nation typically controlled both Congress and the White House. The only exceptions occurred in the 65th and 83rd Congresses when the minority party nationally (in partisan preference among voters) controlled the White House and Congress. Second, the margin between the majority and minority parties was generally small to moderate. In only two of the seventeen Congresses was the margin over 100 seats. The range of margins for these Congresses was from a virtual tie in the 65th Congress to 105 seats for the Democrats over the Republicans in the 77th Congress (with a mean of 57). In contrast, the range of margins for Congresses with restricted minorities was from 29 during the 58th Congress to 244 during the 75th Congress (with a mean of 137; see Table 2.3). Third, minority party unity typically was moderate to strong.

The differences are also worth notice. First, in eight of these Congresses, the president was weak, giving the minority party an advantage. In nine of the Congresses, the president was classified as strong but was limited in some manner in exercising the full force of his power with Congress. In some cases a war crisis was important, in others majority party disunity or stress between the president and

TABLE 6.1
CHARACTERISTICS OF MODERATELY UNRESTRICTED MINORITIES IN THE HOUSE OF REPRESENTATIVES

			EXTERNAL CONDITIONS				INTERNAL CONDITIONS				
Congress	Minority party	Temper[a]	Majority-minority combination[b]	Minority party unity	President[c]	Procedure	Margin[a]	Majority leadership	Minority leadership	Years in minority	Minority party in Senate
60	D	2	16	Moderate	Strong (TR)	No changes	Moderate	Strong	Moderate	12	Restricted
69	D	2	16	Moderate	Weak (CC)	No changes	Moderate	Strong	Moderately weak	6	Moderately unrestricted
76	R	4	1	Strong	Strong (FDR)	No changes	Moderate	Moderate	Moderate	8	Restricted
77	R	5	1	Strong	Strong (FDR)	No changes	Large	Strong	Moderate	10	Restricted
81	R	2	1	Moderately weak	Moderately weak (HST)	Minor changes	Moderate	Strong	Moderate	0	Moderately unrestricted

a For key, see Table 4.1.
b See Table 2.1.
c See Table 2.2.

TABLE 6.2
CHARACTERISTICS OF UNRESTRICTED MINORITIES IN THE HOUSE OF REPRESENTATIVES

			EXTERNAL CONDITIONS			INTERNAL CONDITIONS					
Congress	Minority party	Temper[a]	Majority-minority combination[b]	Minority party unity	President[c]	Procedure	Margin[a]	Majority leadership	Minority leadership	Years in minority	Minority party in Senate
61	D	3	16	Moderate	Weak (WHT)	Major changes	Small	Strong	Moderate	14	Moderately unrestricted
65	R	5	12	Moderately weak	Moderately strong (WW)	No changes	Small	Moderately weak	Weak	6	Moderately unrestricted
68	D	1	16	Moderate	Weak (WGH, CC)	Minor changes	Small	Moderate	Moderately weak	4	Moderately unrestricted
70	D	1	16	Moderate	Weak (CC)	No changes	Small	Strong	Moderately weak	8	Unrestricted
71	D	4	16	Moderate	Moderately weak (HH)	No changes	Large	Strong	Moderate	10	Unrestricted
78	R	5	1	Strong	Strong (FDR)	No changes	Small	Strong	Moderate	12	Moderately unrestricted
79	R	5	1	Strong	Strong (FDR)	Major changes	Moderate	Strong	Moderate	14	Moderately unrestricted
82	R	2	1	Moderate	Weak (HST)	Minor changes	Small	Strong	Moderate	2	Unrestricted
83	D	2	5	Moderately weak	Moderately weak (DDE)	No changes	Small	Moderate	Strong	0	Unrestricted
87	R	2	1	Strong	Moderately strong (JFK)	Minor changes	Moderate	Weak	Strong	6	Moderately unrestricted
88	R	2	1	Strong	Moderately strong (JFK, LBJ)	Minor changes	Moderate	Moderate	Moderate	8	Moderately unrestricted
90	R	5	1	Strong	Moderately strong (LBJ)	Minor changes	Moderate	Moderate	Moderate	12	Moderately unrestricted

a For key, see Table 4.1.
b See Table 2.1.
c See Table 2.2.

his congressional party leaders weakened the majority party. A second difference is in the leadership advantage of the majority party over the minority party. The majority party had a clear advantage in leadership in ten Congresses, though their leaders were not always strong. During the other seven Congresses, the two parties either had leadership of approximately the same strength or the minority party had the advantage (as in the 83rd and 87th Congresses). The most favorable conditions for the minority party are: a weak president (partly caused by party disunity), relatively weak majority party leadership, strong minority party leadership, and a small margin between the two parties. Although none of these Congresses exactly fits all of these conditions, the 83rd comes closest and will bear careful examination. Another important difference is the variation in the temper of the times among these Congresses, ranging from the war crises of Franklin D. Roosevelt Congresses to the relatively pacific Congresses in the 1920's.

RANGE OF STRATEGIES

Congresses in this category can be discussed in blocks. They will be examined in the following order: (1) the unrestricted Congresses with strong or moderately strong presidents, notably the war Congresses (65th, 77th–79th) and the 87th and 88th Congresses and (2) the unrestricted Congresses with weak or moderately weak presidents, notably the Taft, Harding, Coolidge, and Hoover Congresses as one block (61st, 68th–71st); the Truman Congresses (81st–82nd) and the Eisenhower Congress (83rd) as another block.

For each of these Congresses, the principal effort will be to determine: (1) the extent to which the political situation allowed the minority party to be flexible in adopting strategies in policy making and (2) the extent to which the minority party did in fact adopt these strategies. Obviously, the minority party could be technically (that is, by the conditions identified here) quite free to adopt a number of strategies — including those which take the initiative from the majority — and yet do little but offer partisan opposition. When this happens, it is clear that other limiting conditions are significant, e.g., the minority party mentality.

THE WAR CONGRESSES. The war Congresses mark an interesting strategic situation for the minority party, one wrought with conflicting expectations. On the one hand, the minority party might be expected to support the president and his efforts to conduct war. On the other hand, the minority party could be expected to search for bases of opposition so as to achieve the ultimate goal of majority party status. In comparing the war Congresses (65th, 77th–79th), the minority party had somewhat greater flexibility under Wilson than under Roosevelt. In the 1916 elections, the Republicans had actually won more seats in the House than the Democrats, but enough independents joined the Democrats so that the Republicans remained in the minority. Further, Wilson had won a very narrow victory over Hughes, hardly comparable to Roosevelt's triumph in 1940. And finally, the Republican Party remained the majority party among voters during the Wilson administrations. Thus, the minority party Republicans were considerably stronger in Congress than during the Roosevelt war Congresses. Though they did offer support for war measures, Republicans also opposed certain war efforts by President Wilson and countered with proposals of their own. Historian Seward E. Livermore seriously challenges the thesis that politics was adjourned during the 65th Congress:

> The pre-election [1918 election] image carefully fostered by Republican propaganda of selfless and wholehearted cooperation in the war effort has remained undisturbed, and statistics are frequently drawn from this source to demonstrate that as many, if not sometimes more, Republicans as Democrats voted for military appropriations and other war measures. Statistics alone, however, do not convey any idea of the bitter and prolonged struggles that preceded the adoption of many of these measures, indeed all of the major ones, and gave a strong partisan coloration to the proceedings despite all the solemn disavowals to the contrary.[2]

Though a potent force in the House, the minority Republicans continued to fight among themselves. The war split them even further. Some old-line conservatives joined Theodore Roosevelt in calling for intervention; others opposed the war. In the House, Minority Leader Mann called for bipartisan support of Wilson's early peace efforts and was bitterly criticized.[3] Despite disunity, Livermore documents

---

[2] Seward W. Livermore, *Politics Is Adjourned: Woodrow Wilson and the War Congress, 1916–1918* (Middletown, Connecticut: Wesleyan University Press, 1966), p. 3.

[3] *Ibid.*, p. 11.

a range of alternatives employed by the House Republicans, indicating that the minority party had greater flexibility than during the subsequent war Congresses.

In some respects, the 77th, 78th, and 79th Congresses bore some relation to the early depression Congresses. With the nation at war, the president could depend on an important source of power: public belief that the chief executive deserved full support. In addition, Roosevelt continued to receive large majorities at the polls, capturing the electoral vote in thirty-eight states in 1940 and in thirty-six states in 1944. The Republicans were recovering, however, and this period marked their return as a viable second party. Beginning with the 76th Congress, when the Republicans gained 80 seats, the minority party could begin to offer more than support or inconsequential opposition to the president's program (particularly in view of the growing recalcitrance among southern Democrats). Though they continued to lose seats whenever Roosevelt ran for reelection (1940 and 1944), the losses were not great and their midterm gains were sizable. In the four elections from 1930 to 1936, House Republicans had a net loss of 178 seats, losing seats in every election. In the four elections from 1938 to 1944, House Republicans had a net gain of 101 seats, gaining a total of 127 in 1938 and 1942 and losing a total of 26 in 1940 and 1944. House Republicans were encouraged by these results and began to harbor false hopes that they would soon reassert themselves as the majority party nationally. The 1946 election results further stirred these hopes.

In general, the pattern of minority party strategy during the Roosevelt war Congresses can be explained by the conflicting expectations mentioned above. For the most part, the party supported the president in the war effort but adopted various strategies on domestic policy to defeat him and build their own record. The president associated as much domestic policy as possible with war defense, exploiting the war as a source of power.

Efforts were made very early in the war to minimize partisan conflict. The two national committee chairmen, Edward J. Flynn for the Democrats and Joseph W. Martin for the Republicans, exchanged communications in which Martin pledged that Republicans would not permit "politics to enter into national defense." [4] Pro-

---

[4] Roland Young, *Congressional Politics in the Second World War* (New York: Columbia University Press, 1956), p. 13.

fessor Roland Young points out, however, "no ground rules were established for 'adjourning politics' or for keeping politics out of national defense." [5] Certainly, the vague moratorium was not as extensive as that in Britain where a coalition government was established. And, as will be illustrated, partisanship and hostility between Congress and the president increased steadily during the war years.

Though less potent overall than the minority Republicans during the 65th Congress, the House Republicans during the early 1940's were more unified and enjoyed stronger leadership. Joseph W. Martin, Jr., not only served as minority floor leader during this period, but also served as Republican National Committee Chairman from 1940 to 1942.[6] The House Democrats, too, were favored with stronger leadership than during the 65th Congress. The team of Rayburn and McCormack served throughout this period.

As a practical matter, Congress could not be involved in strictly military strategic decisions and the executive needed broad discretion in spending. Congress was kept busy, however, principally with economic matters. In his study, Young notes six major areas of activity: organizational matters (for conducting the war), price control, taxes, profits, manpower (including labor legislation and the draft), and production.[7]

As the war progressed, the president had an increasingly difficult time with Congress on matters not directly involved with the war effort. The end-of-session analyses by Floyd Riddick in the *American Political Science Review* reflect the development of strained relations between the two branches:

> *77th Congress, 1st session:*
> Congress seems to have fallen under more control by the Administration than in the past several years, perhaps more than ever before.

> *77th Congress, 2d session:*
> In the case of "strict war measures," the President continued to request what was wanted and got it; in the case of noncontroversial measures, the results were practically the same; but on many other counts *there was an estranged feeling between the two arms of government.* . . . Congressmen had

[5] *Ibid.*, p. 14.
[6] See Joseph W. Martin, Jr., *My First Fifty Years in Politics* (as told to Robert J. Donovan) (New York: McGraw-Hill, 1960), Chs. 7, 8.
[7] See Young, Ch. 1, and *passim.*

begun to feel the support of public opinion in opposition to
the way things were being done in Washington. . . . For
the first time, Representatives and Senators became deliberate
in their fight against Administration requests.

78th Congress, 1st session:
When he recommends legislation, and works for it, he usually
gets it; as a rule, the only time he fails to get legislation that
he really works for is when fundamental sectional issues are
raised which force a coalition of the Republicans and the
Democrats representing the section of the country involved.

78th Congress, 2d session:
*Strained relations between the President and Congress were
perhaps more manifest than in the last several years.*
Time and time again during the session, senators and repre-
sentatives accused the Administration of flaunting the will of
Congress in administering the laws.

79th Congress, 1st session:
*The strained relation between Mr. Roosevelt and Congress
had been growing increasingly tense during the last several
years;* it is probable that only the defense program eliminated
the possibility of a complete break between the two arms of
the government. Congress had been rejecting more and more
items of the President's domestic program.[8]

As the president's party maintained its majority during these Congresses, his defeats were a result of Republican unity and Democratic disunity. In the last years of the war, a frequent vote split
found 50 per cent of the Democrats joining all the Republicans
against the president. Often, in fact, the southern Democrats led the
opposition to the president's domestic and "fringe-war" proposals.
Roosevelt faced a situation somewhat like that of the Republican
presidents during the 1920's, with the major opposition frequently
coming from within his own party.

Congressional Republicans were faced with the dilemma of discovering issues on which they could legitimately be partisan. They

[8] Floyd Riddick, "The First Session of the 77th Congress," *American Political
Science Review*, Vol. 36 (April, 1942), p. 300; "The Second Session of the 77th
Congress," Vol. 37 (April, 1943), p. 302; "The First Session of the 78th Con-
gress," Vol. 38 (April, 1944), p. 313; "The Second Session of the 78th Con-
gress," Vol. 39 (April, 1945), p. 334; "The First Session of the 79th Congress,"
Vol. 40 (April, 1946), p. 256. (Emphasis added.)

were somewhat neutralized by the war and yet encouraged by their return as a viable second force. Finding those issues on which they could legitimately be partisan would be difficult if the Democrats remained unified. The frequent defection of many southern Democrats, however, provided the Republicans with more options. Republicans could support the president, join the southern Democrats in opposition, support southern Democratic alternatives, cooperate with southern Democrats in developing alternative proposals or in forming a majority in partisan opposition to the president, or offer alternatives of their own. Thus, *the defection of many in the president's own party provided the Republicans with the legitimacy they needed for opposing the president.*

A few cases will serve to illustrate the flexibility of the minority party during these Congresses. The Republicans offered support and occasional inconsequential opposition on defense matters. On matters peripheral to the war, however, considerable southern Democratic–Republican cooperation in the early stages of the legislative process often resulted in legislation contrary to the wishes of the president. In some cases, the president vetoed the legislation only to have his veto overridden. For example, the Smith-Connally Act was passed in 1943 with broad bipartisan support in the House. Roosevelt vetoed the bill but the House overrode the veto by a larger margin than the bill had received initially. Southern Democrats and Republicans also combined on legislation providing for voting by the military. But perhaps the greatest flexibility for the minority party came on price control legislation. Not only could the Republicans expect support from Democrats in curbing price control, criticizing existing price control policy, and harassing the Office of Price Administration, but they could depend on considerable public support for their position as well.[9]

Despite the minority party's flexibility, which increased as the war continued, the party was not very innovative. The Republicans occasionally offered alternatives, or supported southern Democratic alternatives, but these were normally in the form of cutbacks and would not be classified as innovative ideas designed to solve a particular problem.

Professor Young offers interesting evidence to illustrate the increasing Republican success on floor votes during the war years. In the

[9] See Young, Ch. 4.

House, a majority of Republicans were on the winning side on roll calls more frequently than the Democrats in 1943 and 1944, and as nearly as often in 1942.

Year	Majority of House Democrats on winning side of roll calls (%)	Majority of House Republicans on winning side of roll calls (%)
1941	92	51
1942	87	86
1943	65	83
1944	71	85
1945	87	62

The ratios of House Democratic victories to Republican victories, where a majority of one party was voting against a majority of the other party, were: 7 : 1 in 1941; 1 : 1 in 1942; 1 : 2 in 1943; 1 : 2 in 1944; and 3 : 1 in 1945.[10]

THE MINORITY PARTY AND JFK. President Kennedy's view of the presidency was in the tradition of Wilson and Roosevelt, but he did not have their sources of strength. No pervasive crisis dominated national politics in 1960, Kennedy's margin over Nixon was extremely narrow, Republicans had increased their numbers in both houses over 1958, Republicans were generally unified, and Democrats were plagued by disunity. Kennedy's greatest sources of power seemed to be his energy in producing new ideas (or renovating old ideas) for solving public problems, and the fact that so little had been accomplished in the 86th Congress. In Neustadt's words, Kennedy could rely on "the expectations of those other men regarding his ability and will to use the various advantages that they think he has." [11] President Kennedy took a very broad view of the presidency.

> Whatever the political affiliation of our next President, whatever his views may be on all the issues and problems that rush in upon us, he must above all be the Chief Executive in every sense of the word. *He must be prepared to exercise the fullest powers of his office — all that are specified and some that are not.*[12]

[10] *Ibid.*, pp. 224–25.
[11] Richard E. Neustadt, *Presidential Power: The Politics of Leadership* (New York: Wiley, 1960), p. 179.
[12] *The New York Times*, January 15, 1960, p. 16 (emphasis added).

With the exception of a procedural change in the House, internal conditions also tended to favor the minority party. For the first time since 1952, in 1960 Republicans increased their numbers in the House of Representatives. The Democrats still had a commanding majority — 263 to 174 — but with probable Democratic disunity on some measures, Republicans could expect some success in building negative majorities so as to defeat the president's proposals. The president was successful in effecting a procedural change of some significance. The House Committee on Rules had become an antiadministration device and could be expected to cause considerable procedural difficulty for the president's program. In a major power struggle between Chairman Howard W. Smith and Speaker Rayburn, Rayburn won (with the critical support of twenty-two Republicans) and the Committee on Rules was enlarged by three members. Though enlargement did not result in the committee's loss of power and independence, it did represent a major defeat for those who had relied on it to curb the majority and it opened the door to more drastic reforms.[13]

The House party leadership situation in the 87th Congress was almost the reverse of what it was in the 85th Congress. The Republicans were much stronger, the Democrats much weaker. Rayburn, McCormack, and Albert continued to lead the Democrats, but the long-time speaker was apparently losing his touch. As one senior Democrat put it:

> Rayburn died at a propitious time. During the last three to five years, things were getting out from under his control. And during the last two years people really had no idea, but it was distressing to sit there with his group of about fifteen, and see him trying to grapple with bills like the foreign aid bill when he had lost his touch.[14]

McCormack was elected speaker after Rayburn died in November, 1961.

---

[13] A number of excellent studies have been written about this struggle. See Robert L. Peabody and Nelson W. Polsby, eds., *New Perspectives on the House of Representatives* (Chicago: Rand-McNally, 1963), Chs. VI and VII; William R. MacKaye, *A New Coalition Takes Control: The House Rules Committee Fight of 1961* (New York: McGraw-Hill, 1963); Neil MacNeil, *Forge of Democracy: The House of Representatives* (New York: McKay, 1963); James A. Robinson, *The House Rules Committee* (Indianapolis: Bobbs-Merrill, 1963). It should be noted that further changes were made in 1965 to reduce the power of the Committee.

[14] Personal interview, a senior House Democrat, June, 1963.

The Republicans changed leadership in 1959. Joseph W. Martin was in poor health and had lost contact with many of the younger members of the party. The 1958 election, in which House Republicans lost forty-seven seats, served as a catalyst for change. The new minority leader, Charles A. Halleck, was less a friend of Rayburn and could be expected to be more partisan than Martin had been. Though he was not the first choice of many House Republicans who had pressured for a change in leadership, they generally considered him superior to Martin. As it turned out, he was to serve as interim leader only, until the insurgents could muster enough support to get someone more to their liking. At the time Halleck was elected, House Republicans also reorganized their party. The most significant change was to separate the floor leadership and Policy Committee chairmanship posts. This change was made at the insistence of the insurgents. Though the reorganized Policy Committee by no means satisfied those House Republicans who desired more vigorous and imaginative policy leadership, it did give them more access to decision-making and served to unify the party.

The range of strategies available to the Republicans in the 87th Congress was impressive and can be illustrated briefly. Many bills in the 87th Congress illustrate partisan opposition by the minority party. In some cases, unified partisan opposition found enough support among Democrats to defeat the legislation. The federal aid to education bill in 1961, the attempt to establish a Department of Housing and Urban Affairs in 1962, and the first farm bill in 1962, all were defeated by the combination of a cohesive minority and defecting Democrats. The total House Republican vote on these three bills was 20 in favor and 480 against (an overall index of cohesion of 92).[15]

In other cases, House Republicans offered constructive opposition on the House floor following unsuccessful efforts in committee to have their proposals adopted.[16] That is, efforts were made on the floor to amend the legislation and/or recommit it with instructions to accept Republican changes. One such effort, on the Area Redevelopment Act of 1961, was inconsequential. Many House Republicans

---

15 Relying on Stuart Rice's index of cohesion in *Quantitative Methods in Politics* (New York: Knopf, 1928).

16 "Constructive" means that the Republicans were offering an alternative. That alternative may well have been "destructive" from the president's point of view.

defected to vote against recommittal and for the bill. Other efforts came close to victory. The recommittal motion on the Omnibus Housing Act was defeated 215 to 197 and on the Tax Reform Act the recommittal motion was defeated 225 to 190. House Republicans were actually successful in substituting their pared-down version of a minimum wage bill on the House floor in 1961 — an important defeat for the Kennedy Administration. The president recovered, however, by a victory for his bill in the Senate. The Conference Committee adopted the Senate bill and their report was approved by the House only because 33 Republicans supported the president.

Many other patterns of strategy characterized the 87th Congress. On the important Trade Expansion Act of 1962, there was considerable Republican cooperation and support during the formative stages of the legislation in the Committee on Ways and Means. The legislation split the House Republican Party, however, and many conservative Republicans opposed the bill. Because of this division, no Republican position was adopted. The minority party withdrew on this legislation. The House Republican Policy Committee took no position, allowing members to vote as they wished. The results showed 80 House Republicans in favor, 90 opposed.

The Communications Satellite Act of 1962 is an example of cooperation in the formative stages followed by support on the House floor. The Manpower Development and Training Act of 1962 is an example of innovation followed by support on the House floor. The Subcommittee on Special Projects of the House Republican Policy Committee conducted a general study of employment in the United States, one section of which examined manpower retraining. Many of the recommendations contained in this study eventually found their way into the Manpower Development and Training Act.

This flexibility for the minority party in the 87th Congress carried over into the first session of the 88th Congress. The president gained an important victory in the midterm elections in that the Republicans had a net gain of only two House seats. The average loss for a president in midterm elections previously was between 35 and 40 seats, depending on how far one goes back in making calculations. But maintaining the status quo in 1962 was not a happy prospect for the president, and the minority Republicans continued to select among various options in congressional policy making. The assassination of President Kennedy appeared to be an important catalyst for enacting much of the program he had been unable to get through

Congress. The second session of the 88th Congress was vastly different from the first. The minority party was more restricted in its role; the initiative was with the new chief executive. This is not to say that the minority party did not have options available. For example, northern Democrats and Republicans cooperated in the development of civil rights legislation and the minority party supported the bill on the floor. But overall the minority party had a more restricted role than during the previous three sessions of the Kennedy administration.

WEAK PRESIDENTS AND LOST OPPORTUNITIES. The first group of Congresses under relatively weak presidents, the 61st and 68th–71st, have much in common in addition to executive impotence. In each case, the Democrats were in the minority by the four measures used here (both houses of Congress, the White House, and nationally among the voters). These Congresses represent the largest block of sessions in which the Democrats were in the minority and therefore provide the best opportunity in this century for studying the Democrats in that role.

Another significant characteristic of these Congresses, and one which is important in explaining the weakness of the president, was the disunity among majority Republicans. Beginning with the 61st Congress, the Progressives made their presence apparent in the Republican Party. From that point on, when they were in the majority, regular Republicans often had to contend as much with members of their own party as with the Democrats.

For the most part, minority party Democrats were limited in achieving the full benefit from their strategic situation during these Congresses because of weak party leadership in the House. In each case, majority party leadership was stronger. During the 61st Congress, the Democrats were led by the amiable Champ Clark, who was no match for Speaker Cannon and his formidable organization. During the Harding-Coolidge-Hoover Congresses, the Democrats were led by Finis J. Garrett of Tennessee (68th–70th) and John N. Garner of Texas (71st). Garrett was unimpressive in leading his party, while Garner had greater sources of power and a more distinguished record. The Republicans had a very weak "transition" speaker, Frederick H. Gillett of Massachusetts, when they regained the majority in the House in the 66th Congress (just as had the Democrats following the 1910 revolt), but in the 69th Congress House Republicans elected Nicholas Longworth of Ohio speaker and John Q. Tilson of Connecticut majority leader. The Longworth-Tilson team was strong and did much to recentralize party leadership in the House.[17]

The Democrats in both periods, 1909–1910 and 1923–1930, had ample opportunity to grow accustomed to their minority position. During the 61st Congress they were serving their thirteenth and fourteenth consecutive years in the minority; during the 68th–71st Congresses they were serving their fifth through twelfth consecutive years in the minority.

There were also some important differences between these two sets of Congresses. The Taft Congresses were characterized by serious decline for the Republican Party. Although Taft won the presidency in 1908, his margin was far below that of Roosevelt in 1904 and the Republicans in both the House and Senate suffered a net loss of seats. In 1910, the Republicans lost control of the House and suffered a net loss of ten seats in the Senate, the greatest shift in many decades. Further, Speaker Cannon's control in the 61st Congress was so strong that it led to open revolt within the Republican Party, and provided the Democrats with a strategic opportunity to contribute to the downfall of the Republicans.

During the 1920 Congresses, though the presidents were weak and the majority party still divided, the Republicans continued to win control of both houses. The very fact that party leaders did not have the prerogatives that Cannon had may have prevented a more important role for the minority. If Gillett, Longworth, and Tilson had been as assertive as Cannon, the Progressives might have had more reason than they already had to join with the Democrats in policy making. Longworth, in particular, had the ability to lead with strength while recognizing and respecting the limits of leadership in the House. Eventually, the domestic crisis brought on by the depression defeated the Republicans. Their own disunity was a considerably more remote cause for their defeat than in 1910.[18]

In illustrating the strategies available to the minority party, it is

[17] Rather than note the biographies of House and Senate leaders, we refer the reader to the listing in Charles O. Jones and Randall B. Ripley, *The Role of Political Parties in Congress: A Bibliography and Research Guide* (Tucson, Arizona: University of Arizona Press, 1966).

[18] Of course, one could argue that the disunity in the Republican Party was one of the principal causes of the depression in that the party was unable to develop workable proposals for averting economic disaster. But this argument is based on the highly questionable assumption that the party — knowing that a depression was possible — would have developed such proposals had it been unified.

helpful to recall the earlier discussion of the context in which strategies are adopted (see Chapter two). The range of strategies is based on the general assumption that the minority party will be reacting in various ways to the majority-building efforts of the president and his party. Only the strategy of innovation is not of this type. What if the president's view of his office is limited, however? Each of the four Republican presidents discussed here held a restrained view of his responsibilities. Harding's views on this subject have already been discussed. Taft's views are well-known. He contrasted himself sharply with Theodore Roosevelt in stating that:

> The true view of the Executive functions is, as I conceive it, that the President can exercise no power which cannot be fairly and reasonably traced to some specific grant or power or justly implied and included within such express grant as proper and necessary to its exercise. Such specific grant must be either in the Federal Constitution or in an act of Congress passed in pursuance thereof. There is no undefined residuum of power which he can exercise because it seems to him to be in the public interest.[19]

Coolidge, to a considerable extent, and Hoover, to a somewhat lesser extent (particularly following the stock market crash) accepted Taft's interpretation of the president's powers. Coolidge, called "the quiet president" in a recent biography by Donald H. McCoy, saw no great need for extensive legislation. Professor Macmahon's summary analysis of the second session of the 69th Congress had broader applicability in this period:

> Neither in his message nor in the less formal types of influence did the President show the inclination and ability to lead the recent session in a positive way. "No great amount of new legislation is possible," read the message of December 7; and its dozen and a half items of recommendation were of very uneven importance and for the most part either defensive statements or glancing and vague suggestions.[20]

Professor McCoy suggests that the president's limited view of his

---

[19] William Howard Taft, *Our Chief Magistrate and His Powers* (New York: Columbia University Press, 1916), pp. 139–40.

[20] Arthur Macmahon, "The Second Session of the 69th Congress," *American Political Science Review*, Vol. 21 (May, 1927), pp. 308–9.

office was dictated by his interpretation of his role, that of representative of the people.[21] The quiet president behaved as he did because he thought the people wanted him to. As Justice Holmes wrote after the 1924 election: "While I don't expect anything very astonishing from Coolidge, I don't want anything very astonishing." [22] An "astonishing" event forced Hoover to take a somewhat broader view of the presidency, but his nature was in the tradition of Taft, Harding, and Coolidge.

Men who subscribed to this restrained view of the president's role would not be likely to produce any great outpouring of legislative proposals. Sandwiched on either side of Woodrow Wilson were presidents who, for the most part, allowed Congress to do what it wanted to do (and then expressed surprise and dismay when they experienced trouble getting their few proposals enacted into law). Normally, if Congress is allowed to do whatever it wants, it will do very little. Congress is not equipped to initiate action on all public problems.

In his survey of major legislation in the last decade of the nineteenth century and the first forty years of this century, Professor Chamberlain categorizes ninety pieces of legislation into four categories: presidential influence preponderant, congressional influence preponderant, joint presidential-congressional influence, and pressure group influence preponderant. During the five Congresses under discussion (61st, 68th–71st), Chamberlain counted only ten major pieces of legislation. Of these, three were classified as congressional influence preponderant, four as joint presidential-congressional influence (three of which passed during the first Hoover Congress), and three as pressure group influence preponderant. None were characterized by presidential influence preponderant.[23] In contrast, Chamberlain listed nineteen major bills for the eight years of the Wilson administrations, nine of which were characterized either by presidential influence or joint presidential-congressional influence. During the first eight years of the Franklin D. Roosevelt administrations (73rd–76th Congresses), Chamberlain counted twenty-four major

[21] Donald R. McCoy, *Calvin Coolidge: The Quiet President* (New York: Macmillan, 1967).

[22] Quoted in a review of *Calvin Coolidge: The Quiet President* by Francis Russell, *Christian Science Monitor*, April 14, 1967.

[23] Lawrence H. Chamberlain, *The President, Congress and Legislation* (New York: Columbia University Press, 1946), pp. 450–52.

bills, twenty-two of which were characterized either by presidential influence or joint presidential-congressional influence.

The minority Democrats thus had a major opportunity to produce proposals of their own and attempt to build majorities for them. The opportunity to do so was enhanced by the division of the Republicans during these Congresses between the regulars and the Progressives. But the Democrats failed to take advantage of this opportunity. Indeed, it is of some significance to this study that the minority within the majority, the Progressives, made more of an effort to innovate than did the minority party Democrats.

During the 61st Congress, the principal legislation was a new tariff bill, the Payne-Aldrich Tariff. The Republican Party had pledged in 1908 to reduce the tariff and President Taft intended to see that this pledge was carried out. Taft relied on private rather than public persuasion, however, and the result was that "his efforts were largely ineffectual for by refusing to speak out he failed to take advantage of a strong public opinion which would have given him almost solid backing." [24] The original Payne bill did follow Taft's recommendations, but this bill never emerged from the House Committee on Ways and Means. It was developed during the lame-duck session of the 60th Congress primarily to ward off an alliance between the insurgents and the Democrats. Once the regular Republicans were successful in organizing the House, however, major concessions were no longer necessary and the Cannon cabal made the necessary minor accommodations to ensure victory for an essentially protectionist bill. In this and other legislation, the Democrats did have strategic options available but were outmaneuvered by the Republican leadership. The potential for a Democratic–insurgent Republican alliance was seldom realized on substantive matters before the House. When it did surface, it was the result of insurgent leadership rather than Democratic leadership. For example, on the Mann-Elkins Act of 1910, F. H. Dixon indicates that the most valuable provisions were the result of insurgent leadership and Democratic backing.[25]

Of course, the 61st Congress is most remembered for the major procedural changes that occurred in the House. Speaker Cannon and his loyal lieutenants were well advised to proceed with care during

---

[24] *Ibid.*, p. 102.
[25] F. H. Dixon, "The Mann-Elkins Act, Amending the Act to Regulate Commerce," *Quarterly Journal of Economics*, Vol. 24 (August, 1910), p. 631.

the early days of the 61st Congress. Twelve insurgents refused to vote for Cannon for speaker at the opening of the special session called by Taft to consider the tariff. A combination of insurgents and Democrats then defeated the motion to adopt the rules of the preceding Congress. Minority Leader Champ Clark followed this victory with a resolution that would have expanded the Committee on Rules from five to fifteen, removed the speaker from the Committee, and denied the speaker his power of appointing committees (except the Committee on Ways and Means). With insurgent cooperation, the Democrats had ample votes to effect these changes. The effort failed, however, because twenty-two Democrats, led by John J. Fitzgerald of New York, refused to support the resolution. Fitzgerald then introduced a compromise which passed. The compromise established a unanimous consent calendar and a motion of recommittal (for use by the minority), and increased the majority needed to set aside Calendar Wednesday.[26]

The insurgents felt denied in 1909 and waited for another opportunity to trim the speaker's power. The significance of the defeat of Clark's resolution during the organizational period of the special session was that the insurgents and Democrats were successful in preventing the adoption of the rules. Therefore, amendments to the rules were in order, without having to seek prior approval from the speaker, who scheduled the business for the House through his Committee on Rules. Such an opportunity might not arise again during a session. It was a tribute to the ingenuity of George Norris (R-Nebraska) that he was able to discover another opportunity during the second session. An attempt was made by the leadership to dispense with the newly adopted Calendar Wednesday on March 16, 1910, in order to consider the "constitutional question" of taking the census. Speaker Cannon ruled that, as a constitutional question, the resolution dealing with the 1910 census was privileged, the rules of the House to the contrary notwithstanding. Fitzgerald, who had introduced the compromise establishing Calendar Wednesday, appealed the decision to the House and won.

Norris saw in this series of events an opportunity for again introducing the resolution which would remove the speaker from the Committee on Rules. He sought recognition from the speaker,

---

[26] See Paul Hasbrouck, *Party Leadership in the House of Representatives* (New York: Macmillan, 1927), Ch. 1, and Joseph Cooper, "Congress and Its Committees" (unpublished Ph.D. dissertation, Harvard University, 1961).

saying, "Mr. Speaker, I present a resolution made privileged by the Constitution." If Cannon could rule that a census resolution was privileged because the Constitution called for a decennial census, Norris reasoned that a change in the House rules would also be in order because the Constitution gave the House authority to establish rules. The situation was marvelous. Norris was reasoning on the basis of Cannon's ruling, which had been overturned by the House, and which Norris himself had opposed. Thus began one of the most significant debates in the history of the House (thoroughly recorded in a number of sources).[27] Of principal interest to this study is the fact that the insurgents and minority Democrats eventually were able to make major changes in the House rules, removing the speaker from the Committee on Rules and enlarging the Committee. The Democrats remained united on all roll calls involving the change and were joined by 35 to 40 Republicans (depending on the vote).

This flexibility on procedural matters might well have carried over to substantive matters if the Democrats had been more united and able to agree on policy. As it was, however, cooperation between them and the Progressives was limited to the overthrow of Speaker Cannon.[28]

The 68th–70th Congresses all had similar characteristics. Coolidge was hesitant about introducing legislation, the Republicans were divided, the Progressives frustrated, and the Democrats inactive. Of the ten pieces of legislation which Chamberlain discusses for the five Congresses under consideration here (61st, 68th–71st), only four were before Congress during these six years (1923–1929). Thus, very little was done, not because the minority party Democrats were effective in curbing the majority party's program, but because the president had little to offer and the Democrats countered with less.

---

[27] A number of sources can be consulted on the Cannon overthrow. In particular see Hasbrouck; Chang-wei Chiu, *The Speaker of the House of Representatives Since 1896* (New York: Columbia University Press, 1928); William R. Gwinn, *Uncle Joe Cannon, Archfoe of Insurgency: A History of the Rise and Fall of Cannonism* (New York: Bookman Associates, 1957); Kenneth Hechler, *Insurgency* (New York: Columbia University Press, 1941); George R. Brown, *The Leadership of Congress* (Indianapolis: Bobbs-Merrill, 1922); Charles R. Atkinson, *The Committee on Rules and the Overthrow of Speaker Cannon* (New York: Columbia University Press, 1911); Charles O. Jones, "Joseph G. Cannon and Howard W. Smith: An Essay on the Limits of Leadership in the House of Representatives," *Journal of Politics*, Vol. 30 (August, 1968), pp. 619–46; plus the several biographies and autobiographies of those who participated.

[28] Since the Democrats were in their fourteenth consecutive year of minority status, their failure to develop an innovative policy program is not surprising.

The Democrats had their greatest flexibility during the 68th Congress, when the Republicans were led by Frederick H. Gillett of Massachusetts, serving his third term as speaker. Gillett, who never exerted strong leadership in the House, has been categorized as a "figurehead Speaker" by Randall B. Ripley.[29] At the start of the 68th Congress, despite the Republican majority in the House, Gillett could not get the necessary majority to be elected speaker. For two days, the House was deadlocked among four candidates, the two party Caucus nominees (Gillett and Garrett) getting about the same number of votes, and the Progressives voting for Henry Cooper of Wisconsin and Martin Madden of Illinois. The Progressives were pressing for rules changes and the deadlock was finally broken when the regulars agreed to have the Committee on Rules consider amendments to the rules during the first thirty days of the session. Minor rules changes were later adopted (one of which was proposed by the Democrats and supported by the Progressives). With the narrow margin of Republicans over the Democrats, the Progressives holding the balance of power, weak leadership in the House, and a "reluctant" president who had succeeded to the presidency rather than having been elected, the minority party Democrats had favorable conditions for exerting considerable influence in the policy-making process. But their own disunity, weak leadership, and the lack of mood for action among the public, prevented them from taking the initiative.

During the 69th and 70th Congresses, House Republicans were led with strength by Nicholas Longworth and John Q. Tilson.[30] Though the number of major bills passed did not increase, the Republicans had a larger majority and were more unified than in the 68th Congress. An attempt was made to gather insurgents back into the fold. As Professor Macmahon observed in his review of the first session: "Leadership in the House was integrated and nearly effective in so far as it knew its mind; Speaker, floor leader, and steering committee merged almost indistinguishably with the chairman of the rules com-

---

[29] See Randall B. Ripley, *Party Leaders in the House of Representatives* (Washington, D.C.: The Brookings Institution, 1967), p. 16.

[30] Gillett left the House for the Senate in the 69th Congress. Longworth, the majority leader in the 68th Congress, was elected as Gillett's successor over Martin B. Madden, 140–85, in the Republican Caucus. See Arthur W. Macmahon, "The First Session of the 69th Congress," *American Political Science Review*, Vol. 20 (August, 1926), p. 606.

mittee as an instrument." [31] During the 70th Congress, Longworth even got the vote of the insurgent Wisconsinites for speaker. He was properly grateful:

> The Speaker gave a genial wave to Wisconsin as he took the chair: "I am particularly pleased to have received the votes of gentlemen who have been seated on my party's side of the aisle for the past four years, but who on two previous occasions have preferred to vote for a candidate for Speaker other than the one proposed by the Republican majority. I welcome your return to the Republican Party, where you rightfully belong." [32]

Clearly the most important issue during these three Congresses was farm relief. In a period of general economic prosperity, the farmers were suffering. Several attempts were made to pass a major farm relief bill; the McNary-Haugen bill, a complicated proposal guaranteeing a fair price for farm commodities, was significant in all three Congresses. Five McNary-Haugen bills were acted on between January, 1924, and April, 1928. The first three were defeated in Congress, the last two were vetoed by the president. The farm relief issue cut across party lines and thus was not a major test of minority party strategy. As neither the president nor the majority party in the House was attempting to build coalitions of support for this legislation, and the Democrats themselves were split on the issue, the minority party role was ambiguous. [33]

Professor Chamberlain does provide one example of leadership by President Coolidge. The president not only pressed for railway labor legislation but took an active role in getting labor and management involved in drafting the bill. The Railway Labor Disputes Act of 1926, was, as Chamberlain notes, a cooperative measure "written entirely outside any governmental agency or committee." The president could take considerable credit for the bill:

> President Coolidge was identified to a most unusual degree with the measure. Contrary to his ordinary custom of silence he had been vocal in support of such legislation since his

[31] *Ibid.*, p. 608.

[32] Quoted in Macmahon, "The First Session of the 70th Congress," *American Political Science Review*, Vol. 22 (August, 1928), p. 652.

[33] For a brief summary of action on this legislation, see Chamberlain, pp. 245–48. See also Murray Benedict, *Farm Policies of the United States, 1790–1950* (New York: Twentieth Century Fund, 1953).

elevation to the presidency. . . . He followed words with action by using his good offices to bring together the representatives of the parties concerned in the working out of the details of the bill. . . . The contribution of the President in this case was genuine and important.[34]

The final Congress in this block is the 71st, Hoover's first. Because of the circumstances, but also because of his demeanor, Hoover was more active than his predecessor. As a result, the minority party Democrats had more to react to and were more active. The strength of the House Republican leaders, and their willingness to use this power, was demonstrated in this Congress. On many occasions, it appeared as though the days of Cannon for the Republicans and Underwood for the Democrats had returned. Congress had emerged from its long period of inactivity and therefore majority and minority strategies were somewhat more distinguishable.

Generally the president could expect more support, and less disunity, in the House than in the Senate. Hoover called a special session of Congress shortly after his inauguration to consider farm relief legislation. This very act indicated more presidential interest in the farm problem than had been evident in previous administrations. Hoover was closer in style to a Coolidge than to either Roosevelt, but his action, plus his clarity in advising the Congress what he would not accept in farm legislation, led to the passage of the Agricultural Marketing Act of 1929. The House Committee on Agriculture prepared legislation before the opening of the special session to reflect the president's wishes. Though the legislation was not as strong as farm groups would have liked, "the members [of the House] were seemingly glad to be able to vote for any measure which had some plausible chance of success and which the President was willing to sign." [35] House Democrats were drawn into this process and supported the bill in final passage.

House Republican leaders were less generous with regard to tariff revision. In 1929 and 1930, the Congress treated itself to one last "tariff orgy" before giving the president wide authority in this area. This last fling was magnificent. The Committee on Ways and Means

[34] Chamberlain, pp. 158–59. In his biography of John N. Garner, Marquis James recounts a victory for Minority Leader Garner in getting his version of the tax bill enacted in the 70th Congress. See James, *Mr. Garner of Texas* (Indianapolis: Bobbs-Merrill, 1939), pp. 101–7.

[35] Chamberlain, p. 252.

held extensive hearings before the special session. At the conclusion of the hearings, the Republicans excluded their Democratic colleagues and divided themselves into fifteen subcommittees — one for each of the schedules of the bill. The result of this process was generally in line with Hoover's request for limited revision. Compromises had to be made before the bill was reported to the floor, however, in order to get full support of the Republican Party. The Republican Conference approved the bill 206–24 and supported a strict rule for debate on the House floor.[36] More conciliations were made on the House floor and the bill deviated even further from that originally developed by the Republican subcommittee in Ways and Means. The bill passed with strong Republican support and strong Democratic opposition. It later received similarly rough treatment in the Senate.

Despite minimal influence on the Hawley-Smoot Tariff of 1930, the minority party Democrats in the 71st Congress were beginning to react both to the president and to the economic conditions following the stock market crash. The House Democrats were particularly active in pressing for farm relief and banking legislation.[37]

THE TRANSITION CONGRESSES OF TRUMAN AND EISENHOWER. The 81st–83rd Congresses are three of the most interesting in this century from the point of view of minority party analysis. The Republicans had assured themselves of victory in 1948. Their confidence was based on their majority in the 80th Congress, what they considered to be a solid record of achievement in that Congress, the serious split in the Democratic Party, and the polls which predicted that Thomas E. Dewey would win handily over President Truman in the upcoming presidential election. Truman's upset victory was a serious blow to the Republicans, resulting in much internal party reorganization. But certain hazards ensue for the victor in an upset election. Immense problems are likely to surface and limit the power of the president. As the sessions progressed, President Truman had increasing difficulty

[36] See Arthur Macmahon, "The First Session of the 71st Congress," *American Political Science Review*, Vol. 24 (February, 1930), pp. 38–59. The Republicans apparently used the caucus in much the same manner as Underwood had in the 63rd Congress in order to build support for the tariff. See Ch. 4.

[37] In his memoirs, Claude Bowers notes that, on the sugar schedule, the minority Democrats were "in absolute control of the Republican House." "The old regime had just about reached the end of its string." Bowers, *My Life: The Memoirs of Claude Bowers* (New York: Simon and Schuster, 1962), pp. 221–22.

with Congress, both with the Republican Party and with his own party. The minority party Republicans found that their strategic options increased steadily with each passing year of the Truman administration.

In the 83rd Congress, the Democrats were in the minority in the House for the second time since 1930. President Eisenhower's victory was most impressive, with over 55 per cent of the popular vote and over 83 per cent of the electoral vote. It was evident that the Republicans had discovered a record vote-getter, a man so popular that the minority party Democrats in the 83rd Congress sought to avoid serious conflict with him. In Neustadt's terms, Eisenhower had one major source of power: how other decision-makers perceived his public image. The 83rd Congress was characterized by "shadow boxing" as two potent forces, a strong congressional minority party temporarily out of power and a popular minority party president with a slim majority in Congress, sparred cautiously.

There were several differences between the Truman and Eisenhower Congresses. President Truman had the initial advantage of his upset victory and a moderate margin in the House. He could also rely on strong leaders in the House, Rayburn and McCormack, and a measure of disunity among the Republicans, who spent the early months of 1949 blaming each other for the defeat. In the House, for example, moderate Republicans were calling for more representation in party decision making. Many were critical of Minority Leader Martin and held him partly responsible for the net loss of seventy-five House seats in the 1948 elections. It was in this atmosphere that the House Republican Policy Committee was created.

To win at the polls in 1948, President Truman found it necessary to commit himself publicly to an extensive program of legislation, much of which was bound to be controversial in Congress. In his careful study of congressional voting during the 81st Congress, Professor David B. Truman summarizes the president's dilemma:

> Truman was almost inevitably a prisoner of the kind of campaign he had conducted. Following the "coup" at the Philadelphia convention he had embraced the civil rights program with renewed vigor, and his attacks on the Republicans had all but obliged him to seek repeal of the Taft-Hartley Act and passage of legislation on public housing, rent and price controls, education, and farm prices, to list only the most conspicuous domestic matters. The diversity and controver-

siality of these commitments were a standing threat to the solidarity of an already divided party, and the size of the program meant that the most favorable conditions would be required if legislative action were to be taken on any considerable number of items.[38]

An early move by administration forces in the House was to change the House rules so as to permit committee chairmen to bypass the potent Rules Committee. The new procedure was as follows: When a bill had been reported by a standing committee, and a resolution requested from the Rules Committee, a committee chairman could seek recognition from the speaker to call for immediate consideration of the resolution if the Rules Committee had not acted in *twenty-one calendar days after the request for a rule had been made.* The 21-day proposal was endorsed by the Democratic Caucus, the first called since 1935 (except on organizational matters), by a vote of 176–46 — not a very impressive victory in a party caucus.[39] The rules change passed by voice vote on the floor following a motion to close debate which passed on a crucial roll call vote 275–143 (D:225–31, R:49–112, Ind:1–0). Since this rules change was a direct attack on a power base of the southern Democrats, the success of this move could only increase the animosity between that wing of the party and the president.[40]

The 21-day rule was used sparingly during the first session of the 81st Congress — only three times successfully. In his study of the Rules Committee, Lewis J. Lapham concludes that it was quite successful as a threat, however.[41] At the start of the second session, Eugene E. Cox (D-Georgia), an opponent of the 21-day rule and second-ranking member of the Rules Committee, introduced a resolution repealing the rule. The Republican leadership favored repeal but faced a dilemma. The Fair Employment Practices Commission bill was scheduled to be debated under the 21-day rule just three days after the vote on the 21-day repeal resolution. To vote for repeal

[38] David B. Truman, *The Congressional Party: A Case Study* (New York: Wiley, 1959), pp. 17–18.

[39] Christopher Van Hollen, "The House Committee on Rules (1933–1951): Agent of Party and Agent of Opposition" (unpublished Ph.D. dissertation, Johns Hopkins University, 1951), p. 258.

[40] For details on this change, see James A. Robinson, *The House Rules Committee* (Indianapolis: Bobbs-Merrill, 1963); Lewis J. Lapham, "Party Leadership and the House Committee on Rules" (unpublished Ph.D. dissertation, Harvard University, 1954); and Van Hollen.

[41] Lapham, p. 211.

might be interpreted as opposing FEPC. Cox's resolution was defeated 183–236 (D:85–171, R:98–64, Ind:0–1), but the potency of a southern Democratic–Republican coalition was amply demonstrated. Clearly, if the Republicans had remained unified, they could be a very effective force in defeating the president's program.

The 21-day rule situation illustrates the potentialities for the minority party in the 81st Congress. After recovering from the stunning defeat of 1948, the House Republicans discovered that they remained a potent force for negating much of the president's program. As David B. Truman found, the House Republicans were slightly more cohesive than the House Democrats but were more "fractionated." That is, the Democrats divided rather clearly between northern and southern Democrats; the Republicans split among various blocs, but the blocs were closer together in their voting.[42]

As one reviews various aspects of President Truman's program in the 81st Congress, the Republicans appeared to select rather freely among the strategies designed to defeat or support the president, but were unable to adopt the more positive and innovative strategies.[43] Typically, they adopted either consequential partisan opposition, support of the southern Democratic efforts to modify or defeat a presidential program, or support of a popular presidential program. During the first session, House Republicans attempted to defeat the Housing Act of 1949 (though thirty-four Republicans provided crucial support for the bill) and tried unsuccessfully to have the Trade Agreements Act recommitted. They also successfully supported Representative Albert Gore's (D-Tennessee) attempt to substitute an extension of rigid price supports for the administration's farm bill. During the second session, House Republicans attempted, unsuccessfully, to delete the authorization to initiate President Truman's Point Four program, but offered important support for FEPC (124–42). They also provided significant support for legislation favoring independent producers of natural gas (79–57), which Truman opposed and later vetoed, and for the Internal Security Act of 1950 (126–2), which passed over the president's veto.

During the 82nd Congress, House Republicans were even more flexible in adopting strategies. The Democratic margin in the House

---

[42] Truman, Ch. 5.

[43] Much of the analysis contained in the following pages is based on the descriptions of legislative action in various volumes of the *Congressional Quarterly Almanac* and the Congressional Quarterly publication *Congress and the Nation, 1945–1964.*

was reduced considerably by the 1950 elections, from 92 seats to a mere 35. Further, the Democrats were increasingly divided as President Truman became more and more unpopular in his own party. Not even the Rayburn-McCormack leadership team could remedy the serious internal party disorders. The Republicans, on the other hand, showed increasing unity as their prospects of victory in 1952 brightened. Again, if they could not agree on a definite program of their own, they could agree on measures to defeat the president's program, or embarrass him by supporting congressional Democratic alternatives to his program.

The first clear indication of the strength and flexibility of the minority, particularly when working with the southern Democrats, occurred very early in the session. Eugene E. Cox (D-Georgia) and Clarence J. Brown (R-Ohio), both members of the Rules Committee, fashioned an impressive majority to repeal the 21-day rule. Ninety-one Democrats, virtually all of them from the South, voted with 152 Republicans for repeal. This vote, and the manner in which it was collected, indicated what was to come in a Congress in which leadership was diffused between three minorities — southern Democrats, northern Democrats, and Republicans.

Illustrations abound for virtually every strategic situation in the 82nd Congress. In some cases the Republicans were successful in having their own legislative preferences enacted (this would fit the category of consequential constructive opposition). One such instance, which had "destructive" consequences for the administration, occurred with the passage of the Trade Agreements Extension Act of 1951. Richard Simpson (R-Pennsylvania) had tried unsuccessfully in 1949 to have "peril points" reinserted in the law. As the name suggests, peril points are established in advance of tariff negotiations as minimums below which the tariffs should not be set. In 1951, Simpson had more success. His amendment to restore peril points passed 225–168. Since he received nearly 98 per cent of the Republican vote, he needed only modest support from southern Democrats for victory.

There are countless other instances of minority party success in a Congress in which the majority-building efforts of the president virtually collapsed. A coalition of southern Democrats and Republicans passed a submerged lands act by a large majority (265–109) and enacted the Immigration and Nationality Act of 1952 over the president's veto with votes to spare (278–113).

In other cases the minority party was successful in fashioning majorities to defeat the president, with no alternatives proposed. B. Carroll Reece (R-Tennessee) succeeded in moving recommittal of the Mutual Security Act of 1951, with instructions to reduce the aid allotment to Europe by $350 million. The bill had already been reduced in committee. In 1952, a bill establishing universal military training was killed when Dewey Short (R-Missouri) moved recommittal "for further study." In other instances, particularly on agriculture, the Republican Party adopted the withdrawal strategy because they themselves could not agree on the issue at hand.

President Truman had increasing difficulty in building majorities to support his legislative program, and the minority party Republicans had considerable flexibility in choosing among strategies. But the House Republicans tended to select the more negative strategies — defeating or modifying the president's program — rather than offer definite Republican alternatives. No doubt this pattern was motivated by the feeling that there was more to be gained in 1950 and 1952 from defeating President Truman, and emphasizing the internal division in his party, than from suffering legislative defeats themselves. The southern Democratic–Republican alliance existed, after all, on the basis of mutual opposition to the president. Republican attempts to take the policy-making initiative from the president and enact policy proposals could get little support from southern Democrats and may well have divided the minority party.

The 83rd Congress represented what Republicans thought was denied them in 1948 — a return to power in Washington. The victory was not as complete as it should have been, however, if Republicans were to take full charge. While the president enjoyed a tremendous personal triumph, his party's margin in the House was only eight seats. In the Senate, the Republicans had a precarious one-seat margin. Thus, the minority party Democrats had it within their power not only to create havoc with the president's program but also to take the initiative in policy making. On the basis of the margins alone, the 83rd Congress represented a situation for maximum minority party activity.

A number of factors prevented the Democrats from realizing the full potential of the situation, however. First, Eisenhower was immensely popular and one can discern similarities with the early Franklin D. Roosevelt Congresses, if not in the situation which brought the two men to power. Just as the impotent Republicans lent support to Roosevelt, the considerably more potent Democrats offered support to Eisenhower. Second, the Democrats remained internally divided. Third, the president proceeded very cautiously, always conscious of his narrow majority in Congress. He constructed his majorities very carefully in support of legislation that was generally conservative. The fact that the president himself was not partisan, and had large bipartisan support from the public, made it difficult for the Democrats, even if united, to offer strong partisan opposition or take the initiative in policy making. The result was that the Democratic minority was considerably less vigorous in pursuing the role of opposition than a review of the political conditions in the 83rd Congress might suggest.

These conclusions may be supported in a number of ways. The Congressional Quarterly began computing presidential success scores with the 83rd Congress. During his first year in the White House, Eisenhower had a phenomenally high acceptance score for his legislative requests — 72.7 per cent enacted into law.[44] But he made a total of only 44 requests. (By contrast, during his first year in office after being elected, President Lyndon B. Johnson made 469 requests of Congress.) Clearly Eisenhower was proceeding very carefully, both in developing a program and in building the necessary majorities for its enactment. In answer to a letter inquiring how he would approach the task, particularly in view of the internal divisions in both parties, the president wrote:

> People like to think of Mr. Roosevelt as a leader; in the situation where his own party was delighted to hear a daily excoriation of the opposite political party, his methods were adequate to his time and to the situation. As of today, every measure that we deem essential to the progress and welfare of America normally requires Democratic support in varying degrees. I think it is fair to say that, in this situation, only a leadership that is based on honesty of purpose, calmness, and inexhaustible patience in conference and persuasion, and refusal to be diverted from basic principles can, in the long run, win out.[45]

Consequently, the president attempted to establish an elaborate communication link between Congress and the executive.

The pace increased considerably during the second session. Eisen-

[44] *Congressional Quarterly Almanac*, Vol. 9, 1953, pp. 87–89.
[45] Dwight D. Eisenhower, *Mandate for Change, 1953–1956* (Garden City, N.Y.: Doubleday, 1963), p. 193.

hower made 232 requests and was able to maintain a high acceptance score — 64.6 per cent enacted.[46] As expected, the acceptance scores dropped dramatically when the Democrats regained control in the 84th Congress. The average acceptance score for Eisenhower during the next six sessions was 41.2.[47]

An examination of the key votes during the 83rd Congress supports the conclusions of this book regarding the role of the minority party in this Congress. A typical voting pattern showed 75 to 100 per cent of the House Republicans voting with 25 to 50 per cent of the House Democrats to give the president most of what he wanted. Though House Democratic support was usually necessary for passage, there were instances when, owing to defection among House Republicans, more than the usual number of Democratic votes were necessary. For example, many House Republicans traditionally have been wary about relaxing tariff restrictions. When the president asked for an extension of the Trade Agreements Act, members of his own party, led by protectionist Richard Simpson (R-Pennsylvania), sought to pass more restrictive legislation. The issue split the Republicans in half, but a sizable number of Democrats, over 70 per cent of those voting, supported the president and the Simpson bill was recommitted. Other proposals requiring Democratic support included immigration legislation and the creation of the St. Lawrence Seaway Development Corporation.

The minority party Democrats in the House during the 83rd Congress were more limited in adopting strategies than might have appeared on the surface. They offered considerable support to the president even though they easily could have scuttled much of his program. On the other hand, they were not in a position to adopt the more positive role of seeking to build majorities for their own programs. Internal divisions, their perception of the president's strength among the public, the unlikelihood of Republican support for a Democratic program, and the lack of machinery for developing an alternative program, all precluded a more creative role in policy making.

SUMMARY

The several Congresses discussed in this section illustrate the conditions under which the minority party has more flexibility in adopting

---

[46] *Congressional Quarterly Almanac*, Vol. 10, 1954, pp. 37–46.
[47] See *Congressional Quarterly Almanac*, Vols. 11–16, 1955–1960.

strategies in the process of majority building. The minority party in the House does not always take advantage of what appear to be favorable circumstances for a creative role in policy making. Much depends on the strength and initiative of the president. In general, it seems that the minority party is more active in majority building when the president is active. Most minority party strategies are reactive: leaders seek to defeat the majority party with or without alternatives, support the majority party, or cooperate with the majority party. If the president and his party offer little or no legislative program, the minority party cannot react. And seldom has the minority party taken the initiative when the president has failed to act.

CHAPTER SEVEN

Unrestricted Minorities in the Senate

Since many Congresses had unrestricted minorities in both the House and Senate, and thus the same political conditions explain minority party behavior, it is possible to be somewhat more brief in examining the Senate. As with the House, many of these Congresses have characteristics in common. Eleven of the sixteen were characterized by majority-minority combinations in which one party controlled the House, Senate, and White House and was dominant nationally. In three others one party controlled Congress and the White House but was not the dominant party nationally (63rd, 65th, and 83rd). And in two of the Senates (62nd and 72nd) the Democrats were in the minority but were the majority party in the House. The Senate minority party in these Congresses was typically united — in thirteen of the sixteen unity was moderate to strong. The margin of the majority over the minority was generally small to moderate. The range was from virtual ties in the 70th, 72nd, 82nd, and 83rd Congresses to a 28-seat margin for the majority party Democrats in the 87th and 90th Congresses, with a mean difference of 12. The range for restricted Congresses was from 17 in the 64th Congress to 58 in the 75th, with a mean of 33 (see Table 2.3).

As with the House, the various Senates in this category also differed considerably in terms of the temper of the times, the strength of the presidents, and the nature of Senate leadership. Three were war Congresses (65th, 78th, 79th), one was a depression Congress (72nd), and two (61st and 62nd), though dominated by no single crisis, were influenced by a mood for action among the public. Of the presidents serving with these Congresses, ten fall in the weak category (Taft twice, Harding once, Coolidge twice, Hoover twice, Truman twice, and Eisenhower once), three in the moderately strong

TABLE 7.1
CHARACTERISTICS OF MODERATELY UNRESTRICTED MINORITIES IN THE SENATE

| Congress | Minority party | Temper[a] | EXTERNAL CONDITIONS | | | | | INTERNAL CONDITIONS | | Years in minority | Minority party in House |
			Majority-minority combination[b]	Minority party unity	President[c]	Procedure	Margin[d]	Majority leadership	Minority leadership		
61	D	3	16	Moderate	Weak (WHT)	No changes	Large	Moderately strong	Weak	12	Unrestricted
63	R	3	12	Weak	Strong (WW)	No changes	Small	Strong	Weak	0	Restricted
65	R	5	12	Moderately weak	Moderately strong (WW)	No changes	Small	Weak	Weak	4	Unrestricted
68	D	1	16	Moderate	Weak (WGH, CC)	No changes	Small	Moderate	Moderate	4	Unrestricted
69	D	2	16	Moderate	Weak (CC)	No changes	Small	Moderate	Moderate	6	Moderately unrestricted
78	R	5	1	Strong	Strong (FDR)	No changes	Moderate	Strong	Weak	10	Unrestricted
79	R	5	1	Strong	Strong (FDR)	Major changes	Moderate	Strong	Weak	12	Unrestricted
81	R	2	1	Moderately weak	Moderately weak (HST)	No changes	Small	Weak	Weak	0	Moderately unrestricted
87	R	2	1	Strong	Moderately strong (JFK)	No changes	Large	Moderately weak	Moderately strong	6	Unrestricted
90	R	5	1	Strong	Moderately strong (LBJ)	No changes	Large	Moderately weak	Moderately strong	12	Unrestricted

a For key, see Table 4.1.
b See Table 2.1.
c See Table 2.2.
d For key, see Table 4.2.

TABLE 7.2
CHARACTERISTICS OF UNRESTRICTED MINORITIES IN THE SENATE

			EXTERNAL CONDITIONS					INTERNAL CONDITIONS[a]		
Congress	Minority party	Temper[b]	Majority-minority combination[c]	Minority party unity	President[d]	Margin[e]	Majority leadership	Minority leadership	Years in minority	Minority party in House
62	D	3	15	Moderate	Weak (WHT)	Small	Weak	Weak	14	GOP in minority (participating)
70	D	1	16	Moderate	Weak (CC)	Small	Weak	Moderately strong	8	Unrestricted
71	D	4	16	Moderate	Moderately weak (HH)	Moderate	Weak	Moderately strong	10	Unrestricted
72	D	4	15	Moderately strong	Weak (HH)	Small	Weak	Moderately strong	12	GOP in minority (participating)
82	R	2	1	Moderate	Moderately weak (HST)	Small	Weak	Moderate	2	Unrestricted
83	D	2	5	Moderately weak	Moderately weak (DDE)	Small	Strong	Moderately strong	0	Unrestricted

[a] Since no significant procedural changes were made in these Senates, this condition is omitted.
[b] For key, see Table 4.1.
[c] See Table 2.1.
[d] See Table 2.2.
[e] For key, see Table 4.2.

category (Wilson once, Kennedy once, and Johnson once), and three in the strong category (Wilson once and Roosevelt twice).

Differences in Senate party leadership also show up among these Congresses. Overall the strength of Senate party leaders is not impressive on either side. In six instances, I have judged the minority leaders to be stronger than the majority leaders; in five, the two seem to be equal in strength or weakness; and in five, the majority leaders seem stronger than the minority leaders.

Because of the special nature of the Senate as a legislative body political parties are not as meaningful there as they are in the House — either organizationally or as policy units. The significance of this fact in the discussion of "restricted minority party" Congresses was that though the party overall might be restricted, individual minority party senators could have considerable influence in policy making. In the present discussion, the absence of a strong party organization means that the minority party is never quite able to reach the full potential that favorable conditions might allow. Again, individual minority party senators may be able to be creative, constructive, destructive, and otherwise influential in determining whether and how a majority is constructed for legislation. But the party *qua* party is not likely to be influential very often. As a result, the House minority party and its members are likely both to be more flexible under favorable circumstances and more restricted under unfavorable circumstances than their counterparts in the Senate. The Senate minority party, on the other hand, is likely to be more constant in its role in the process of majority building, always playing the game rather loosely by acting as a communication link and facilitating the individual influence of its members.

These sixteen Congresses represent situations in which the minority party was more flexible in choosing among strategies. In many instances, however, conditions prevented the party from being able to select freely among the full complement of strategies, particularly those which one might label "aggressively positive" strategies (e.g., "innovation" coupled with "support" and "participation"). It seems appropriate, therefore, to discuss these Congresses in terms of *the limits which prevented the party from asserting itself more in the legitimation process in the Senate*, keeping in mind that there are countless examples both of the more "aggressively negative" strategies and of individual minority party senators attempting to be "aggressively positive."

LIMITED BY WAR

The first set of Congresses to discuss are those in which the temper of the times — specifically war conditions — limited the minority party. Three Congresses fit this category: the 65th, 78th, and 79th. In each case, the minority party Republicans were reestablishing themselves after a series of serious losses. In the 65th Congress, 1917–1918, Senate Republicans made their first net gains in five elections. They had suffered a net loss of twenty-two seats over the four previous elections. Thus, they were anxious to reassert themselves in the 65th Congress. The war prevented them from being too partisan, however. As Arthur W. Dunn wrote: "The war in Europe was of great service to the Democratic Party. It was evident that the party in power was going on the rocks when the outbreak in Europe changed the whole course of events." [1] Though overdrawn, and clearly representing anti-Wilsonian views, George R. Brown's description probably represented the attitude of many frustrated Republicans:

> As the war clouds gathered and the business of the American people passed more and more into the keeping of the Executive . . . the majesty of Congress declined. . . .
> The White House obscured the Capitol. Statesmen of both parties responsible for making the laws dared not raise their voices against the encroachments of the invisible Mind which in deep seclusion abode away from all human contact and ran the war on intellect. Senators of sovereign states, and leaders of parties, groveled in their marble corridors, so terrified were they of public opinion. [2]

In his account of the period, Seward W. Livermore observes that Senator Gallinger (R-New Hampshire), the Republican floor leader, responded in frustration to Senator Elihu Root's (R-New York) efforts to rally bipartisan support for President Wilson. Senator Gallinger "deplored the 'Republican gush' over Wilson and complained that 'a Republican victory two years from now cannot be

---

[1] Arthur W. Dunn, *From Harrison to Harding*, 2 vols. (New York: Putnam's, 1922), p. 257.
[2] George R. Brown, *The Leadership of Congress* (Indianapolis: Bobbs-Merrill, 1922), pp. 186–87.

brought about by exalting Wilson, and declaring that he deserves the undivided confidence of the American people.' " [3]

Though Livermore argues convincingly that the war did not keep either House or Senate Republicans from partisanship, the war clearly prevented them from taking a more aggressive stance in 1917–1918. As Livermore himself concludes, the Senate investigation of Secretary of War Newton Baker

> risked causing a reaction which, if allowed to get out of hand, might blast Republican prospects for years to come. Many Republicans therefore welcomed the respite afforded by the end of the investigation and Roosevelt's enforced retirement from the public arena. The wisest, or safest, course now was to consolidate whatever gains had been made at the President's expense and to continue to probe the administration's position for weak spots that did not bear so directly on the war itself as to alienate the voters.[4]

Other factors would have limited the Senate minority party in the 65th Congress, whether there had been a war or not. First, the Republican Party was still suffering considerable disunity. The 1916 elections represented a long step on the road back to reunion, but a number of Progressives were still in Congress. Second, partly as a result of continued division in the party, Senate Republicans lacked leadership. Jacob Gallinger of New Hampshire struggled on as minority leader in the 65th Congress. Never a strong leader, Gallinger was nearly eighty when the 65th Congress convened and he died before it adjourned.

During the 78th and 79th Congresses, the minority party Republicans had reason to be hungrier than in the 65th Congress, and they were less able to satisfy that hunger. They had experienced many lean years and the fruits of victory were long in coming, particularly in the Senate. Typically, the House responded more quickly to voting trends. Whereas Republicans had captured nearly 40 per cent of the House seats in the 76th Congress (nearly doubling their share over 1936), they controlled only 24 per cent of the Senate seats (an increase of just 6 per cent over 1936). It was not until the 78th Congress that the Senate Republican Party had regained a position of strength in numbers. Further, whereas the Republican Party re-

---

[3] Livermore, p. 12.
[4] *Ibid.*, pp. 103–4.

mained the dominant party nationally during the Wilson administration, defeated only by its own disunity, it was definitely the national minority party in every way after the depression.

With 40 per cent of the Senate seats in the 78th Congress, Republicans should have been anxious to defeat the president whenever possible. The fact that the United States was engaged in the war, however, made it difficult for Senate Republicans to find a proper base of opposition. They had to concentrate on domestic issues which were less involved with the war effort and for which popular support could be found for an antiadministration stance. As in the House, Senate Republicans were assisted in their search by Democratic criticism of President Roosevelt. On one notable occasion, the Senate Democratic critics included the distinguished majority leader, Alben W. Barkley from Kentucky. Barkley was so critical of President Roosevelt's veto message of a tax bill in the second session of the 78th Congress that he submitted his resignation to the Democratic Caucus. Barkley interpreted the message as "a calculated and deliberate assault upon the legislative integrity of every member of Congress." He chided the president:

> I dare say that during the past seven years of my tenure as majority leader I have carried the flag over rougher territory than was ever traversed by any previous majority leader. Sometimes I have carried it with little help here on the Senate floor, and more frequently with little help from the other end of Pennsylvania Avenue.

Barkley concluded as follows:

> I thank Heaven that my future happiness does not depend upon whether I shall retain the post of majority leader of the Senate for another hour. As proof of that, Mr. President, and in confirmation of this statement, I have called a conference of the Democratic majority for 10:30 o'clock tomorrow morning . . . at which time my resignation will be tendered and my service terminated in the post at which I now hold at this desk.[5]

The Democratic Caucus reelected him to his post by acclamation.

Overall, the Senate Republicans adopted the sensible strategy of supporting the president in the war effort. At this time the spirit of

[5] Floyd Riddick, *American Political Science Review*, Vol. 39 (April, 1945), p. 322.

bipartisanship in foreign policy was beginning to develop, owing principally to the efforts of the former Republican isolationist, Senator Arthur Vandenberg of Michigan. Democrats and Republicans worked together, with the president, on many foreign policy issues — notably the creation of the United Nations.

Senate Republicans had the most flexibility in regard to certain domestic issues where, as in the House, they could depend upon southern Democratic support or would willingly support southern Democratic moves to defeat the president. The Smith-Connally Act, both in its initial passage and in the vote to override the veto, received major support from Senate Republicans. Various other Senate Republicans were very much involved in other manpower legislation during the 78th and 79th Congresses. And, as in the House, the Senate minority party could concentrate on price control legislation with some expectation of success.

Senate Republicans generally appeared to be less flexible in adopting successful minority party strategies than were their colleagues in the House during these same Congresses. For example, Professor Young's data show that a majority of Senate Republicans were on the winning side on roll calls less frequently than House Republicans (comparable House figures are in parentheses).

Year	Majority of Senate Democrats on winning side of roll calls (%)		Majority of Senate Republicans on winning side of roll calls (%)	
1941	93	(92)	35	(51)
1942	88	(87)	78	(86)
1943	79	(65)	68	(83)
1944	79	(71)	69	(85)
1945	85	(87)	60	(62)

The Senate Republicans also had fewer total victories than House Republicans, where a majority of one party voted against a majority of the other. The ratios of Senate Democratic victories to Senate Republican victories were: 9 : 1 in 1941 (the House figures were 7 : 1); 2 : 1 in 1942 (1 : 1 in the House); 3 : 2 in 1943 (1 : 2 in the House); 3 : 2 in 1944 (1 : 2 in the House); and 3 : 1 in 1945 (3 : 1 in the House).[6]

These differences can best be explained by the fact that there were more House Republicans proportionally than Senate Republicans (48

6 Young, pp. 224–25.

per cent of the House seats were held by Republicans in the 78th Congress, 44 per cent in the 79th Congress), and the difference in the strength of leadership in the two houses. The House Republicans had reasonably strong leadership in Joseph W. Martin. Senate Republicans, however, were led by Wallace White of Maine. White was a lack luster leader, ill-equipped to lead the Republican Party with strength. To the extent that the Senate Republican Party had policy leadership, it was centered in the fast-rising and influential Robert A. Taft of Ohio.

LIMITED BY WEAK LEADERSHIP

Weakness of leadership in the Senate minority party is common and keeps the party from realizing the potential of the unrestricted situation in the policy-making process. This condition is related to the Senate style of individualism. More often than not, "gentlemen" become the elected leaders in the Senate. Although in each of these Congresses a combination of factors prevented the minority party from exercising greater flexibility in policy making, in the 62nd Congress lack of leadership appeared to be a central limiting factor. All other conditions were favorable to a strong and vigorous minority party: the mood was for action, the majority party was seriously divided, President Taft had virtually no sources of strength, the margin in the Senate was small (49 Republicans and 42 Democrats), majority party leadership was weak (Senator Aldrich having retired after the 61st Congress), and the Democratic Party controlled the House of Representatives.

During the first decade in this century, southern Democrats, many of them old men, had passed around the leadership of the Senate Democratic Party. It was normal to change leadership every session of the Senate. A battle over leadership developed with the election of the 62nd Congress and the opportunities it represented. William Jennings Bryan, titular leader of the party, wanted to break the hold of the southern Democrats. He favored a progressive Democrat, but Thomas S. Martin of Virginia was elected, 21–16, over Benjamin Snively of Indiana. Snively was made vice-chairman of the Caucus. Though Martin made a definite effort to represent both wings of the party, even to removing certain high tariff Democrats from the Steering Committee and replacing them with progressive Democrats, he and his colleagues did not represent the mood of the country which had divided the Republican party, given the Democrats control of the House, and increased by ten the number of Democratic senators (the largest increase for either party in thirty-six years).[7] The results of minority party action were, therefore, quite disappointing. Whereas in the House the majority party Democrats were making progress toward developing a program that would be implemented in the 63rd Congress, very little innovation occurred in the Senate. It is significant that when the Democrats won control of the Senate in 1912, Martin was not reelected to his leadership post.

Disunity and weak leadership limited the minority party in several Congresses, though in none were conditions so favorable to aggressive minority party action as in the 62nd Congress. In the 63rd Congress, to the extent that the divided and hapless minority party Republicans offered opposition to President Wilson's program, this opposition came in the Senate. Though on their way out, Senate Republicans retained 44 seats in the 63rd Congress, 7 fewer than the Democrats. They were seriously divided and were led by an old-guard "caretaker" leader, Jacob H. Gallinger of New Hampshire. The Senate Republicans were able to mount effective opposition to the major legislation passed in this Congress, particularly to the Federal Reserve Act where a Democrat, Senator Gilbert Hitchcock of Nebraska, was successful in forcing the Committee on Banking and Currency to report two bills — the president's and one much more favorable to the bankers. With strong Republican support, Hitchcock nearly succeeded in having his bill passed (41–44). The president's bill eventually passed by a comfortable margin.

During the 61st Congress, the minority party Democrats probably had more disadvantages than the minority party in any of the other Congresses listed in Tables 7.1 and 7.2. They were few in numbers, capturing only 32 seats in 1908; suffering from some disunity; led by a group of senior southern Democrats, and facing the strong majority party leadership of Nelson W. Aldrich of Rhode Island. Why not include this Congress among those in which the minority party was restricted? Principally because definite opportunities existed for the Democrats to be more flexible. First, President Taft took a limited view of his responsibilities in relation to Congress and had limited popular support. Second, and more important, though Aldrich remained strong, the insurgents were gaining in strength and conse-

---

[7] See *The New York Times*, April 7, 8, 12, 1911.

quently in voice. As the La Follettes observe in their biography of the Wisconsin senator, "The revolt against 'Cannonism' in the House was based on the same principle as was the opposition to Aldrich rule in the Senate." [8] Aldrich uncharacteristically became "unglued" during the debate on the Payne-Aldrich Tariff, as the Republican insurgents attacked the legislation. "Senator Aldrich . . . met these attacks first with indifference, then with contempt, and finally with white rage." [9] He attacked the insurgents, questioning their party loyalty. Far from bringing them back into the fold, these attacks encouraged them to bolt their leadership.[10] The Democrats might have taken advantage of this situation, since there were occasions when ten or eleven insurgents refused to vote with their party. Typically, the Democrats did not capitalize on situations of this sort, however. Indeed, Aldrich could depend upon many Democrats to support him in his efforts to enact a high tariff and prevent the passage of progressive legislation.

LIMITED BY WEAK PRESIDENTS

The largest bloc of Congresses in this category are those during the Harding, Coolidge, and Hoover administrations when the Senate minority party Democrats had a wide range of favorable conditions. The weakness of the Republican presidents and the continued divisiveness in the Republican Party during this period have already been discussed. In addition, the Senate Democratic Party had sizable representation in all four Congresses (ranging from 39 in the 71st to 47 — 2 short of a majority — in the 70th), and, for the first time since Kern led Senate Democrats under Wilson, the party was able to rely on relatively strong and consistent leadership. Joseph T. Robinson of Arkansas was elected Democratic floor leader in the 68th Congress and remained in that post until his death in 1937.

The minority Democrats in the Senate did little or nothing to fill the vacuum of policy leadership created by the virtual abdication of President Coolidge. There was cooperation among "farm bloc" senators to pass farm relief legislation, but overall, despite their advan-

[8] Belle C. and Fola La Follette, *Robert M. La Follette*, 2 vols. (New York: Macmillan, 1953), p. 270.
[9] John A. Garraty, *Henry Cabot Lodge: A Biography* (New York: Knopf, 1953), p. 267.
[10] See Hechler, *Insurgency;* and Claude Bowers, *Beveridge and the Progressive Era* (New York: The Literary Guild, 1932).

taged situation, the Senate Democrats did no more than their colleagues in the House to offer solutions to pending public problems. As with the House, it appears that one limiting condition for the creative minority party is a weak president who does not offer an extensive program to Congress.

Additional support for this conclusion is provided by the 71st Congress. Hoover was forced to submit to Congress an extensive legislative program, and consequently the minority party was more active. During the 71st Congress, the Senate Republicans were more divided than ever (there had been some reunification in the House under Longworth's leadership). As Professor Macmahon observed in his review of the first session: "It has been easy to laugh." [11]

Senator Charles Curtis of Kansas was elected vice-president in 1928, leaving open the majority floor leadership position. Senator James E. Watson of Indiana was elected to fill the position in the 71st Congress. Watson was one more floor leader in a long line of "amiable personalities" who do not "stir up animosities but placates them." [12] Professor Macmahon observed that "it would be unfair to Mr. Watson . . . to blame him for the deep disharmony in what passes as the Republican Party, or, for that matter, to mistake effects for causes when nature has its way in those loose leagues to capture the presidency which are called national parties in the United States." [13] President Hoover disliked Watson; he had a higher regard for Robinson than for his own floor leader.[14]

The Democrats began to vote rather consistently with certain insurgent Republican Senators in the 71st Congress. There was talk of "the coalition," a group Senator Furnifold Simmons (D-North Carolina) claimed "was not brought about by caucusing, but is a coalition that resulted from a union of minds." [15] Membership included most of the Democrats and various midwestern Progressive Republicans. The coalition was much in evidence during the debate and voting on the Smoot-Hawley Tariff in 1929 and 1930.

[11] Macmahon, *American Political Science Review*, Vol. 24 (February, 1930), p. 38.
[12] Quoted in *ibid.*, p. 41.
[13] *Ibid.*, p. 42.
[14] See Harris G. Warren, *Herbert Hoover and the Great Depression* (New York: Oxford University Press, 1959), pp. 153–54. See also Herbert Hoover, *The Memoirs of Hoover: The Great Depression, 1929–1941* (New York: Macmillan, 1952), p. 101.
[15] Macmahon, *American Political Science Review*, Vol. 24 (February, 1930), p. 51.

But if President Hoover could be accused of talking "around" the economic collapse in 1929, rather than acting decisively to stem the tide, the minority party Democrats in the Senate could not receive credit for doing much more. They began to react at about the same time the president realized that no amount of optimism would halt the economic decline. In 1930, the Democrats came close to capturing control of the Senate and, though often frustrated by presidential veto, the minority party Democrats in the 72nd Congress realized more fully than any of their predecessors the potentialities of the minority party in policy making.

HIGHLY FLEXIBLE SENATE MINORITY PARTIES

President Hoover's second Congress, the 72nd, was most unusual. The only close parallel is the 62nd, under Taft. The temper of the times following the economic collapse of 1929 was dramatically emotional. The 72nd Congress convened with "hunger-marchers" parading outside the Capitol. The election returns in 1930 served as impressive evidence that the public was not satisfied with the majority party. The Republican majority in the House was reduced from 104 in the 71st Congress to 2 in the 72nd. And by the time the first session convened (December 7, 1931), deaths among House Republicans had placed them in the minority. In the Senate, the Republican majority dropped from 17 to 1. Despite their electoral triumph in 1928, all evidence in 1930 pointed to the decline and fall of the Republican Party. The situation was very much like that in the 62nd Congress, where, though from different causes, the Republican Party lost control of the House and had its margin in the Senate reduced. In both cases the Republican Party was obviously in the process of becoming the minority party in the national policy-making institutions. The atmosphere in the 72nd Congress was almost unreal. Not only was the Republican Party in transition between majority and minority status, as distinct from the 62nd Congress, but the transition was to be a permanent arrangement.

During the first session of the 72nd Congress the President had to rely on a Senate Republican Party that was seriously split between the regulars and the insurgents. The party could not even perform the relatively simple task of selecting a president pro tempore. A regular, George H. Moses of New Hampshire, had served in the post since the 69th Congress, but the insurgents refused to support him.

On the twenty-third ballot, the Democratic candidate, Key Pittman of Nevada, received 34 votes; Moses received 23; and Arthur Vandenberg (serving his first term) received the support of 14 insurgents. Since no one had a majority, Moses remained as president pro tempore under an 1890 ruling that the incumbent will serve in the post until a successor is appointed. President Hoover advised Senator Watson, his majority leader in the Senate, to allow the Democrats to organize the Senate so as "to convert their sabotage into responsibility."

> I felt that I could deal more constructively with the Democratic leaders if they held full responsibility in both houses, than with an opposition in the Senate conspiring in the cloak rooms to use every proposal of mine for demagoguery.[16]

Senator Watson did not take Hoover's advice.

After the 1930 elections, the Senate Democrats realized that their party could well be on its way to total victory in 1932. From the point of view of the minority party, conditions could not have been better. This is not to say, of course, that the Democrats relished the economic distress in the nation. They deplored it. But it became increasingly apparent that if conditions did not improve the Democrats could look forward to majority status. It would be ridiculous to expect the Democrats not to take advantage of the situation in adopting policy-making strategies. While Senate Democrats supported some of the president's program for recovery, naturally many of them had different ideas. Close cooperation between the parties in policy making, therefore, was not very likely during the 72nd Congress.

The first session of the 72nd Congress was not totally unproductive. In many instances, the president was given what he wanted, with the support of many Democrats. Though, as Professor E. Pendleton Herring noted in his review of the first session, "unified leadership of a bi-partisan program of reconstruction was well-nigh defeated at the start," [17] some progress was made in coping with the economic disaster. Surely no one expected "unified leadership of a bi-partisan program" anyway. Senate Democrats did not restrict themselves to the strategies of support, constructive opposition, and partisan opposition, however. Particularly in regard to relief legislation, considerable innovation and cooperation with insurgent Progres-

---

[16] Hoover, Memoirs, p. 101.
[17] E. Pendleton Herring, "The First Session of the 72nd Congress," American Political Science Review, Vol. 26 (October, 1932), p. 857.

sives was evident. The chief Democratic innovators were Robert F. Wagner of New York; Edward P. Costigan of Colorado; Hugo Black of Alabama; and Bronson Cutting of New Mexico. They worked closely with Robert M. La Follette, Jr., of Wisconsin; George Norris of Nebraska; and William Borah of Idaho. Wagner in particular began to develop a program of his own. Arthur M. Schlesinger, Jr., summarizes this program:

> His proposals started with $2 billion for public works. He wanted in addition a Federal Employment Stabilization Board for the advance planning of public works, an effective federal employment service, a system of collecting unemployment statistics, and a federal system of unemployment insurance.[18]

As Schlesinger observes: "he could hardly have conceived measures more objectionable to Hoover." [19] Hoover stressed balancing the budget and stabilizing the currency through banking legislation. He was unwilling to support an extensive federal role in public relief legislation. He was willing to assist local and state governments with loans from the Reconstruction Finance Corporation. When more extensive relief legislation was passed in Congress, Hoover vetoed it. Indeed, he called congressional leaders to the White House in advance to warn them of the veto. An innovative Senate Democratic Party was checkmated by the president.[20] And in his veto message, "the President asserted himself as a director of national policy." [21]

The first session of the 72nd Congress was a veritable picnic compared to the second session. The last of the lame duck sessions was nothing short of weird. President Hoover had just suffered a calamitous defeat at the polls, only 117 House Republicans and 36 Senate Republicans were elected. Both houses were filled with lame ducks, making the president the lamest duck of them all. Herring summarizes the situation:

> Here was a Congress, divided in control, weakened by the presence of repudiated representatives, and under the dis-

---

[18] Arthur M. Schlesinger, Jr., *The Crisis of the Old Order* (Boston: Houghton Mifflin, 1957), p. 225.

[19] *Ibid.*

[20] Not all Democrats in the Senate were interested in innovation for solving the problems at hand. Opposition to relief legislation came from southern Democrats — relying on "the pork-barrel, states-rights, self-respect, unbalanced-budget, historical-precedent, morale-weakening, it's-a-dole arguments." See Warren, p. 203.

[21] Herring, *American Political Science Review*, Vol. 26 (October, 1932), p. 855.

credited leadership of a defeated president, but never the less faced with perplexing problems of national and world import arising in a highly critical period. The necessities of the time called for cooperative planning and swift united action, but the exigencies of politics suggested procrastination and obstruction. And the latter considerations prevailed.[22]

It was a session in which the Senate minority party had become the Senate majority party. Plans were laid for cooperating with President Roosevelt when he took office in March but little was done to meet the requests of President Hoover. As Herring concludes: "The record of the session is not to be judged so much in terms of what it did as in terms of what it refrained from doing." [23] With so little time before the new administration was to be inaugurated, Senate Democrats were reluctant to enact legislation which might be credited to Hoover. The chaos and the inaction were advantageous to the Democrats. "If the Congress in this last session 'did nothing in particular,' " observed Herring, "from the viewpoint of the new administration it 'did it very well.' " [24]

The position of the Senate minority party in the 62nd Congress was similar in many respects to that in the 72nd Congress. The Republicans had been dealt a staggering blow in the elections of 1910, losing the House by a much larger margin than in 1930. There was also one of those unreal lame duck sessions in which a thoroughly beaten President Taft continued in the White House while the Democrats prepared to take control of all the national policy-making institutions.

There are differences between these two Congresses too. A mood for action among the public in 1911–1912 was evident, but no all-engaging domestic crisis dominated the scene. Pressed by the dramatic economic collapse, Hoover was forced to work long and hard each day to develop proposals to aid recovery. In the 62nd Congress, Taft did very little even to lead his own party. Further, the Senate minority party had much stronger leadership and greater receptivity to new ideas in the 72nd Congress. Party leadership in the 62nd Congress was extraordinarily weak. And, finally, the cause of Republican defeat in 1930 and 1932 was different than in 1910 and 1912.

Two blocs of Congresses remain for analysis. First, in the three

[22] E. Pendleton Herring, "The Second Session of the 72nd Congress," *American Political Science Review*, Vol. 27 (June, 1933), p. 404.

[23] *Ibid.*, p. 421.

[24] *Ibid.*, p. 422.

Congresses between 1949 and 1953 (81st, 82nd, and 83rd) the Senate minority party had considerable strength. During this interesting period in congressional politics, the Republican Party was enjoying considerable success. In fact, during the six-election period from 1947 to 1959, Republicans averaged 47 seats in the Senate and 207 seats in the House. Three of these Congresses have been discussed — 80th, 84th and 85th — all as characterized by participating minorities. Second, two recent Congresses deserve attention. Despite the fact that Senate Republicans had only 36 seats, they were able to remain quite flexible in adopting strategies in both the 87th and 90th Congresses. (Since the 90th Congress will be discussed in detail in Chapter 8, only the 87th Congress will receive attention here.)

The situation in the Senate during the 81st, 82nd, and 83rd Congresses was very much like that in the House. The Republicans, denied victory in 1948, nevertheless remained strong enough to choose among alternative strategies, particularly in view of the internal division in the Democratic Party. On housing legislation, there was considerable bipartisan support, with Senator Taft exercising impressive influence within his party and within the Senate. Typically agricultural legislation divided the Republicans. They remained united enough, however, to be instrumental in defeating the Brannan Plan [25] and in instituting flexible supports for the future. They also helped override the veto of the Internal Security Act of 1950. On the other hand, Senate Republicans offered strong opposition to some measures, with less success than they enjoyed in the 82nd Congress.

With the exception of support for Korean War measures, the president met with one defeat after another on major legislation in the Senate during the 82nd Congress. On a much reduced scale, the Senate Republicans were in a situation like that of Senate Democrats during the 72nd Congress. President Truman's popularity with the public, and in his own party, was continuing its downward trend. Senate Republicans had every incentive to make the president look bad. After twenty years, the minority party did not want to miss the opportunity of capturing control of the government in 1952. The 1950 elections gave them ample cause to be encouraged. And with the internal divisions in the Senate Democratic Party, Senate Republicans were able virtually to take control of the Senate. Certainly it was not the Senate majority leadership which was in control.

[25] The Brannan Plan authorized a permanent system of high price supports, extended supports to perishables, and instituted a highly controversial "direct payment" plan for support of perishables.

Of the twelve key votes on major legislation during the 82nd Congress (identified by the Congressional Quarterly) [26] seven represented votes in which a majority of Senate Republicans opposed a majority of Senate Democrats. Because of the Republicans' greater cohesiveness, and defections among southern Democrats, the Republicans won *all seven roll calls*. In addition, the tidelands oil bill, opposed by the president and later vetoed by him, was passed with the support of 26 Republicans and 24 Democrats (50 per cent of the Democrats voting) and the Immigration and Nationality Act of 1952 was passed over the president's veto with the support of majorities of both parties. In many instances, these key votes came on amendments introduced by southern Democrats. Very little effort was made by Senate Republicans to adopt the more aggressive positive strategies, however.

The 83rd Congress found the Democrats in the minority, but by the narrow margin of one seat. An unusual number of deaths during the session kept party control continuously in doubt. The Republicans' most serious loss was their majority leader, Robert A. Taft. Elected to replace Taft was William F. Knowland of California. Knowland was no match for Taft's talents, but with the able H. Styles Bridges of New Hampshire in the background Senate Republican leadership was a match for the minority party Democrats. As in the House, the Senate Democrats were careful about offering too strong opposition to America's new-found political idol. A majority of Democrats voted with a majority of Republicans on six of the twelve key votes during the 83rd Congress.[27] On five of the remaining six votes, majorities in the two parties were opposed. The Republican majority *won all five*, but in no case would victory have been possible without Democratic votes. The final key vote came on the censure of Senator Joseph McCarthy (R-Wisconsin) for his communist-hunting tactics; all the Democrats voting joined 50 per cent of the Republicans to censure him. Thus, in the 83rd Congress, the flexibility of the Senate Democratic Party was reduced somewhat by the popularity of the new president, the fact that the party had recently been rejected at the polls, persistent internal divisions, new leadership, and the care with which President Eisenhower formulated his program.

[26] The key votes are those identified by the Congressional Quarterly in *Congress and the Nation, 1945–1964*, pp. 56a–57a.

[27] *Ibid.*, pp. 62a–63a.

The final Congress to consider in this chapter is the 87th, John F. Kennedy's first. This is one of those Congresses in which the minority party was seriously outnumbered — the Democrats had a 28-seat margin over the Republicans. Further, the president had won in a mild upset over his opponent and came to the White House with a program more extensive than that of any other president in history (including Roosevelt). Why include this as a Congress in which the minority was flexible in choosing among alternative strategies? First, the Democrats continued to be plagued by internal division. The Republicans, on the other hand, were reasonably unified. Second, though the Senate Republicans gained only two seats in the 1960 elections, this represented their first gain in four elections. Third, Kennedy's victory was very narrow, denying him the major source of power that comes from the types of victories enjoyed by Franklin D. Roosevelt, Eisenhower, and Lyndon B. Johnson. And finally, because Johnson became vice-president, a new leader had to be selected by Senate Democrats. Mike Mansfield of Montana, who had served as Johnson's assistant floor leader, moved up to assume the position of majority floor leader. A more striking contrast in personalities is hard to imagine. Mansfield relied on the "soft sell." He defined his view of himself in response to criticism on the Senate floor:

> I confess freely to a lack of glamour. . . . I would not, even
> if I could, presume to a toughmindedness. . . . I shall not
> don any Mandarin's robes or any skin other than that to
> which I am accustomed in order that I may look like a major-
> ity leader or sound like a majority leader — however a major-
> ity leader is supposed to look or sound. I am what I am and
> no title, political facelifter, or imagemaker can alter it. . . .
> I do my best to be courteous, decent, and understanding of
> others and sometimes fail at it. But it is for the Senate to
> decide whether these characteristics are incompatible with the
> leadership.[28]

The review of minority party activity on major legislation before the Senate in the 87th Congress suggests that the party was able to choose among the full complement of strategies. In many instances Senate Republicans provided significant support for the president's

---

[28] *Congressional Record*, 88th Cong., 1st sess., November 27, 1963, pp. 21758–59. This was a response to Senator Thomas Dodd (D-Connecticut) who had, on November 6, called on Mansfield to "behave like a leader."

program — notably area redevelopment, minimum wage, trade expansion, communications satellite, and tax legislation. In other instances cooperation between the leadership of the two parties was evident — notably on civil rights and communications satellite legislation. Senate Republicans also offered "constructive" opposition by introducing amendments to major legislation or supporting modifying amendments offered by Democrats which were not favored by the administration (particularly on housing and agriculture legislation). And, of course, Senate Republicans united to offer strong opposition to certain legislation, sometimes successfully, as with medical care for the aged; sometimes unsuccessfully, as with agriculture, education, and housing. The minority party was not as potent in the 87th Congress as in the 82nd Congress, however. For example, despite their problems of cohesion, the Democrats were able to win seven of the ten "key" roll calls when the majority of one party was pitted against the majority of the other. And of those seven victories, only two required Republican votes to win the day.

CONCLUSIONS

Several conclusions develop from this analysis of unrestricted minorities in the House and Senate. First, and most obvious, different types of unrestricted minority parties can be identified, depending on a variety of conditions. Second, minority parties that are relatively unrestricted in choosing among strategies in the process of majority building do not necessarily adopt all the strategic options that appear to be available to them. Indeed, "unrestricted" minority parties seldom choose what I have labeled "aggressive positive strategies." Third, the role of the president, the temper of the times, and the leadership of the minority party are all important in determining the extent of minority party activity when strategic options are more plentiful. Particularly impressive is the finding that the minority party is ill equipped to innovate in the absence of presidential initiative. When the president is weak and takes a restricted view of his role, other conditions may be very favorable to the minority party and yet the party is unable to take advantage of the leadership vacuum. The minority party most aggressively pursues various strategies when the president is active and innovative.

Two other comparative observations can be made. First, though comparing the two parties over time is difficult, on the basis of this analysis the two parties appear to differ little in their role as the minority. Aside from the Republicans in recent years, it seems that, as minority parties, both the Democrats and the Republicans have taken a basically limited view of their policy-making role. Second, the striking differences between the House and Senate in this analysis continue to be demonstrated. The individualism in style in the Senate makes the party role most difficult to reconstruct.

CHAPTER EIGHT

The Minority Party Today

In this chapter we will focus on the second session of the 89th Congress and the first session of the 90th Congress. The justification is simple enough. First, it is useful to "get inside" a session of Congress to flesh out the analysis by examining specific actions. Second, "getting inside" allows more detailed inquiry into the distinction between party activity and party members' activities. Obviously, the two may not always coincide or be based on the same analysis of goals. Third, there have been important developments — particularly in the House Republican Party — in recent years that suggest that the minority party is establishing party machinery so as to adopt the "aggressively positive" strategies. Finally, a more limited focus will assist in clarifying the distinctions between the organization and behavior of the House and Senate minority parties.

ORGANIZATIONAL DEVELOPMENTS SINCE 1959

A number of important organizational developments have taken place in the Republican Party since 1959 which must be reviewed because of their importance in determining the behavior of the minority party in 1966–1967. These organizational moves, including various leadership changes, provided a basis for adopting more positive strategies in majority building. Those responsible for these changes wanted the Republican Party to project a more "positive image." Any organizational changes in a political party are intimately involved with power struggles within the party. The struggle in the Republican Party has generally been between old-line leaders who have accommodated themselves to a political career in the minority party, and younger leaders who want more than minority party status. The results of the many changes suggest the importance of leadership in overcoming the disadvantages of any one minority party situation — e.g., large margin of the majority over the minority, strong presidential leadership, strong majority party leadership, etc. — and suggest potentialities for the minority party in policy making.

HOUSE REPUBLICANS REORGANIZE. The developments in the House are considerably more striking than those in the Senate. These developments began with the revitalization of the House Republican Policy Committee in 1959. Minority Leader Martin agreed to the establishment of the Committee in 1949 but relegated it to the same fate of inactivity as previous steering committees. For ten years the Policy Committee met irregularly and "was more a debating society — a more or less academic procedure to endorse Joe's decisions." [1] Certainly the 1949 Committee did not satisfy the demands of those who wanted it formed. Specifically the younger members were frustrated in an attempt to find some means of expressing their ideas. Several attempted to find an outlet by forming the Response Group in 1956, a group designed to respond to the majority party's program with alternatives developed as a result of research on policy questions. By 1958 these members began to make demands for support of their efforts to strengthen the image of the minority party by asking for staff assistance from the party leadership. Though Martin did not obstruct these efforts, he did little to encourage them.

The devastating defeat in 1958 served as a catalyst for action. Junior members were joined by more senior members in an effort to oust Martin. As Martin explained it in his book, "they began to look for someone to blame for the calamity of election day. Many an eye lighted on me." [2] At first an attempt was made to convince Martin to give up the Policy Committee chairmanship so that members would have this more formal outlet for their activities. Martin refused. Then, on January 6, 1959, he was defeated for the leadership post by his former majority leader, Charles A. Halleck of Indiana. Halleck was by no means the favorite candidate among junior members, but he became the only possible alternative. And he was more acceptable than Martin, partly because he was willing to have a separate chairman of the Policy Committee.

[1] Charles O. Jones, *Party and Policy-Making: The House Republican Policy Committee* (New Brunswick, N.J.: Rutgers University Press, 1964), p. 27.
[2] Joseph W. Martin, Jr., *My First Fifty Years in Politics* (as told to Robert Donovan) (New York: McGraw-Hill, 1960), p. 5.

The new chairman of the Policy Committee in 1959 was John W. Byrnes of Wisconsin, one of those members most seriously considered as Martin's replacement by the insurgents. Under Byrnes's leadership the Policy Committee came to have an important role in the House Republican Party. It met every Tuesday to discuss pending legislation, issued policy statements which were distributed to all members, and hired a staff to do research. The Committee was also more broadly representative of the party after 1959. The revitalization of the Committee resulted in (1) House Republicans meeting on a regular basis to discuss strategy on legislation before the House and (2) efforts, however feeble, to develop policy alternatives to those offered by the majority party. In my study of the Policy Committee, I concluded that the principal function of the Committee under Byrnes was to discover a basis for consensus on policy strategy or that no such basis existed. But efforts were also made by the new Policy Committee to construct consensus on policy positions rather than simply discovering that a consensus existed. Obviously, this is no simple task for a congressional party and it is this experimentation which is of most interest here.

In 1961, the Policy Committee established a Subcommittee on Special Projects, chaired by John J. Rhodes of Arizona. This Subcommittee was a direct outgrowth of the activities by the Response Group. Rhodes in particular tried to find some place in the party structure where a research group might be able to function. He considered the Congressional Campaign Committee but concluded that is was "too mixed with politics." Byrnes agreed in 1961 to attach the research operation to the Policy Committee. The Subcommittee, with the assistance of the Policy Committee staff, attempted to develop long-range policy for the party by intensive and scholarly study on important issues. Efforts were made to effect cooperation between congressional and academic experts.

Though the resources of the Subcommittee were seriously limited — the permanent staff for the full Committee never exceeded three persons — several studies eventually were produced. Typically a task force of congressmen was organized, background papers solicited from experts, and position papers prepared by the staff. A final report was then issued and the results of these efforts were often inserted in the *Congressional Record*. One study, an examination of "Employment in a Dynamic American Economy," resulted directly in legislation. One section of the study dealt with manpower retraining, and many of the recommendations were incorporated in the Manpower Development and Training Act in 1962.

Any objective analysis of the Subcommittee and its work would have to agree with Chairman Rhodes: "I would say that we have lit a very small candle. But for the amount of money which has gone into it, we have had a modicum of success." [3] Not only were most of the studies ignored by the press, but many Policy Committee members were unable to discuss with accuracy the research operations of the Subcommittee. One member noted that the studies were "too scholarly." "It is the impact that is important and this is a problem with these studies." [4] This member's opinion illustrates the problem inherent in this type of effort. Long-range policy-studies — designed to develop consensus among party members on policy alternatives — are not only difficult to produce, given the present structure and resources of congressional political parties, but also difficult to have accepted and understood by party members. Further, and potentially more important, this procedure represents a significant departure from, and a direct challenge to, the existing standing committee–seniority system. The fact that the Subcommittee existed as a party agency is significant because it represents the first attempt by a political party in the House to develop policy responses based on research. The surprising feature of the Subcommittee is not that it had limited success but that it had any success at all, and that it continues to exist (though in different form).

In 1963 the junior Republicans in the House staged another revolt against the leadership. Led by Charles E. Goodell of New York and Robert P. Griffin of Michigan, the group succeeded in ousting Charles B. Hoeven of Iowa as Conference chairman and electing Gerald R. Ford of Michigan in his place. The Goodell-Griffin group actually had in mind capturing both the whip and Conference chairman slots, but Arends represented too formidable a challenge.[5] The group was also successful in gaining more representation on the Policy Committee for younger members.

The defeat of Hoeven, as with the defeat of Martin, is of direct relevance to this discussion because of what the insurgents had in mind. In 1959 they were able to get a revitalized Policy Committee,

[3] Jones, p. 67.
[4] *Ibid.*
[5] The Goodell-Griffin group was first interested in ousting Halleck but determined that any such effort would be futile at that time.

in 1961 they were able to get a research group in the Policy Committee, and in 1963 they were successful in beginning the revitalization
of the Conference. Various members of the group ousting Hoeven
discussed their efforts in interviews:

> Hoeven's post just goes to waste.
>
> We could use it [the Conference] at the beginning of a
> session to present Republican ideas — a sort of State of the
> Union message for Republicans. Then we would organize so
> that we could respond to and discuss the President's state-
> ments. . . . We could have experts from the committees
> come in on specific legislative areas — John Byrnes on taxa-
> tion for instance.
>
> Those of us who pressed for a change thought that the
> Conference was dead and unimaginative. It has greater po-
> tential. Thus our move was more than just symbolic.
>
> There is potential in the Conference. After all, all the
> party power is in the Conference — the whole party organiza-
> tion comes from there. *Seniority doesn't count there* — every
> man has one vote — that is why we went to the Conference.

Not content with their gains, the new Republicans took advantage
of the 1964 defeat at the polls to continue the biennial reordering of
their party.[6] Much of the ferment in 1963 was in fact directed against
Halleck rather than the innocuous Hoeven. As Hoeven himself
prophesied: "I was picked as the lamb for the slaughter. This should
serve as notice to Mr. Arends and Mr. Halleck that something is
brewing." [7] On January 4, 1965, Hoeven's prediction proved accurate.
In the Republican Conference on that day, Gerald R. Ford defeated
Halleck for the minority leadership. Ironically, Joseph W. Martin
attended the Conference to cast his vote against Halleck.

There is no need to describe all the details of Halleck's defeat.
Peabody has done an admirable job of that. What is important for
present purposes is that the struggle in 1965 was one more chapter
in an innovative attempt to reconstruct the minority party so that it

---

[6] This discussion relies heavily on Robert L. Peabody's detailed analysis of the
1965 revolt. See *The Ford-Halleck Minority Leadership Contest, 1965* (New
York: McGraw-Hill, 1966); "Party Leadership in the United States House of
Representatives," *American Political Science Review,* Vol. 61 (September, 1967),
pp. 675–93; and "House Republican Leadership: Change and Consolidation in a
Minority Party" (paper prepared for delivery at the 1966 Annual Meeting of the
American Political Science Association, New York City, September 9–12, 1966).

[7] Jones, p. 155.

could do more than simply select among essentially negative strategies. As one of Peabody's interviewees noted: "I'm tired of always painting ourselves into a corner. I don't like being there all the time." [8]

Victory in 1965 gave this new group of Republicans almost complete control of the party. Having achieved a near rout of the old-guard leadership over a period of six years (Arends continued to demonstrate a remarkable ability to survive), the major reason for unity among insurgents was gone. That is, members from both the conservative and moderate wings of the party had participated in the several revolts against incumbent leaders. It was likely, therefore, that some members would be unwilling to support other members for leadership positions once the old guard was gone. For example, Rhodes had been instrumental in the defeat of Martin in 1959 but supported Halleck over Ford in 1965. In short, as they got closer to the top, internal power struggles among the insurgents themselves were inevitable.

In addition to the floor leader's position, three other party positions had to be filled in 1965: the Conference chairmanship, the whip position, and the Policy Committee chairmanship. The Conference chairmanship was open as a result of Ford's being elevated to floor leader. Arends had been party whip since 1944 and Ford was anxious to have someone else in that spot. Byrnes was Policy Committee chairman but had to step down as a result of a Conference resolution that prohibited party leaders from serving as ranking minority members of congressional standing committees. Byrnes preferred to retain his position as ranking Republican on Ways and Means.[9] In a contest between two Ford supporters, Melvin R. Laird of Wisconsin won the Conference leadership over the moderate-liberal candidate, Peter Frelinghuysen of New Jersey. Ford wanted a member who was "wholeheartedly behind the new legislative strategy of constructive alternatives" as whip.[10] After his impressive showing against Laird, Ford asked Frelinghuysen to be his candidate against Arends. Frelinghuysen agreed but was again defeated as Arends successfully fought to retain his position.

---

[8] Peabody, "House Republican Leadership," p. 3.

[9] Actually Byrnes had indicated he was interested in stepping down before because of the pressure of responsibilities on the Committee on Ways and Means. See Jones, p. 111.

[10] Peabody, "House Republican Leadership," p. 7.

The last contest — that for Policy Committee chairman — is of greatest interest to this study. John J. Rhodes announced his intention to seek the chairmanship. It was a reasonable move for Rhodes in view of his chairmanship of the Subcommittee on Special Projects. Rhodes was not Ford's choice for this slot, however, partly because of Rhodes's close association with Senator Barry Goldwater of Arizona (thus damaging Ford's effort to build a more positive image for the party) and partly because Ford wanted to reward Charles E. Goodell of New York. Rather than face another defeat at the hands of the Party Conference, Ford sidestepped the problem by allowing Rhodes to become chairman without opposition and appointing Goodell to chair a new committee that would serve the Conference. The new Committee on Planning and Research assumed the functions of the old Subcommittee on Special Projects. It would act independently of the Policy Committee and could rely on the newly formed research staff of the Conference under the direction of Dr. William Prendergast. Thus, the two functions of the Policy Committee — discovery of consensus on pending legislative issues and research on policy problems so as to build consensus — were separated. The latter was assumed by the newly formed Committee on Planning and Research.[11]

The procedure of the new research committee was very much like that of the Subcommittee on Special Projects, only on a grander scale. The new Committee had the benefit of the newly formed Conference staff of six full-time people and twelve permanent task forces on the following subjects: agriculture, economic opportunity, education, the Atlantic Community, urban and suburban affairs, platform implementation, voting rights, congressional reform and minority staffing, budget, nuclear affairs, Latin America, and the United Nations. Each task force had a member of the full Committee on Planning and Research acting as liaison between the task force and the full committee.

Goodell made a serious attempt to use the task forces as mechanisms for coordinating House Republican policy statements. During 1965 the task forces issued press releases, held hearings on policy issues, conducted studies (including a white paper on Vietnam), criticized the administration, and developed policy proposals. The task force on the Atlantic Community even went to Paris on a fact-

[11] Certain changes were made in the system of representation on the Policy Committee in 1965; there were other minor changes. See *ibid.*, pp. 15–16.

finding mission. Clearly, much of this activity was directed at the public so as to recapture the House in the 1966 elections. But the overall effort was unprecedented, representing a serious effort on the part of a woefully outnumbered minority party (only six times in this century has the minority party had fewer members) to be more aggressive in pursuing positive strategies in the policy-making process.

It would be too much to expect dramatic results from this audacious effort by House Republicans during the first session of the 89th Congress. President Johnson was still able to ride the crest of his outstanding victory in 1964 and the Party had to accommodate the reshuffling in leadership and organization in 1965. In 1966, however, an impressive record was established. Despite the fact that the Republicans still had only 32 per cent of the seats in the House, they offered formidable, not wholly negative, opposition to the majority party.

Certain changes were made in the Planning and Research Committee's procedure during the first session of the 90th Congress. Fewer task forces were organized and greater emphasis was placed on development of alternatives within standing committees (with staff assistance from the Planning and Research Committee). Only four task forces were organized in 1967: agriculture, crime, east-west trade, and western alliances. All were active but the crime task force was the most successful in terms of influencing the form of legislation on the floor. Task forces were created where it was felt that the Republicans on standing committees could not, or would not, develop alternatives to majority party proposals. In every case, the Planning and Research Committee made an effort to publicize House Republican attempts to influence policy making. Those who had pressed for reform were strongly of the opinion that attempts in the past to be creative had failed in part because feeble efforts were made to publicize what was going on. In large part, the reformers blamed Martin and Halleck, contending that they projected a negative image of the party to the public. The new leaders wanted to present the image of a young party with hard-working members offering new ideas.

Important changes were also made in the Policy Committee procedure following the 1965 revolt and leadership change. Policy statements were more positive than before. Efforts were made in every statement to present rationale for the position taken or the alternative proposed. These statements were given much wider circulation than before, with increased efforts to get press coverage. Further, policy statements were not limited to pending legislation. Attempts were made to urge the administration to deal with certain problems, e.g., the maritime industry, deployment of antiballistic missiles, executive reorganization. Nor did the Policy Committee wait for legislation to be reported by a committee before issuing a statement. In many instances it would urge adoption of legislation which had been introduced by House Republicans and which was pending in a standing committee. Again, as with the Planning and Research Committee, supreme efforts were made to project a more positive image and to make certain that these efforts were highly publicized.

Finally, the Congressional Republicans adopted a technique used by Senate Majority Leader Lyndon B. Johnson during the Eisenhower administration. In 1966 and again in 1967, Senate Minority Leader Dirksen and House Minority Leader Ford presented the Republican version of the "State of the Union." As with the presidential State of the Union address, the minority leaders presented specific legislative proposals — to my knowledge an unprecedented action for a minority party.

The organizational changes in the House Republican Party since 1959 are the most important developments in the role of the minority party in policy making in this century. By certain subjective measures of what party reformers think the minority party should be, these efforts may seem feeble, halting first steps. But by comparison to the organization, leadership, and actions of congressional minority parties in this century, the efforts are remarkably innovative.

SENATE REPUBLICAN ACTIVITIES. The development of mechanisms for constructive alternatives is considerably less clear-cut in the Senate Republican Party. This is to be expected, given the differences in structure, organization, and functions of political parties in the House and Senate. Still the Senate adopted policy committees in its version of the Legislative Reorganization bill of 1946. When the House deleted this provision, the Senate amended the First Supplemental Appropriations Act for 1947 (passed in 1946) to provide appropriations for Senate policy committees. Since 1947, therefore, the Senate has had policy committees in both parties which receive appropriations from Congress.

The reformers' intentions in recommending policy committees for congressional parties in 1945 and 1946 were quite clear. The committees were to "plan the legislative program, coordinate and guide committee activity, focus party leadership, and strengthen party responsibility and accountability." [12] These lofty goals have never been achieved by the policy committee of either party. The exact function of the Senate minority party policy committee, according to Hugh A. Bone and Malcolm E. Jewell, depends upon who is chairman.[13] Senator Robert A. Taft served as chairman of the Republican Committee during the first six years of its existence. Taft viewed the Committee as a device for "committing the Senate Republican Party to a program" but specifically to a program which was "in accord with his own views of public policy." [14] Taft believed that the minority party should present alternatives, and he tried to accomplish this goal through the Policy Committee.

> Robert Taft was probably the only leader of a policy committee who tried to make it a vehicle for formulating policy. During his six years as chairman (1947–1952), Taft dominated the Republican Policy Committee; in [William] White's words, "It became, and pretty correctly so, the custom to consider Taft *as* the policy committee." He dominated the committee because of his detailed knowledge of legislative measures and the force and persuasiveness with which he argued for adoption of his views. When there was near unanimity on the committee and its members sensed a high level of consensus in the senatorial party, the committee often took a formal stand on a measure or an amendment, and this stand was sometimes publicized.[15]

One long-term minority staff member noted that "everyone in the Policy Committee would say, 'What does Bob Taft think?' He had an answer on everything. Everyone relied on him." [16]

Senator H. Styles Bridges apparently was a strong leader of the

---

[12] George B. Galloway, *The Legislative Process in Congress* (New York: Crowell, 1953), p. 335.

[13] See Hugh A. Bone, "An Introduction to the Senate Policy Committees," *American Political Science Review*, Vol. 50 (June, 1956), pp. 339–59, and Malcolm E. Jewell, "The Senate Republican Policy Committee and Foreign Policy," *Western Political Quarterly*, Vol. 12 (December, 1959), pp. 966–80.

[14] Malcolm E. Jewell and Samuel C. Patterson, *The Legislative Process in the United States* (New York: Random House, 1966), p. 191.

[15] *Ibid.*, p. 194.

[16] I conducted interviews with several staff aides in 1965 to determine how Republican senators organized their work and to examine the role of the party and party leaders in the daily activities of minority Senate offices.

Policy Committee too, but more partisan and negative than Taft. In interviews with minority party staff personnel, comparisons were made between Bridges and the then chairman, Bourke B. Hickenlooper of Iowa. Bridges was characterized as being "much more partisan — blasting the Democrats and calling the Republicans angels. 'Hick' isn't like this." At the same time, however, Bridges was more fully in command of the Committee and its staff, using both to advantage in pressing the Republican advantage in the Senate.

> Bridges had them [the Policy Committee staff] doing research for speeches which he would make. He used the staff in a more political way than Hickenlooper uses them. And Bridges was likely to use them to serve him as chairman and his concept of what the Policy Committee ought to be.

Under Chairman Hickenlooper the Policy Committee rarely met as a committee. Since nearly half the total membership served on the Policy Committee (fifteen members in the 90th Congress),[17] it was practically as easy to have a meeting of all senators as to have a meeting of the Policy Committee. Thus, under Hickenlooper, Tuesday policy luncheons open to all Republican senators were held. Attendance was high (80 to 100 per cent) and party leaders often raised important policy matters, attempting to reach agreement on a Republican position. Minority Leader Dirksen often held a press conference following the luncheon. When Bridges was Policy Committee chairman, the Policy Committee would meet on Monday before the Tuesday lunch, thus giving him considerable influence in the Tuesday meeting. Hickenlooper did not try to extend his influence in this way.

Policy statements from the Committee have been rare (six or seven in four years) but when issued, they were carefully worded. Hickenlooper apparently went over every word, framing the statement very carefully, "with attention to the law, the legal aspects of the issue." He then circulated the statement to get consensus, which could take weeks. Again the contrast between Hickenlooper and Bridges is striking: "Bridges presented a proposal and had a vote on it."[18]

---

[17] The membership has usually been small, ten to fourteen members, but was twenty-three members in 1956 when all Republican senators up for reelection were placed on the Committee.

[18] Interview with Senate staff aide.

The staff of fifteen to twenty persons serves the Committee, the Conference, and the Calendar Committee. Thus, they serve all Republican senators and the distinctions between serving the Policy Committee and the Conference are not very clear, particularly if the chairman is less assertive. One staff member, David Kammerman, served the Calendar Committee in the period studied. He reviews the calendar every day to determine whether legislation might be objectionable to the minority or controversial in any way. He also makes certain that senators who want to amend legislation are alerted to the progress of the legislation and arrangements are then made for the amendment. Because of his job, this staff member becomes an important source of information for Republican senators on the details of legislation. Apparently Bridges used the Calendar Committee more than Hickenlooper. According to knowledgeable staff personnel, "he used it to do some dealing on bills. The calendar was gone over very carefully and then he would do some trading on legislation by warning that he would object to certain legislation. In so doing he was able to get things." This tactic has not been relied on either by Hickenlooper or Dirksen and therefore the Calendar Committee chairmen, Milward L. Simpson of Wyoming in the 89th Congress and Paul J. Fannin of Arizona in the 90th Congress, have been less aggressive. As one staff aide noted, "Dirksen simply doesn't work this way."

The staff works principally on requests from senators, though they may also be asked for information by the Republican National Committee or outside groups (e.g., the League of Women Voters). The requests are for research on issues, speeches for individual senators, and bill drafting. In many ways, they serve as a standing committee staff since the minority has less staff than the majority. The requests vary from 125 to 150 a month and all work flows through the staff director, Fred Rhodes in the 89th and 90th Congresses. Though each professional staff member has special interests and abilities, staff members get a wide variety of work assignments.

Considerable criticism was expressed of the Policy Committee, Chairman Hickenlooper, and the staff. In interviews with Senate staff personnel, principally administrative and legislative aides to individual senators, relatively few said that they used the Policy Committee staff frequently and many were critical of the staff and its work. Staff personnel from twenty-three offices (of thirty-two) were interviewed. Of these, six reported frequent use of Policy Committee staff, eleven reported "some use," and six said that they had virtually no contact at all with the Policy Committee staff. The attitudes regarding the Policy Committee and its staff varied widely among these three groups. Those who used the staff frequently relied on them for research, information on scheduling of legislation and other legislative matters, speech writing, and as a means for communicating good ideas to other senators.

> We have frequent contacts. They are a capable bunch down there. I often call Dave Kammerman on problems of legislation. I can get quick answers to questions down there because they have an extensive library. Sometimes they draft speeches for the Senator, sometimes statements, and, of course, I give suggestions to them.

> I have had a lot of contact with the Policy Committee — especially Dave Kammerman. Then we have also had contact through them for research on problems. We ask them for information if we want to develop a speech on, let's say, area redevelopment. They might do the background research. Then their vote summaries are useful to us. We have never used them to write speeches, though I guess some do.

> We give them all kinds of ideas and suggestions. We send them all our speeches, all of our press releases, and they can use what they want of them. Once in a while we need research and they do an adequate job.

The second group — those who had few contacts with the Policy Committee — were more critical in their remarks. The criticisms resulted from their discussions of why they did not rely more on the Policy Committee.

> Frankly, I don't find them of much value. I have tried to use them but they seem more interested in referral than research — that is, referring me to somebody else. We've tried to use them and never had much success.

> I must frankly volunteer the information that the Policy Committee staff is not the best in the world. They put themselves in the position of trying to accommodate everybody, trying to keep everybody happy. They could put out lots of stuff, but they try to reach the lowest common denominator. We had an item for their memorandum [a weekly newsletter] recently but they thought it would offend the big-city sena-

tors. So they don't get involved in as much as they should.

We can't ask them for a speech, because it just wouldn't be his [the Senator's] type. He's not the partisan type and they are. They are not used to doing non-partisan type speeches. We will draw on them for information which they send over and we occasionally suggest studies to them. But overall we don't call on them a great deal.

We don't have too much contact with them. They contact us more than we contact them. An example of how we use them occurred today. I just got a letter from a constituent. I first checked with the standing committee staff which was concerned with the problem and then I double checked with the Policy Committee to find out how the senators actually felt about this problem. The Policy Committee then becomes a kind of center of communication and a double check for information.

The last group — those who virtually never use the Committee staff — were, as expected, most critical.

We call the Library of Congress when we need studies — we have had some fine studies done over there. They [the Policy Committee Staff] have written a speech or two when it was necessary to have a straight political speech, but the Senator doesn't make many of those. When it does come up, that he has to give a straight political speech, I say, "Well, the Policy Committee boys can do that. Let's turn it over to them."

I do not have a high opinion of the Policy Committee staff. The staff director was a bad selection. If you stop him and ask him, he doesn't know anything on issues at all. He's a back slapper and goes from office to office slapping backs. The Policy Committee can put out a massive report and that's all right but it's not very useful to individual members. It's never specific enough. And they don't generate any ideas or any programs or policies over there. It's more or less a holding operation. And it should be much more dynamic. It should be a place where there are ideas developed. They get requests to do a lot of things, but these are very minor things.

I would like to get a hold of that policy committee down there and use them, and I know a lot of others who would like to as well. You can't expect much out of Hickenlooper. You can't communicate good ideas to him and good ideas

don't come from him. The present staff director is nice
enough but he isn't doing much as far as I can see.

Much of the criticism of the Policy Committee staff had sym-
pathetic overtones. That is, though many of the senatorial staff
assistants did not view the Policy Committee as a major source of
research and information, and were therefore critical of its operations, these critics generally did not question the ability of the staff.
The problem was more in the nature of the Policy Committee structure under Hickenlooper. The Committee staff must serve many
masters, with no one really in charge. As one staff aide noted: "I
doubt very much whether any committee staff can work for a variety
of people. I wonder if it wouldn't be better to have a strong leader
who uses the committee directly for purposes of the Republican
Party, as he sees those purposes [apparently more on the model of
the Taft and Bridges operation]."

Many of the special studies requested from the Policy Committee
staff are intended for partisan use, as one would expect from a party
committee. Few of these studies get any more than limited attention
and use, nor are they the basis of constructive alternatives offered by
the Republican leadership. Two recent studies deserve special consideration, however. The first of these is the report on Vietnam
released in May, 1967. This report got national attention because the
impact of its "factual account" was to blame the Democrats for the
Vietnam war. Though intended for partisan purposes, the report was
generally acknowledged to represent a realistic appraisal of the entire
situation. Following its premature release, it became obvious that
there would be adverse reaction and that not all Republican senators
agreed with the implications of the report. Several leaders disasso-
ciated themselves from the report and, typically, the Policy Committee staff was blamed for producing it. The procedures for research in
the Policy Committee suggest that the staff could not have initiated
the study. Research follows requests from senators. Indeed, the most
frequent criticism of the staff is that they do not come up with ideas
of their own.

For our purposes, the Vietnam report illustrates the problems of
the Policy Committee and its staff. In an attempt to discover a basis
for criticism and constructive alternatives on a major issue, the
Senate Republican Party has great difficulty in developing consensus.
One is asking for agreement among many individuals who have access to the national communications media. The Policy Committee

is composed of fifteen senators, but all Senate Republicans participate. The lack of specialization of senators, compared to House members, means that every Republican senator wants to review any policy statement from his own party committee. With the release of the Vietnam report, many Republican senators issued statements presenting their reactions; few supported the report. The result was a public preview of what would have happened behind the scenes had the report not been prematurely released. Without the strength of a leader such as Taft or Bridges, the Policy Committee has little or no function and the staff is limited to providing background papers, speech material, information for the partisan purposes of a single senator, and performing routine administrative tasks. Certainly the staff cannot do any more than reflect the desires and designs (or lack thereof) of their masters.

Another report that merits attention is entitled "Where the Votes Are" and was issued in July, 1966. This report represents one of the most realistic analyses of the status of the Republican Party, the trends in American society, and the relation between the two. It reviews facts about population growth, urbanization, education, agriculture, air and water pollution, labor, transportation, and Negroes. The report could well serve as a basis for offering constructive alternatives in the Senate Republican Party — and probably will, but, as always, through individual Republican senators rather than through the party or through individual senators working with the party.

In summary, though much remains to be described of the actual workings of the Senate Republican Party as a minority party, there appear to be virtually no outstanding organizational developments which parallel those in the House Republican Party. Certainly no attempt has been made in the Senate Republican Party to develop mechanisms which could eventually build consensus on policy issues. The greater individuality of senators, and their access to national media, have been identified as reasons why such mechanisms are difficult to develop.

But another factor surely is the leadership of the Senate Republican Party. In the case of the House, Ford's election represented a triumph of those forces which wanted to develop means by which the House Republican Party could offer constructive alternatives. The late Senator Dirksen, however, had a leadership style which was unlikely to accommodate any such mechanisms. Dirksen preferred to remain flexible on policy issues before the Senate. He did not want to be tied to one position when negotiating in the majority-building process in the Senate. In general, his style was one of remaining vague on an issue, or taking an initial position from which he could negotiate: bargaining with the majority party, the president, and his own colleagues, and eventually accepting a compromise. Senate staff aides were generally quite perceptive in describing this style. They variously described his style as follows:

> He's a real charmer, and we probably need this type of leader.

> Dirksen is a charmer, the man with the honeyed word.

> He is able to cajole, talk, persuade. Dirksen never pressures anybody to do anything. He leads principally through talking and bringing people together and listening to people, and then trying to work out something in the legislation itself.

This ability to persuade, compromise, and bargain, should not imply, however, that he lacked knowledge about the legislation itself. Most staff members agreed that Dirksen was "extremely knowledgeable on legislation — up to snuff on all the details of legislation."

Dirksen's manner obviated having a firm Republican position in advance. Staff aides were well aware of this fact, and many were accordingly critical. Taft, according to one staff aide, "had a line which was well made. He had logical thoughts, was more reliable, and his position could be predicted. You can't predict Dirksen." Other aides noted, "Republican positions aren't set forward very clearly," and "there is a lack of affirmative notions establishing party policy." Some described these characteristics in detail:

> He tends to be against something in the beginning. He doesn't have much foresight as to what is a major issue and how to solve it. Then the band wagon will come along and it becomes obvious it's going to pass and because Dirksen is a showman, and because he can speak well, he will actually appear to be out in front pulling the bandwagon when he wasn't even on it before.

> He is very pragmatic. He tries to do what's possible, and everybody enjoys him. Since Mansfield took over it really means that there's a void of leadership in the Senate — Dirksen tries to fill that void. An issue will come up and Dirksen will say, "well, I don't know. Let's hold up on that. Let's look at it very carefully." Then everybody will wait to see what he's going to do and pretty soon people start to say, "he holds the balance."

Of course, this procedure can make other senators suspicious. Dirksen would collect support for a vague position so as to retain flexibility. One staff aide noted that his office was very careful on such matters:

> Dirksen wants to accommodate people if he can. He and my senator get along fine together. Dirksen did not try to pressure my senator on the _____ issue. When Dirksen first asked my senator about _____, we said, "well, we want to see the text — the actual language." We've learned to ask for the text on something before we agree with Dirksen. We learned this from sad experience. Dirksen would say something about what he was going to do by way of putting something in a text, and then the language itself would come out hazy or unclear and then you would have given him your word that you were going to support it. Senator _____ had done this on the _____ issue but we didn't.

What is the result of this style of leadership? A surprisingly high percentage of those interviewed had serious reservations about the effectiveness of the style for the Republican Party. The attitudes ranged from "he is the single most influential senator in the Senate," to "Dirksen is pretty much helping Dirksen — I doubt that Dirksen's leadership is helping the Republican Party very much." The latter opinion was more prevalent than the former among Senate Republican staff aides and took various forms:

> Dirksen is more personal, but Taft was more party oriented.

> He doesn't really push for partisan causes. He is effective but not partisanly effective.

> Dirksen does not present a loyal opposition picture. He tends to agree with the Democrats too much. So the image which is projected is that of a minority agreeing with the majority, and this is bad for the party. It may be good for Dirksen, but not good for the party.

> We don't ever seem to get our end of the bargain. We don't ever seem to win.

> We seem to be unified on matters only if Dirksen is interested. And there is more Dirksen projected than the Republican Party. We aren't organized enough.

Dirksen's supporters argue that the opinions expressed above do not take into account the weak position of the Republican Party. As one noted:

> When Al Lopez was coaching the Chicago White Sox, it was said that he could squeeze everything out of the ball players. Well, Dirksen is like this. He squeezes everything out of the minority and makes them much more effective than they would be otherwise.

Individuality of senators and leadership style were two principal reasons for differences between the structure and operation of the minority party in the House and Senate in 1966 and 1967. Also, the Senate Republican Party did not have the influx of young members that the House had. The clash between the old and the new had not yet developed.

THE OLD AND THE NEW — BATTLING THE MINORITY PARTY MENTALITY

In a legislative body where seniority is an important determinant of power, junior members naturally will be frustrated. Newly elected, able, and intelligent young members of Congress soon discover, that they must serve a long apprenticeship before they can have impact. Thus a rift exists between energetic junior members and complacent senior members. One of the principal critics of the system, former Representative John V. Lindsay (later mayor of New York City), summarized the attitudes of his junior colleagues:

> It is a little difficult to say with pride that ours is a government of laws and not of men when power and prestige in Congress are not won, as they should be, through diligent, intelligent achievement, but are rather "awarded" to the winners of the continuing race against time.[19]

In the minority party, this gap between old and new members can have some dysfunctional consequences. Senior members tend to develop a "minority party mentality," accepting minority party status as a fact of life and accommodating themselves to their fate.[20] Hold-

---

[19] Mary McGinnis, ed., *We Propose: A Modern Congress* (New York: McGraw-Hill, 1966), p. 32.

[20] The "minority party mentality" is not a new phenomenon. Evidence suggests it has characterized the minority party outlook in Congress throughout the period of this study.

ing senior positions on committees, they tend to pursue personal rather than party goals. Any mechanism such as an active policy or research committee, which is designed to formulate innovative party policy, threatens these entrenched senior members who frequently have made accommodations with standing committee chairmen. Therefore, it is no coincidence that the revitalization of the Policy Committee in the House was the result of pressure from below. Interviews with junior members of the House Republican Policy Committee elicited many complaints and suggestions for reforms. All of these reforms were directed toward getting more representation on the committee and developing a procedure for offering constructive alternatives. Interviews with the senior members revealed that they sought no reforms and doubted the utility of offering "constructive alternatives." One senior member, who was ranking on a major committee and serving in a party leadership position, said he saw no need for reforms and, in response to the question of whether he had heard others suggest reforms, noted further: "No, I don't think so. Of course, there are the certain few who always bellyache about things, but you get to know who they are and don't pay much attention to them." He was later overthrown.

There are other examples of the minority party mentality among senior House members. When asked who benefited most from membership on the Policy Committee, one senior member said: "The freshmen. It is novel for them. They keep in touch with their group — tell them what went on at the meetings: The older members are saturated in the process and don't have to talk to others." Another noted: "I don't go [to the meetings of the Policy Committee] to make up my mind anyway. I have generally made up my mind and the older I get the less I want to argue." [21] This same member contrasted the Eisenhower and Kennedy administrations by saying, "It's more fun now." That is, under Eisenhower, "you had to keep your mouth shut if you opposed," and this member frequently opposed.

Junior members wanted reforms in the Policy Committee that would help develop a *"majority* party mentality."

> The Policy Committee is overweighted to the negative. I am not a liberal myself, but the committee is not positive enough. This is a result of its being overweighted to senior members. It would be more useful if we represented all views

[21] Jones, p. 105.

in the House. This is not a conservative-liberal split — I am
talking about people who want to offer constructive alternatives.[22]

These members had specific ideas about how the Committee should
be reorganized; most of them were implemented in 1965. Of course
the 1965 revolt in the House offered an opportunity to make many
changes reducing the effect of the minority party mentality. Many
changes were made possible because an unusually large number of
senior members were defeated in the 1964 election.[23] Despite the
considerable reduction in numbers, the time was ripe for revolt in
1965. As one Ford supporter observed:

> Many of our members have a minority psychology, partic-
> ularly the older ones, the ones who survive every storm. But
> the majority of our members have been elected in the last six
> years and they don't feel that way. They don't want to
> remain a minority party forever.[24]

The success of the insurgents in 1965 represents the culmination of
their efforts from 1959 to 1965 and is a milestone in the role of the
minority party in Congress.

What of the Senate? Two major factors make minority senators
even more susceptible to the "minority party mentality" than are minority representatives: the lesser role of party overall and the greater
role of individual senators, and the slowness with which Senate elections respond to changes in the electorate. A *minority party senator
may well be able to satisfy his personal goals as easily as a majority
party senator.*[25] Thus he has no great incentive on most issues to
work through the party in developing policy alternatives. In the 1966
election, the House Republicans increased their numbers from 32
per cent of the House seats to 43 per cent; the Senate Republicans
increased their share of the Senate seats from 32 per cent to 36 per
cent. This simply means that the sort of revolt staged in the House
— based as it was on an influx of young members — is more difficult
to effect in the Senate.

[22] *Ibid.*, p. 107.

[23] See Peabody, *The Ford-Halleck Minority Leadership Contest, 1965,* p. 10.

[24] Peabody, "House Republican Leadership," p. 3.

[25] William S. White, in his celebrated work, *Citadel: The Story of the U.S.
Senate* (New York: Harper, 1957), developed the thesis that the Senate is oper-
ated by an "inner club" made up of senators from both parties. One does not
have to accept the thesis to acknowledge the high degree of extra-partisan bargaining in the Senate.

There are other significant differences between the Senate and House Republican parties. The Senate Republican Party in the 89th and 90th Congresses was older on the average than the House Republican Party and considerably more "top-heavy" in terms of when members were elected. The average age of Senate Republicans in the 89th Congress was 60.5. Even with the election of five new senators in 1966, two of whom replaced older Republican senators (Brooke for Saltonstall in Massachusetts and Hansen for Simpson in Wyoming), and the election of one appointee replacing a Democrat (Griffin of Michigan), the average age was reduced only slightly in the 90th Congress — to 59.3. If these new, younger senators had not been elected, the average age of Senate Republicans in the 90th Congress would have increased to 62.5, retirement age for many occupations. In both Congresses, the average age of Republican senators exceeded that for all senators — by nearly three years in the 89th Congress and by over one and one-half years in the 90th Congress.

In striking contrast, the average age of House Republicans in the 89th Congress was 49.6 and in the 90th Congress 48.9, over ten years younger on the average than Senate Republicans. Further, in both Congresses, the average age of House Republicans was less than that of all House members, over a year younger in the 89th Congress and nearly two years younger in the 90th Congress.

Dramatic differences between the longevity of Republican members in the two houses are also apparent (see Table 8.1). During the 89th Congress, half of the House Republicans had been elected since 1959 and 90 per cent had been elected since 1949. The comparable figures for Senate Republicans are considerably lower. Even more dramatic are the figures for the 90th Congress, again reflecting the greater degree of recovery in the 1966 elections for House Republicans. Whereas two thirds of the House Republicans had been elected since 1959, nearly two thirds of the Senate Republicans had been elected before 1960. In fact, prior to the influx of new blood in 1966 (six senators with an average age of forty-six) only nine new Republican senators had come into the party since 1960. One of these (Strom Thurmond of South Carolina) changed parties, and it is doubtful that he could be considered "new blood" under any circumstances.

Although the House Republicans have changed their party structure dramatically and taken measures to conquer the minority party mentality, the Senate Republican Party remains a moribund instru-

TABLE 8.1
LONGEVITY OF HOUSE AND SENATE REPUBLICANS,
89TH AND 90TH CONGRESSES [a]

	89th Congress		90th Congress	
Year of first service	Senate Republicans	House Republicans[b]	Senate Republicans	House Republicans
Before 1950	7 (22%)	14 (10%)	6 (17%)	11 (6%)
1950–59	16 (50)	56 (40)	16 (44)	52 (28)
Since 1959	9 (28)	70 (50)	14 (39)	124 (66)
	32 (100%)	140 (100%)	36 (100%)	187 (100%)

[a] Compiled from data in the *Congressional Quarterly Weekly Reports*, Jan. 1, 1965, and Jan. 6, 1967.
[b] Includes members who had some previous experience in the House. The beginning of the present service is used in this table.

ment in policy making. The minority party mentality, though perhaps never as extreme as it has been at times in the House, nevertheless remains a significant factor in the Senate Republican Party. There are signs of change, however. Several new senators elected in 1966 have given indications that they expect the Senate Republicans to be offering reasonable alternatives to administration programs. And at least one member of this new group, Griffin of Michigan, was one of those who was instrumental in effecting the revolution in the House Republican Party.[26] After serving his apprenticeship, he may well have designs for the Senate Republican Party which could conceivably receive the support of successive infusions of new blood in 1968 and 1970. The Senate party may be reorganized as a result of the same process of reorientation that occurred in the House.

STAFFING THE MINORITY PARTY TODAY

In his book, *Professional Staffs of Congress*, Professor Kenneth Kofmehl concludes that:

> Every proposal for earmarking part of each committee staff for the minority must be appraised against the prevailingly nonpartisan operation of most committees. According to the

[26] In this connection, freshman Senator Griffin challenged Dirksen by moving to nullify a provision in the education bill favored by the minority leader. Dirksen himself noted, "What the Senator from Michigan is proposing to do is to gut the amendment that I have offered today." Griffin's move was successful. See *The Washington Post*, December 10, 1967, p. A2.

staff members interviewed, there was little — if any — cleavage along party lines or interjection of partisan issues in the proceedings of an overwhelming majority of the committees during the period covered.[27]

Whether accurate or not, Professor Kofmehl's interpretation differs considerably from that of many House and Senate Republicans. In 1963 House Republican Conference Chairman Ford appointed a Subcommittee on Increased Minority Staffing, chaired by Fred Schwengel of Iowa. This Subcommittee made serious efforts to gain more committee staff for the minority Republicans because:

> To deny the Minority in Congress access to adequate representation on Committee staffs eliminates the opportunity for a minority to act responsibly after a careful examination of the problems under consideration. . . . What is needed are professional staff members separately responsible to the majority and the minority.[28]

A minority party will find it difficult to employ a wide range of strategies in policy making if it does not have adequate staff. In particular, the more positive strategies are virtually precluded without reliable staff. Representative James C. Cleveland of New Hampshire summarized the minority Republican view:

> We Republicans . . . are often accused of mere obstructionism and are charged with failure to come up with constructive alternatives. . . . When the majority party not only controls all committee personnel but, as is the case at present, has exclusive access to the vast resources of advice, information, and power in all the federal agencies, the minority party is at a terrible disadvantage. . . . The ability to reach sound policy decisions for the nation, both in foreign and domestic affairs, is critically hobbled in this circumstance.[29]

He also observed that "nowhere in the House does the minority party have guaranteed to it an unobstructed conduit to information vital to the success of its adversary role under our two-party system." [30]

Professor Kofmehl's analysis led him to recommend that earmark-

---

[27] Kenneth Kofmehl, *Professional Staffs of Congress* (West Lafayette, Indiana: Purdue University Press, 1962), p. 52.

[28] McGinnis, p. 6.

[29] *Ibid.*, p. 8.

[30] *Ibid.*

ing committee staff for the minority "should be avoided wherever possible." [31] But the minority itself can be expected to react negatively to Kofmehl's analysis for two reasons: (1) they do not accept the statement that committee staffs that are responsible to the majority are nonpartisan, and (2) even if the staffs were nonpartisan, this would not satisfy the minority. The minority, it is argued, must have staff assistance for purely partisan goals, that is, for developing viable (and data-based) strategies in the majority-building process. The pursuit of partisan goals, they contend, ultimately is beneficial to the system.

What staff resources are available to the minority? Is Representative Cleveland correct in his assertion that the minority party does not have a guaranteed information source? On the House side, a minority party has the following sources of information and research: personal staffs of members; standing committee staffs (including those assigned to the minority party); the Legislative Reference Service of the Library of Congress; the staffs of the Congressional Campaign Committee, the Policy Committee, and the Conference (including the Committee on Planning and Research); the bureaucracy; various private foundations and institutions; and universities. This is rather impressive, but the utility of each source is minimal. The personal staffs of the members are primarily involved with constituency service matters and publicity. In his review of staff work based on a mail questionnaire, Professor John S. Saloma found that the average staff for a congressional office spent less than 15 per cent of their time on legislative support for the member.[32] This conclusion found support among members who participated in the Brookings Round Table discussions on the problem of the two-year term.

> The principal job of the staff is to handle the mail and to answer these inquiries.

> My office is almost 100 per cent oriented to doing things that will please constituents, so they will vote for me. And frankly, if you give me twice the staff, they would all be doing the same thing in my district, and in my office.

> Most of the work of my staff is devoted to running the errands, contacting the departments, sending out literature,

---

[31] Kofmehl, p. 68.

[32] John S. Saloma, "The Job of a Congressman: Some Perspectives on Time and Information," unpublished paper, February, 1967, p. 28.

answering inquiries. A minimum of their time is spent on legislative work.[33]

Thus, given the pressure of constituency-related matters that are handled in a congressional office, and the importance of constituency service for reelection, it is unlikely that members can expect much assistance from personal staffs.

The member can expect only limited assistance from standing committee staffs. Too little staff is assigned to the several minority committee members to be of much assistance and it is unlikely that the majority will be anxious to assign other staff for developing alternatives to their proposals. Further, since the minority staff on standing committees is assigned to the ranking minority member of the committee, he likely will want to use it himself rather than turn it over to party leaders.[34]

The Legislative Reference Service is of great assistance to Congress. Their staff and facilities are vastly overtaxed, however. In 1965 the LRS answered a total of 113,628 requests with a staff of about two hundred.[35] More than half of the inquiries originated with constituents.

The various party committee staffs represent a definite source for developing the research, background information, and planning that are necessary if the minority party is to realize the full potential of strategic situations. These staffs are small, however. And, in the case of the very able staff of the Congressional Campaign Committee, they may be otherwise preoccupied. The present combined staff of the Policy Committee and the Conference (assigned to the Committee on Planning and Research) is normally around ten persons. Even this staff is a recent innovation; neither unit had staff before 1959. No specific funds have been appropriated for these staff personnel in recent years. They are hired from monies diverted from clerk hire allowances of individual members or from staff positions allotted to the minority (e.g., Dr. William Prendergast, until recently the staff

[33] Charles O. Jones, *Every Second Year: Congressional Behavior and the Two-Year Term* (Washington: The Brookings Institution, 1967), pp. 89–90.

[34] On congressional committee staffing see Samuel C. Patterson, "Congressional Committee Professional Staffing: Capabilities and Constraints," unpublished paper presented at the Planning Conference of the Comparative Administrative Group Legislative Services Project, Planting Fields, New York, December 8–10, 1967.

[35] McGinnis, p. 308.

director of the Committee on Planning and Research, was officially the "Minority Sergeant at Arms").[36]

Other information sources vary in importance, but none are significant for the minority party. The bureaucracy provides data that may serve as a basis for developing policy alternatives, but ultimately, of course, the bureaucracy serves the president and his party. The minority party has never tapped fully the potential of research and information from private and academic sources. But this is not the complete answer either. First, what is needed is staff on hand, not consultants in Boston, Chicago, and San Francisco. Second, professional staff assistance of this type is expensive.

Virtually the same sources are available on the Senate side, with certain qualifications as to real value. The Senate minority party can depend more on the personal staffs of senators because they are larger; on committee staffs because, while usually not larger than their counterparts in the House, they have fewer members to serve; and on the Policy Committee staff because of its greater size.

To what extent does the minority use available staff sources? Despite considerable complaining about lack of staff, many members do not use all of their clerk hire allowance each month. On the House side, a minority staff aide checked with the disbursing office and discovered that *half of the House Republicans were turning back clerk hire monies each month.* On the Senate side, *two thirds* of the Senate aides interviewed said (1) they *did have* adequate staff in their office, and (2) *they did not use all of their clerk hire allotment.* All of the Senate offices in which aides were interviewed had legislative assistants, and in some cases the senator's legislative assistance staff was extensive.

Regarding committee staff, on the House side the few minority staff are generally available to all members of the committee and are physically located in the committee staff offices so as to be approachable by all members. Three committees — Armed Services, Science and Astronautics, and Un-American Activities — have no minority staff as such, though majority staff are assigned to assist the minority. On the Senate side, where the minority is generally allotted more staff assistance, the availability of these staff personnel for all mem-

---

[36] In 1963, a committee was established in the House Republican Party to determine how best to utilize the few appointments available to the minority. See Peabody, "House Republican Leadership," p. 7, and House Republican Conference, "The House Republican Conference and Committees of the Conference in the United States House of Representatives," 90th Congress, 1967.

bers varies. In many instances the staff appointee of a ranking Republican is physically located in the office of the senator who appointed him rather than in the committee office. Obviously another senator, or his staff assistant, will be reluctant to go to the ranking member's office in order to use the minority staff personnel. Further, in some cases, the appointing senator may be using the minority staff for purposes other than that committee's work. Under these circumstances the minority staff personnel of a standing committee come to be viewed as the appointing senator's staff. Senate staff aides discussed this problem in interviews:

> Committee staff people who are appointed by a chairman or a ranking minority member think of him as the boss man. You can go to them and get some help from them, but still the boss man is the man who appointed them and that creates some problems.

> Our appointments are located down at the committee room. [My Senator] thinks this is very important. They can't be used effectively if they are actually in the office of the senator.

This tendency, plus the tendency to appoint staff personnel who reflect the appointing senator's views, results in minority members doing the work in their own offices or in going to the majority staff personnel.

> The _____ Committee staff is not very good for our purposes. We do everything ourselves there. Most minority staff are no help at all and so we don't call on them. In some cases we will even use Democrats rather than minority staff. For example, when my senator was on _____, we used the Democratic staff people rather than [the ranking Republican's] people. It's simply too much for the senator, who is a liberal Republican, to get anything out of them.

> We do have some cordial relationships with the majority staff people and they are quite helpful. We go to the minority staff but they are [the ranking Republican's] people and that's the way we look at them. On the _____ Committee, the minority staff people there aren't very able and so we go to the majority.

> On _____ Committee, the relationships are not good. [The ranking Republican] had two appointments on minority staff. The previous man worked for [the ranking Republican] directly and was not very satisfactory because he didn't do

much for the rest of the members of the committee. The new man is much better, and more able. The ———— Committee staff ought to be nonpartisan but it turns out to be very partisan. It's very tough to deal with the majority staff. It is all right if you just want straight information, but even there the staff director is very political and he puts a political construction on everything.

The party committee staffs are used extensively in the House. Despite their preoccupation with congressional elections, even the Campaign Committee staff is used for policy-making purposes. Indeed, some of the research units can trace their origins to Campaign Committee activities. Senate minority party use of their large Policy Committee staff has not facilitated greater flexibility of strategy choice for Senate Republicans.

Of the other sources, the Legislative Reference Service is used too much by everyone, given the staff size. The bureaucracy is relied on extensively but principally for handling constituents' problems. The House Republicans have relied on private and academic sources to a considerable extent in recent years. The Senate Republicans as a party have not, though individual senators have relied extensively on these sources.

In summary, the staffing situation for the minority party today is better than it has ever been. On the House side, however, the minority party has very limited staff. What exists is "jerry-built" from a variety of sources. In a sense, the very fact that a party staff has been assembled in this fashion illustrates an important difference between the House and Senate parties. House party leaders wanted a staff to serve the party in policy making and, despite a lack of appropriated funds, they were successful in establishing one. On the Senate side, however, party leaders have shown no similar interest. Ironically, there have been funds appropriated for a policy staff for the party since 1947 in the Senate. Senate minority party leaders would probably not have provided for such a staff without the impetus of legislation.

POLICY-MAKING STRATEGIES
IN THE HOUSE, 1966–1967

The new emphasis reflected in many organizational changes between 1959 and 1965 resulted in efforts to adopt more positive strategies in the policy-making process in the House. One measure of the

TABLE 8.2

SUMMARY OF HOUSE REPUBLICAN POLICY COMMITTEE POSITIONS,
1961, 1962, 1966, 1967 [a]

Policy position	1961	1962	1966	1967
Oppose (no alternative)	12 (52%)	6 (40%)	6 (26%)	1 (4%)
Amend	5 (22)	4 (27)	9 (39)	7 (28)
Support administration	2 ⎫	2 ⎫	2 ⎫	5 ⎫
Support GOP proposal	3 ⎬(26)	2 ⎬(33)	2 ⎬(35)	6 ⎬(68)
Support other	1 ⎭	1 ⎭	4 ⎭	6 ⎭
Totals	23	15	23	25

a Compiled from various policy statements issued by the House Republican Policy Committee.

strategies employed by House Republicans is the policy position taken in the House Republican Policy Committee. The Committee issued a total of sixty policy statements in 1966 and twenty-five in 1967. The other statements were general in nature.

The fact that the House Republicans have in recent years attempted to adopt more of a positive posture is illustrated by Table 8.2. The specific policy positions of the Committee are summarized for four years — 1961–1962, when statements were first issued, and 1966–1967. Most striking, of course, is the increase in the number of positive statements which have been adopted in recent years. Table 8.2 shows a steady increase in the number of statements in support of legislation and a steady decrease in the number of statements which simply oppose during the years 1961, 1962, and 1966. In 1967 there is a sharp increase in positive statements (to 68 per cent) and a sharp decrease in purely negative statements (to 4 per cent). In addition, the statements themselves have been much more elaborate in recent years. Whereas a statement in 1961 frequently would present only the position taken (e.g., "The Republican Policy Committee went on record as favoring H.R. 5560, the Minimum Wage Bill, as introduced by Congressman William Ayres, as a substitute for the committee bill"), lengthy discussions and rationales for action were offered in 1966 and 1967.[37]

Additional evidence for the shift in strategies following several reorganizations is provided by an analysis of the various combinations of strategies employed by the House Republicans on legislation (see

37 The House Republican Policy Committee supplied me with all statements issued for these four years.

TABLE 8.3

SUMMARY OF HOUSE REPUBLICAN STRATEGIES ON SELECTED
LEGISLATION, 1961, 1962, 1966, 1967 [a]

Negative strategies[b]	1961		1962		1966		1967	
1. Inconsequential partisan opposition	8		1		4		1	
2. Consequential partisan opposition	4		4		3		0	
3. Constructive opposition ⟶ inconsequential partisan opposition	1	(65%)	2	(53%)	2	(39%)	2	(12%)
4. Constructive opposition ⟶ withdrawal	2		1		0		0	

Positive strategies								
1. Cooperation and/or innovation ⟶ constructive opposition ⟶ withdrawal	0		0		2		1	
2. Constructive opposition ⟶ support	1		1		1		0	
3. Cooperation and/or innovation ⟶ constructive opposition ⟶ support	1	(35%)	1	(47%)	3	(61%)	1	(88%)
4. Cooperation and/or innovation ⟶ support	3		3		7		15	
5. Innovation	3		2		1		5	
Totals	23		15		23		25	

[a] Legislation on which the House Republican Policy Committee issued statements.

[b] For definition of strategies, see Chapter two.

Table 8.3). The same trends are repeated — an increase in the more positive strategies (with a sharp upturn in 1967) and a decrease in the more negative strategies (with a sharp decline in 1967). And there were instances in 1967 when the combination of "cooperation and/or innovation followed by support" actually resulted in the passage of Republican-sponsored legislation.

The House Republicans were somewhat more confined in adopting strategies in 1966 than in 1967, being outnumbered by 155 seats. But the new House Republican leadership in the 89th Congress refused to accept the role of a dormant opposition and laid much of the groundwork for the legislative success of 1967. Further, House Republicans were often successful in shaping legislation in committees (with the result that they endorsed the legislation occasionally) and in offering major alternative programs to those offered by the administration.

In 1967, bolstered by impressive gains in the 1966 elections, House Republicans had several notable legislative victories. In some cases they won negative victories, as with the initial attempt by the administration to enact a debt limit increase. The Republicans maintained perfect cohesion on the vote and were joined by 8 northern Democrats and 27 southern Democrats. The administration was forced to revise the legislation and resubmit it.[38]

House Republicans were notably successful in building majorities for their own proposals in 1967 — a remarkable achievement for a minority party. On occasion it appeared that the Republicans were the majority and the Democrats the minority. House Republicans were moderately successful in having their way on the Elementary and Secondary Education bill. In the 1967 Republican State of the Union Message, Minority Leader Ford had strongly emphasized Republican support for decentralization of decision making in education through "tax sharing." The purpose was "to return to the States and local governments a fixed percentage of personal income taxes without federal control." [39] A strong effort was made to incorporate this principle in the education bill of 1967. Albert H. Quie of Minnesota introduced legislation that would provide the states block grants for education. Unsuccessful in committee, Quie offered his proposal on the floor as a substitute for the administration measure. The Quie proposal lost 168–197, on a teller vote, but the administration was sufficiently concerned about Quie's legislation to postpone debate on the bill for nearly a month.[40] After Quie's defeat, the House Republicans announced support for a major amendment offered by a northern Democrat on the Committee on Education and Labor, Mrs. Edith Green of Oregon. The Green Amendment fit the Republican guidelines because it gave state departments of

[38] The revised administration bill passed, 217–196.

[39] For full text of the Republican State of the Union address by Representative Ford and Senator Dirksen, see *Congressional Quarterly Weekly Report*, January 27, 1967, pp. 130–34.

[40] A significant religious question emerged in connection with the block grant approach. It was argued by Democrats that the Quie approach would upset the compromises on the parochial aid question which were established in 1965 and create an "unholy war" between the school systems in the states. See *Congressional Quarterly Weekly Report*, May 26, 1967, p. 859.

education (or public instruction) responsibility for supplementary education centers under Title III of the bill instead of the Office of Education of the Department of Health, Education and Welfare. This amendment passed 230–185 with the support of House Republicans and southern Democrats. Mrs. Green also introduced other amendments that had the effect of decentralizing responsibility. These too had the support of House Republicans (though Republican cohesion was uniformly low on all votes).

But the principal House Republican victory came on the amendments to the Law Enforcement and Criminal Justice Assistance bill. House Republicans were even successful in changing the title of the bill, originally proposed by President Johnson as the Safe Streets and Crime Control Act. Though generally in favor of legislation in this area, House Republicans favored decentralization by allocating funds to state planning agencies appointed by the governors and strengthening the legislation in many respects. Their efforts to reconstruct the bill were almost totally successful. The key vote on the floor came on an amendment by William T. Cahill (R-New Jersey) providing block grants to the states instead of the categorical grants to local governments in the administration bill. The Cahill amendment also authorized the governors to establish planning agencies for reviewing projects and developing a state-wide comprehensive plan for law enforcement improvement. The amendment passed by a large margin, 256–147, receiving support from 172 of the 176 Republicans voting, 16 northern Democrats, and 68 southern Democrats. One House Democrat who supported the president was quoted as saying: "It [the amendment] changes the entire character of the bill." [41] Three other significant Republican floor amendments were passed on teller votes. Only one Republican amendment was defeated — one which would have increased the authorization by $40 million rather than the $25 million offered in a Democratic amendment. The Republican amendment was defeated by two votes on a teller vote.

The victory for House Republicans on the anticrime bill represented a high point for the minority party in 1967. It was the result of coordinated efforts among party leaders, the task force on crime of the Committee on Planning and Research (chaired by Richard H. Poff of Virginia), the Republican members of the Committee on the Judiciary (four of whom were members of the task force on

[41] *Christian Science Monitor*, August 12, 1967.

crime), and the Policy Committee. Party leaders were able to get the backing of most governors and attorneys general for their proposals. By the time the legislation got to the floor, the House Republicans had virtually assumed control of its fate. The outcome was all the more remarkable in view of the fact that the ranking Republican on the Committee on Judiciary, William M. McCulloch of Ohio, favored the administration bill and voted against the Cahill amendment.

Republicans were also successful in passing measures that captured the mood of the House of Representatives concerning the riots of 1967, and amending the continuing appropriations bill to set ceilings on fiscal 1968 expenditures. And House Republicans supported much administration-backed legislation (see Table 8.2), often contributing to its development in the standing committees.

Finally, House Republicans made a greater effort than ever before to garner support for legislation sponsored by members of their party. The Policy Committee issued statements in support of six such programs in 1967 that received little or no attention in the House. These ranged from support for congressional reorganization to a broad Republican program for coping with the problem of unemployment, the Human Investment Act of 1967. A congressional reorganization bill passed the Senate in 1967 but was stalled in the House Committee on Rules. House Republicans were very active in shaping legislation to reform Congress; the task force on congressional reform and minority staffing of the Committee on Planning and Research even published a book on the subject in 1966, *We Propose: A Modern Congress.* The essays were written by various House Republicans.

It is too early for a complete appraisal of minority party efforts in 1966 and 1967. It may well be that in ten years the experiment of adopting aggressive policy-making strategies will have been merely that — one more experiment. It is clear, however, that the House minority party in these two sessions attempted to take greater advantage of its strategic position than ever before in this century. This is not to say that minority party members have not been innovative or clever or positive in the past, but the minority party itself never had organized to the extent that it did in these two sessions to influence the process of majority building. It is difficult to contrast the two parties in this respect, of course, as the Democrats have been a "flexible" minority party only once since 1930 in the House. The

House Republican Party is continuing to organize to maximize its role in policy making in an innovative, perhaps even radically innovative, manner. Further, these efforts, twice begun after devastating defeats at the polls (1958 and 1964), have had the effect of reducing the "minority party mentality" in the House to a minimum.

POLICY-MAKING STRATEGIES
IN THE SENATE, 1966–1967

It is more difficult to identify policy-making strategies of the Senate Republicans. No policy statements are issued on specific legislation by the Senate Republican Policy Committee, nor is there any unit analogous to the task forces of the Committee on Planning and Research of the House Republican Conference. Typically individual Republican senators had considerable influence in the shaping of some legislation, but with one notable exception the party as such seldom made an effort to develop a Republican alternative.

Thus, it is not possible to conduct the same type of analysis as for the House. Without some indication of Senate Republican Party positions, the best one can do is rely on roll-call analysis to determine when it was that the Party appeared to be supporting or opposing legislation. Examination of Senate Republican voting on issues on which the House Republican Policy Committee took a stand and on certain other key issues (as identified by the *Congressional Quarterly*) reveals several outstanding features. First, owing again to differences in size and procedure between the Senate and House minority, senators are more likely than representatives to offer amendments. The result is more roll calls on most bills than in the House. On many of these votes, the Senate Republicans split among themselves. For example, on a series of four amendments offered by Minority Leader Dirksen to the Elementary and Secondary Education bill in 1966, the combined total vote of Senate Republicans was 44 in favor of the amendments, 41 opposed (an overall index of cohesion of 4).[42]

Second, Senate Republicans "withdrew" on the final roll-call vote more than House Republicans. That is, Senate Republicans were so seriously divided on the final vote that no serious effort was made, or could be made, to unify the party in favor or against the particular

---

[42] Relying on the index of cohesion developed by Stuart A. Rice in *Quantitative Methods in Politics* (New York: Knopf, 1928).

bill in question. Of the forty-four legislative issues categorized for 1966 and 1967, nineteen (43 per cent) were in the "withdrawal" category (see Table 8.4). The combined index of cohesion for Senate Republicans on these nineteen issues was 2. On several of these bills, amendments by Senate Republicans received considerable support from party members, but once the amendment failed (as it usually did) party unity disappeared.

TABLE 8.4

APPARENT SENATE REPUBLICAN POLICY STRATEGIES ON
SELECTED KEY ISSUES, 1966, 1967 [a]

	1966	1967
Opposition	4	2
Withdrawal	9	10
Support	8	11
Total	21	23

[a] Determined by examining cohesion and direction on roll-call votes on those issues on which the House Republican Policy Committee had taken a stand plus key votes as determined by the *Congressional Quarterly*.

Many of the issues that divided Republicans concerned urban problems and/or problems of poverty. In 1966, Senate Republicans were seriously split on the following bills: education, demonstration cities, rent supplements, unemployment compensation, and minimum wage. In 1967, they were seriously split on aid to Appalachia, redistricting, rent supplements, and the poverty bill.

Aggregate analysis of all roll calls on which the majority of one party voted against the majority of the other party shows that House Republicans were more unified than Senate Republicans in both 1966 and 1967. As calculated by the *Congressional Quarterly*, the party unity scores for 1966 were 68 per cent for House Republicans and 63 per cent for Senate Republicans. In 1967, the gap between the two was by far the largest since the *Congressional Quarterly* began computing the scores in 1949 — 74 per cent for House Republicans and 60 per cent for Senate Republicans. On the other hand, and consistent with the results on party unity, Senate Republicans offered more support to presidential programs than did their colleagues in the House. The scores for Senate Republicans in 1966 and 1967 were 43 per cent and 53 per cent respectively; for House Republicans, 37 per cent and 47 per cent respectively. The differences between the party unity scores and presidential support scores are consistent because *higher minority party unity normally would mean less presidential support.* In the Senate, therefore, the party defection was in the direction of support for the president. Both sets of scores tend to support the generalization made on the basis of an examination of voting results on the key issues selected above.

Of course in 1967 there were fewer Republican senators proportionately than Republican representatives. It is possible that the relatively little emphasis on party in the Senate is the result of accommodation on the part of Republican senators to the fact that there have been so few of them since 1958. This view can be sustained only if one can find evidence of strong party influence before 1958. Such evidence is, in fact, exceedingly difficult to find.

Although the Senate Republicans as a party had no success equal to that of the House Republicans on the crime bill,[43] there was one striking instance in 1967 of Republican initiative. Freshman Senator Charles H. Percy (Illinois) proposed a housing program to enable low-income families to purchase homes. The legislation would establish a Home Ownership Foundation to float bonds and use the proceeds to make loans to local nonprofit housing sponsors (churches, labor unions, civic organizations). The local sponsors would purchase and then rehabilitate old houses for eventual resale to low-income families.[44] Many minority party senators introduce innovative legislation. The significant characteristic of the Percy housing bill was that it was cosponsored by all thirty-six Republican senators. It became the Senate Republican housing program in 1967.

Percy worked carefully to build support for his proposal within his party in both houses. The measure was introduced in the House by William B. Widnall (New Jersey), ranking Republican on the Committee on Banking and Currency (which has jurisdiction on housing legislation). It was actively supported by 106 of the 187 House Republicans. Thus, here was an important piece of innovative legislation on which party support was constructed in the Senate before the committee stage.

The Percy effort received considerable publicity — indeed, a spectacular amount in view of the fact that Percy was a freshman senator in a minority party. It received attention from the Johnson adminis-

[43] The crime bill did not pass the Senate in 1967.
[44] See *Congressional Quarterly Weekly Report,* April 28, 1967, p. 687, for details of this legislation.

tration in the form of a nine-page denunciation of the proposal issued by the Department of Housing and Urban Development. In some ways, the administration reaction resembled minority party responses to new programs sponsored by the president. The minority party took the initiative in proposing legislation, and the majority party (through the president) denounced the proposal.[45]

The Percy housing proposal clearly indicates the potential for innovative strategy in the Senate minority party. Proposals can be developed that will receive broad support from the party. An infusion of new blood in the Senate Republican Party may have results similar to those in the House. The Senate Republican Party has an advantage in that it has a well-established policy staff funded by Congress.

SUMMARY

The House minority party in recent years has consciously developed organizational units, procedures, and a mentality for more flexibility in adopting strategies in majority building. These developments, if they continue to mature, have the potential of reducing the effect of many of the external and internal limiting conditions discussed throughout this book.

The Senate Republican Party may be changing, too. The next four to six years will be crucial in determining whether such changes will come about. Many Republican senators are at retirement age. Potential turnover may make the party relatively young and vigorous. The effect of youth and energy on the party apparatus could be profound.

What does all of this analysis suggest about the Democratic Party as minority party? Not very much. The Democratic Party may have to go through many painful developments before "maturing" as a minority party. Perhaps the Republican experience will be of some value to them.

[45] For details on the administration's denunciation, see *Christian Science Monitor*, May 9, 1967; and *The New York Times*, April 22, 1967.

CHAPTER NINE

Creativity and the Minority Party

The minority party has periods of greater or lesser potential for an aggressive role (positive or negative) in the process of majority building in Congress. A considerable catalog of political conditions is significant in determining how flexible the party can be. This study has shown that under objectively good hypothetical circumstances, the minority party might well not act aggressively to adopt the full range of strategies that seem available. Indeed, the overall record of the minority party in this century is not impressive if one uses productivity under "ideal circumstances" as a measure. The minority party frequently failed to take advantage of such circumstances. How can one explain the disparity between expectations of behavior, based on logically deduced political circumstances for the minority party, and actual behavior in specific Congresses?

In the first place, it became apparent in analyzing the minority party in the thirty-four Congresses in this century that different political conditions are dominant at different times. Major crises such as war and depression can influence the role of the minority party, limiting its strategic options, regardless of whatever favorable conditions may exist simultaneously. The man in the White House is obviously relevant to the specific role of the minority party. The impact of the president varies considerably, and sometimes surprisingly. As expected, when the president has power as a result of a national crisis (e.g., war or depression), the minority party is limited in its range of strategic responses. When the president is weak and initiates very little legislation, it might seem logical that the minority party would have many strategic options. In fact, given the dependence of Congress on executive initiative, historically the minority party has not adopted the more aggressive positive or negative strategies under these circumstances. And, as has been illustrated in detail, strategic options are narrow when the minority party has a man in the White House. The minority party appears to have approached its potential (as defined by political conditions) when the president has been aggressive and relatively strong (in other than crisis situations). The role of the minority party must be one of response. When the president is vigorously pursuing a program and the minority party has strength in numbers and leadership, the minority party is more likely to pursue the full range of strategies in the majority-building process.

Party disunity can also have an overriding effect on the role of the minority party in Congress. The Republicans between 1910 and 1920, in particular, were so divided that efforts toward reunification had to take precedence over adopting an aggressive posture in congressional policy making.

Second, despite the sometimes overpowering influence of certain external political conditions in determining the role of the minority party, it is conceivable that minority party leadership can modify the effects of such conditions through vigor, imagination, and resourcefulness. The minority party has seldom enjoyed the kind of able leadership that might reduce the effects of powerful external political conditions. Indeed, frequently in this century, even when external political conditions were favorable, minority party leadership was weak. Thus, the leadership was unable either to expand minority options beyond those available in basically restrictive situations or to realize the options available when external political conditions allowed more flexibility.

Third, and perhaps most important, the legislative system in Congress simply is not structured to encourage or facilitate an aggressive or creative minority party. Even under the most favorable political conditions, the minority party seldom will structure itself to employ the full range of strategies in the majority-building process.

In his thought-provoking article on functionalism in the analysis of political parties, Theodore Lowi hypothesizes that "in a party system, innovation is a function of the minority party." [1] The evidence in this book casts doubt on the validity of his hypothesis for the minority party in Congress. Party leaders face a dilemma if they

---

[1] Theodore Lowi, "Toward Functionalism in Political Science: The Case of Innovation in Party Systems," *American Political Science Review*, Vol. 57 (September, 1963), p. 571.

decide to accommodate various expectations of the minority party. Perhaps the most frequent complaint about the minority party is that it only opposes, it does not offer alternatives. But offering alternatives may only lead to continued success for the majority party. What are the rewards for adopting the more aggressive, positive strategies (innovation, cooperation, constructive opposition, support)? Except under unusual circumstances, the party will probably not get public credit for such contributions. Without public credit, adopting these strategies probably will not contribute significantly to electoral success for the minority party. With such minimal rewards for the party, as distinct from rewards for individual party members, the party has little encouragement to innovate in policy making.

In a parliamentary system, adopting all strategies available, including the more positive and creative strategies, might have at least two beneficial effects for the minority party: (1) preparing an opposition policy stance which could then form the basis for proposals when the minority became the majority; and (2) preparing party leaders to govern as future cabinet ministers by forcing them to study the issues of the day and to develop an innovative mind-set. Ours is not a parliamentary system, however. If anything, constitutional conditions discourage an aggressive and innovative minority party. The party cannot determine the policy stance of the national party in the next election or when the party wins the White House. And, of course, not only are minority party leaders unlikely to be future cabinet leaders, they may not even lead the House and Senate when their party wins the presidency.

So what are the rewards for a minority party that seeks to be "responsible"? And why should a minority party seek to achieve the potential of hypothetically good political circumstances, as defined here? Why should the minority party seek to be creative? The fact is that there is a rather strong pull toward the "minority party mentality." When a party becomes the minority party it stays that way for a long time. Its experiences as the majority party are infrequent. Minority party members do get instruction in survival, however, often from senior members who have, over a period of years, accommodated themselves to being in the minority party. No member of the Republican Party in either the House or Senate today has had any but the most limited experience in serving in the majority. The eight years of the Eisenhower administration provided some experience in working with the executive, but for many members the experience was unpleasant.

Are there differences between the House and Senate in regard to the role of the minority party? The structural differences between the two bodies are significant in determining the extent to which the minority party is likely to adopt aggressive and creative strategies in policy making. The structure and norms of the Senate seem more accommodating to creativity among individual minority party members and less accommodating to creativity within the minority party as such. The House is not particularly accommodating to either, though because of the greater emphasis on organization and procedure in the House, minority party organizations that seek to develop unified party stances are possible.

Are there differences between the two political parties when serving as the minority party in Congress? The long periods of one-party dominance make comparisons difficult. A comparison of the Democrats during the first three decades of this century and the Republicans during the last four decades, however, suggests no notable differences between the two parties. Both have been limited in their strategic responses — limited either by the variety of constitutional and political conditions of the day or by their own view of their role.

What factors would lead toward a greater realization of potential for the minority party? The recent experience in the House Republican Party suggests that it is possible for the minority party to employ a wide range of strategies successfully even when the party is at a considerable numerical disadvantage. It is too early to judge whether the recent policy-making experiments of the House Republicans will produce any lasting lessons, but it is interesting to speculate about the reasons why these efforts were made. An analysis of these efforts may provide clues for determining the future role of the minority party and for suggesting under what conditions innovation might be a function of the minority party.

House Republican Party activity in the 89th Congress, second session, and the 90th Congress, first session, was exceptional. Minority parties in previous Congresses varied from being severely restricted to unrestricted (a few were classified as "participating") in the strategies which might be adopted in congressional policy making. But none of the Congresses prior to 1966 were characterized by as much minority party policy-making organization and activity as in

1966 and 1967. This emphasizes the usefulness of the political conditions identified in Chapter Two for classifying the minority parties in various Congresses. Not until the 89th and 90th Congresses was one led to inquire whether there might be circumstances in which the minority party could overcome the limitations of political conditions to adopt a more assertive posture than would be expected by the conditions. In previous Congresses the question was why the minority party was *not* taking advantage of the potential of its political circumstances.

At least three complementary factors are helpful in explaining recent developments in the House Republican Party. First, many junior members discovered their strength in numbers. In many interviews among House Republicans concerning developments in the past few years, young members pointed out that they were finally in the majority in their party. As Charles E. Goodell (R-New York), a leading insurgent who later served out Robert F. Kennedy's Senate term, wrote to his constituents in justifying the overthrow of Charles B. Hoeven (R-Iowa) as Conference chairman in 1963, "We are a YOUNG Party in Congress." [2] Professor Robert L. Peabody also noted the importance of the "bottom-heavy structure of the House Republican Party" in his study of the Ford-Halleck leadership battle in 1965. As he notes, almost 58 per cent of the House Republicans in the 89th Congress had been elected in 1958 or subsequent elections.[3] A check of postwar Congresses indicates that *in every case* the junior members (defined as those with *three terms* experience or less) have been in the majority in the House Republican Party. On two occasions, the 82nd and 83rd Congresses, members with two terms experience constituted a majority. Thus, at least in the postwar period, had junior members been so inclined, they could have made changes in House Republican leadership and organization.

Beginning in 1959, these junior members began to overthrow the existing leadership and reshape the party structure. Compromises were made by each successor to the minority leadership post. Halleck found it necessary to agree to a separate Policy Committee chairman. Ford found it necessary to create a strong Conference organization, including a Committee on Research and Planning. A collegial pattern of leadership developed — the second factor explaining develop-

[2] "Letter to Constituents," January 23, 1963.
[3] Robert L. Peabody, *The Ford-Halleck Minority Leadership Contest, 1965* (New York: McGraw-Hill, 1966), pp. 9–10.

ments in the House Republican Party. The third factor was simply the competition among young members who wanted power. In competing for power, men like Ford, Laird, Goodell, Rhodes, Frelinghuysen, Curtis, and others developed ideas about how the House Republican Party might project a more positive role in congressional policy making.

These three complementary developments — junior members' awareness of their strength; collegial leadership pattern; and competition among a new corps of leaders and potential leaders — suggest that it is possible for the minority party to structure itself for more flexibility in congressional policy making, regardless of restrictive political conditions.

How permanent are the changes in the House Republican Party? How likely is it that similar changes will occur in the Senate and/or in the Democratic Party? It is impossible to answer the first question with any certainty. If a single leader emerges with strength in the House Republican Party he may reestablish a more hierarchical organization and return to the pattern of a relatively restrictive view of the role of the minority party. It seems more likely, however, that the developments of the past ten years have in fact taken hold. In the first place, they have already lasted longer than anyone predicted. In the second place, any return to the old pattern would take time because the party is aware of its youth and its record has been impressive.

In regard to the second question, developments similar to those in the House may occur in the Senate Republican Party. An old party is becoming younger and young senators are demanding to be heard. The Senate Republican Party may have reached a maximum average age in the 89th Congress. The average age is bound to go down in the next few elections.

Predicting for the Democratic Party is somewhat more complex. Democratic Party leadership in both houses has tended to be more centralized and the party has been in the minority infrequently in the past four decades. On the other hand, certain developments suggest that the Democratic Party as minority party would follow a pattern similar to that of the House Republican Party. The Democratic Study Group in the House has developed great strength in the past decade. If these members survived an election in which the Republicans won a majority (and many would be vulnerable to defeat since they come from more marginal districts), they might use the opportunity to reorganize their party. In the Senate many Democratic members are young. The average age of Senate Democrats in the 90th Congress was fifty-seven, but in the next few years a significant turnover likely will reduce this average age. In the 90th Congress, eleven Democratic senators were seventy years of age or older and seventeen were sixty-five years of age or older. Retirements, deaths, or defeat could add considerably to the influence of the large number of young Democratic senators (nineteen are fifty or younger, eleven are under forty-five).

One other important consideration may contribute to a more aggressive and positive role for the minority party. The pressure of events — foreign and domestic — in the post-World War II period is such that the political system may not be able to afford the luxury of a minority party that seeks merely to maintain itself in waiting. A more active, aggressive, and creative opposition may be necessary because new ideas are essential and because programs developed by the majority require challenge for perfection.

On January 10, 1967, President Lyndon B. Johnson delivered his State of the Union address to a Congress vastly different from that he faced in 1965. The Republicans had gained an impressive 47 seats in the House and 4 seats in the Senate. Midway through the message, the president turned to his left, broke into that familiar benign smile, and spoke directly to the Republicans:

> I should like to say to the members of the opposition whose numbers, if I am not mistaken, seem to have increased somewhat — that the genius of the American political system has always been best expressed through creative debate that offers choices and reasonable alternatives. Throughout our history, great Republicans and Democrats have seemed to understand this. So let there be light and reason in our relations. That is the way to a responsible session and a responsive government.

The president's historical analysis regarding the role of the opposition was considerably less impressive than his political sagacity in attributing to the minority party a role it has seldom assumed. Great Republicans and Democrats, as individual minority party members, have realized the genius of the American political system through creative debate and by offering reasonable alternatives. But the minority party *qua* party of opposition has seldom reached the heights attributed to it by the president. Throughout the period studied here, the minority party has normally not had the organization, the drive, the leadership, the inclination, or the demands to be a creative instrument in Congress.

It is not necessary to end on a pessimistic note, however. If the former president is not a historian, he may be a prophet. Those who value constructive criticism and opposition now see many encouraging signs — more evidence that democratic government is still emerging in this nation.

Index